MEGACHANGE

OTHER ECONOMIST BOOKS

Guide to Analysing Companies
Guide to Business Modelling
Guide to Business Planning
Guide to Economic Indicators
Guide to the European Union
Guide to Financial Management
Guide to Financial Markets
Guide to Hedge Funds
Guide to Investment Strategy
Guide to Management Ideas and Gurus
Guide to Managing Growth
Guide to Organisation Design
Guide to Project Management
Guide to Supply Chain Management
Numbers Guide
Style Guide

Book of Isms
Book of Obituaries
Brands and Branding
Business Consulting
Business Strategy
Buying Professional Services
The City
Coaching and Mentoring
Doing Business in China
Economics
Emerging Markets
Marketing
Modern Warfare, Intelligence and Deterrence
Organisation Culture
Successful Strategy Execution
The World of Business

Directors: an A–Z Guide
Economics: an A–Z Guide
Investment: an A–Z Guide
Negotiation: an A–Z Guide

Pocket World in Figures

The
Economist

MEGACHANGE

The world in 2050

Edited by

Daniel Franklin
with
John Andrews

THE ECONOMIST IN ASSOCIATION WITH
PROFILE BOOKS LTD

Published by Profile Books Ltd
3a Exmouth House
Pine Street
London EC1R 0JH
www.profilebooks.com

Typeset in EcoType by MacGuru Ltd
info@macguru.org.uk

Printed in Italy by L.E.G.O. S.p.A. - Lavis (TN)

A CIP catalogue record for this book is available from the British Library

Hardback ISBN: 978 1 84668 563 7
Paperback ISBN: 978 1 84668 585 9
ebook ISBN: 978 1 84765 805 0

FSC
www.fsc.org
MIX
Paper from
responsible sources
FSC® C023419

Contents

Contributors

Barbara Beck is *The Economist's* special-reports editor.

Geoffrey Carr is *The Economist's* science and technology editor.

Philip Coggan is the Buttonwood columnist and capital-markets editor of *The Economist*. He is the author of *The Economist Guide to Hedge Funds* and, most recently, *Paper Promises: Money, Debt and the New World Order*.

Simon Cox is *The Economist's* Asia economics editor, based in Hong Kong.

Tim Cross is a science correspondent at *The Economist*.

Kenneth Cukier is *The Economist's* data editor. Previously he was the newspaper's Japan business and finance correspondent, based in Tokyo.

Martin Giles is *The Economist's* US technology correspondent, based in San Francisco. He has covered business for the newspaper from New York, Paris and London.

Anthony Gottlieb is a New York-based writer. A former executive editor of *The Economist*, he is the author of *The Dream of Reason: A History of Philosophy from the Greeks to the Renaissance*.

Robert Lane Greene is *The Economist's* professional-services correspondent, based in New York. He also edits "Johnson", *The Economist's* blog on language, and is the author of *You Are What You Speak: Grammar Grouches, Language Laws, and the Politics of Identity*.

Charlotte Howard is *The Economist*'s health-care correspondent, based in New York. She was previously the newspaper's Midwest correspondent, based in Chicago.

Laza Kekic heads the Economist Intelligence Unit's regional team of analysts covering central and eastern Europe. He is also director of the EIU's Country Forecasting Service.

Edward Lucas edits *The Economist*'s international section. A former Moscow correspondent, he is the author of *The New Cold War: How the Kremlin Menaces Russia and the West* and, most recently, *Deception*, a book on east-west espionage.

Zanny Minton Beddoes is *The Economist*'s economics editor, based in Washington, DC.

Oliver Morton is *The Economist*'s briefings editor and was previously energy and environment editor. He is the author of *Eating the Sun: How Plants Power the Planet* and *Mapping Mars: Science, Imagination and the Birth of a World*.

John Parker is *The Economist*'s globalisation editor. His previous roles include bureau chief in Washington, Moscow and Brussels.

Matt Ridley is a former science and technology editor, Washington bureau chief and United States editor of *The Economist*. He is the author of several books, including, most recently, *The Rational Optimist: How Prosperity Evolves*.

Ludwig Siegele is *The Economist*'s online business editor. He was previously the newspaper's London-based technology editor.

Matthew Symonds is *The Economist*'s defence and security editor. His previous roles with the newspaper include industry editor and political editor.

Paul Wallace is *The Economist*'s European economics editor. He is the author of *Agequake: Riding the Demographic Rollercoaster Shaking Business, Finance and our World*.

Adrian Wooldridge is *The Economist*'s management editor and Schumpeter columnist. He is co-author of several books and, most recently, the author of *Masters of Management: How the Business Gurus and Their Ideas Have Changed the World – for Better and for Worse.*

The editors

Daniel Franklin is executive editor and business-affairs editor of *The Economist*. He is also the editor of *The Economist*'s annual publication on the year ahead, *The World in...*.

John Andrews has written for *The Economist* for more than 30 years and is deputy editor of *The World in ...*. He is the author of *The Economist Book of Isms.*

Introduction: meet megachange

Daniel Franklin

IT WAS 250,000 YEARS BEFORE the world's population reached 1 billion, around 1800. But it took only a dozen years for mankind to add its latest billion, passing 7 billion in October 2011, by the United Nations' official count. This is megachange: change on a grand scale, happening at remarkable speed. It is all around us. Technology is spreading astonishingly fast – think of the internet, mobile phones and the oceans of information now captured on computers or transmitted via social networks such as Facebook and Twitter. The global economy is tilting towards Asia in front of our eyes. All this is having a deep impact on people's lives, businesses' strategies, countries' politics and the planet's prospects.

One of the twin aims of this book is to identify and explore the great trends that are transforming the world, in everything from its health to its wealth. The idea is to cut through the usual clutter, topic by topic. What emerges with refreshing clarity is the big picture, the helicopter view.

The other aim is to look into the future, at how these developments might shape the world in 2050. This is, on the face of it, absurdly ambitious. History is littered with prophecies that turned out to be utterly wrong, as Dan Gardner damningly documents in his book *Future Babble*. "It is as certain as anything in politics can be, that the frontiers of our modern national states are finally drawn," wrote a British journalist, H.N. Brailsford, in 1914. "My own belief is that there will be no more wars among the six Great Powers." Soon afterwards the first world war broke out. "I expect to see the stock market a good deal higher within a few months," forecast Irving Fisher, an American economist, a week before the 1929 crash.

How can anyone know what the future holds? It is hard enough to predict what the weather will be like tomorrow, let alone in four decades' time. By then, the world will have witnessed successive flocks of "black swans", as Nassim Taleb, a writer on randomness, calls unpredictable developments.

Yet it is still worth having a guess. Looking ahead to 2050 is, strangely enough, easier than predicting what will happen next week or next year. Even Taleb is happy to peer a generation or so ahead: over such a period, he reasons, "anything fragile today will be broken." To return to the analogy of the weather, the forecast for next month is unlikely to be terribly reliable; but it would be downright irresponsible not to ask how weather patterns might change by 2050.

Besides, some pretty important aspects of the coming decades can be forecast with a fair degree of confidence. Take demography: though not quite destiny, it comes pretty close. It is an excellent starting point for thinking about the future. Indeed, it is where this book begins, with John Parker's magisterial overview of population trends.

Those trends reach into many of the other topics tackled in these pages. The 20 chapters, each written by a journalist from *The Economist* or a member of its extended family, cover a wide range of subjects, grouped into four broad categories: people, the planet, the economy and knowledge. Running through all of them are not only the theme of megachange but also a number of shared ideas about the future (including an appropriate humility about the fallibility of forecasts).

2050 vision

First, the contributors take more or less the same approach: to look ahead, you have first to look back. This helps to provide a clear idea of the nature and scale of change. It also gives a sense of the momentum behind it.

But that momentum may meet resistance. Hence a second common thread: a willingness to envisage disruption down the road, not simply a straight extrapolation of the past into the future. Nothing might seem more certain than continued destruction of the environment, yet Matt Ridley looks forward to a period of extensive ecological restoration and Oliver Morton explores the profound shifts that could follow from an alternative, risk-management way of thinking about climate change. Despite the flowering of faith in recent times, Anthony Gottlieb argues that religion will eventually weaken in the developing world. Charlotte Howard expects revolutions in genomics and health-care delivery to alter the dynamics of disease. Disruptive social change will flow from rapid development in the emerging world and, as Barbara Beck describes, from the rise in education and opportunities for women. Edward Lucas predicts that, strangely, over the next four decades democracy will advance in authoritarian countries but retreat in free ones.

As for economic matters, the rise in inequality in the rich world now seems relentless, yet it may well go into reverse in the coming decades, reckons Zanny Minton Beddoes. On current trends, states will become ever more bloated because of the rising costs of providing health care and pensions, but Paul Wallace expects reforms will eventually make states smarter and fitter. China's stunning surge is now taken for granted year after year, but by 2050, says Simon Cox, its annual growth rate will be around 2.5%.

That said, the rise of Asia in general, and China in particular, is a third strand that runs through much of this book. A great shift towards the East is taking place. This really is a case of back to the future: as Laza Kekic points out, by 2050 Asia will account for more than half the world economy, which is what its share was back in 1820 and for centuries before that. This will profoundly affect everything from the environment to the balance of military power and the centre of gravity of the global economy. Yet don't expect China to dominate everything by 2050. Mandarin, reckons Robert Lane Greene in his chapter on culture, will not replace English as a world language. Nor will Chinese scientists lead the world, believes Geoffrey Carr – or at least not unless China's political system changes to accept the sort of liberal intellectual environment that allows science to flourish.

Fourth, the authors tend to paint a picture of progress, in contrast to much of the predictions industry, which likes to wallow in gloom. Not that they see the future through rose-tinted crystal balls; far from it. They see enormous challenges ahead, from managing climate change and controlling conflicts over scarce resources such as water to feeding 9 billion people by 2050 and coping with the multitude of new security threats described by Matthew Symonds in his chapter on the future of war. Yet the pages that follow are, on the whole, optimistic. Or, at least, confident that with the right policies progress is possible on most fronts.

In other words, there is every chance that the world in 2050 will be richer, healthier, more connected, more sustainable, more productive, more innovative, better educated, with less inequality between rich and poor and between men and women, and with more opportunity for billions of people. The world will certainly be more urban (nearly 70% of its population will live in towns and cities, compared with just over half today), considerably older (the median age will rise from 29 to 38) and more African (roughly half of the planet's extra 2.3 billion people will be in Africa). Much of this change will come with wrenching upheaval. But as Adrian Wooldridge concludes, in contemplating the future of business: "The storms of creative destruction are blowing us to a better place."

New technologies will help – some as yet unimaginable but others already coming into view. Manufacturing may be revolutionised by "additive" techniques or three-dimensional printing that will make it routine to produce your own car parts. Medical miracles are likely to come from genetically targeted drugs, vaccines that do not need refrigeration during transport and stem cells that grow new tissues. Biology and robotics could combine to make it possible to revitalise paralysed limbs. As the boundaries between the real and virtual worlds blur, learning could be democratised by near-universal access to virtual Oxbridges and Harvards. Science fiction could even become 2050 fact: the rebirth of an extinct species is a distinct possibility. What's more, according to Tim Cross, the discovery of alien life is a pretty good bet.

These are just some of the possibilities to look forward to, and they point to one other thing these chapters have in common. They are brimming with (often counter-intuitive) ideas and data: myriad glimpses of a future that many will find surprising. By 2050, for example, France will be overtaking Germany in population, China's population will on average be older not only than America's but even than Europe's, while a booming Muslim Middle East could be reaping the economic benefits of a "demographic dividend". Nearly 400m Nigerians will be well on the way towards outnumbering Americans – and Nigeria could by then be one of the few big emerging markets to be growing at the sort of pace now associated with the BRICs (Brazil, Russia, India and China).

At a strategic level, NATO by 2050 may have gone out of business as a serious defensive coalition, and drones will have replaced manned aircraft for the majority of missions. Among the sciences, biology will rule, in fertile collaboration with nanoscience and information science. In the markets, the world will have witnessed more than one cycle of the sort described by Philip Coggan. For individuals, having your genome sequenced may be as common as having a blood test today. Learning a foreign language could be a little-used skill, almost as outdated as calligraphy, thanks to progress in computer translation. Individual intelligence will routinely be supplemented by collective intelligence, suggests Martin Giles, as a result of constant connectivity to social networks. Indeed, Kenneth Cukier argues, ubiquitous computing – chips in everything – will bring about the biggest change in how people live over the next four decades. In a world in which telecommunication has in effect killed distance, will physical location still matter? More than you might imagine, argues Ludwig Siegele.

All this is why the chapters that follow will stimulate and provoke a wide variety of readers. Corporate strategists, government policymakers and students of everything from biosciences to business will find rich pickings here. More broadly, this book will fascinate anyone with an interest in seeing today's news in its deeper context and with a curiosity about the possible news of the future.

That future does not have to be nearly as grim as prophets of doom would have you believe. Despite the many perils ahead and the undoubted difficulties of adjusting to megachange, the world in 2050 may not be such a bad place. If you are not convinced, turn to the final chapter, on predictions and progress. It will brighten your day, if not your decades.

PART 1

People and relationships

The dynamics of demography, health and culture

1 Not quite destiny

John Parker

**The population of the world is certain to increase – but is the
world prepared for the consequences?**

ON OCTOBER 31ST 2011, the world celebrated – if that is the term –
the birth of its seven-billionth living person. The United Nations had
declared that day to be the one on which the global population would
reach 7 billion and happy parents and publicity-seeking governments
rushed to claim the title for a particular newborn: Nargis Kumar, for
example, born at 7.25am local time in Mall village, in India's largest
state of Uttar Pradesh, or Danica May Camacho, born at the stroke of
midnight in Manila.

Adnan Nevic, who had been born in the Bosnian capital of
Sarajevo on October 12th 1999, was then two weeks past his 12th
birthday. He had been declared the six-billionth living person and
the dozen-year interval between his birth and that of baby Nargis
and baby Diana was the shortest-equal on record – equal, that is, to
the time that it took for the global population to rise from 5 billion to
6 billion between 1987 and 1999.

On this measure, the world's population is increasing faster than
it has ever done in human history. It took 250,000 years to reach
1 billion, more than a century after that to reach 2 billion (in 1927) and
33 years more to reach 3 billion. By 2050, the world will have over
9 billion people in it and the number will still be rising (see Figure 1.1).

The growth in certain countries has been and will continue to
be astounding. Nigeria in 1970 had 57m people. By 2050, unless its
fertility rate falls unexpectedly fast, it will have 389m – almost the
population of the United States then. Tanzania is growing faster still,

FIG 1.1 **People power**

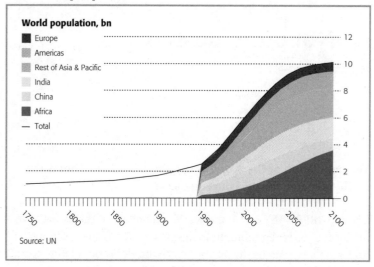

Source: UN

from 14m in 1970 to 139m in 2050. By 2100, they will be the third- and fifth-most-populous places on Earth.

Conversely, some national populations that are now among the world's largest will have hit their peak and be in decline. Russia's numbers have been falling since 1995. Japan's peaked at 126m in 2010. China's will peak at 1.4 billion in 2025, declining thereafter. Even India's population – the largest in the world in 2050 – is nearer its maximum size than most people realise: its peak, when it reaches 1.7 billion, will occur around 2060, declining thereafter.

Different growth rates will shift the weight of population living in different parts of the world. Asia will remain the most populous continent, with just over half the planet's people. But that is a significant drop from 2000, when two-thirds of mankind lived there. In 2000, sub-Saharan Africa and Europe had roughly the same number of people. By 2050, Africa will be almost three times Europe's size. Of the 2.3 billion increase in the world's population between 2010 and 2050, about half will be in Africa.

The global population in 2050 will be considerably older, as well as larger (see Figure 1.2). The segment aged over 65 will more than

Projections: how much salt to be added?

The population projections in this chapter come from the United Nations' population division, using the median forecasts published in 2011. They assume a continuation of the demographic trends of the past few decades. Unless the trends veer off unexpectedly, the projections for 2050 have a reasonable chance of accuracy. However, small differences in assumptions can have a big impact when compounded over many decades. The UN's high variant – which assumes higher fertility rates – projects population numbers about 12% above these figures. The low-variant projections are 8% below. Projections beyond about 2050 need to be taken with a bigger amount of salt.

double, from under 8% of the total in 2010 to over 16% in 2050. The so-called median age (the age at which exactly half the population is older and half younger) will rise by a full nine years in 2010–50, to 38, an increase that is unprecedented in terms of size and speed. In rich countries, many people will have a life expectancy of 100.

This older, larger population will also be much more urbanised (see Figure 1.3). Half the world's people lived in cities in 2010. By 2050 the share will be close to 70% and the cities of the world will contain about 6.5 billion people, the size of the whole world in 2005. Even by 2025, there will probably be 30 megacities of 10m people or more (in 1950 there were just two, the New York–Newark metropolitan area and Tokyo – see Figure 1.4). But the fastest growth will be in cities of 10m or fewer residents. McKinsey, a consultancy, reckons more than 400 such cities will lead growth in developing countries.

These trends will have the most profound effects both on people's family lives (mostly for the better) and also on their economic circumstances (not always for the better). In 1950 the world contained two distinct groups of countries in terms of life expectancy and family size: rich and poor. People in poor countries had much shorter life expectancies (only 37 years on average) and much larger families, often with six or more children. By 2050 there will still be

FIG 1.2 **Ever older**

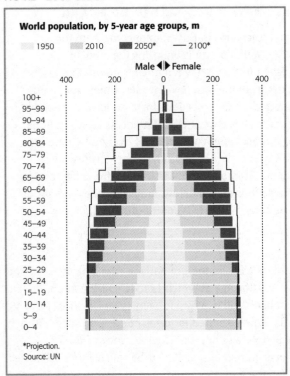

World population, by 5-year age groups, m

1950   2010   2050*   —— 2100*

Male ◀▶ Female

*Projection.
Source: UN

rich and poor countries, but in terms of life expectancy and family size there will no longer be two distinct groups. The world will have converged, with two-child families and life expectancies over 70 the near-universal norm.

This will transform what governments do and impose big new demands on public services. And it will change everything from business innovation and financial markets to the balance of power between the world's two most populous nations.

Comte and Malthus

Demography is destiny, said Auguste Comte, a French philosopher. But there is a big difference between demography meaning changes

FIG 1.3 **Going to town**

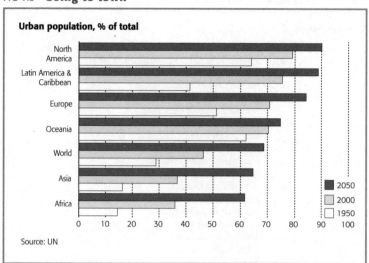

in the overall size of the population and demography in the sense of changes in the constituent parts of the whole – in the relative age and size of population groups, for example.

For many people, the important questions about population concern those overall numbers. Will the world be able to feed 9 billion mouths in 2050? Will the presence of so many people exceed the "carrying capacity" of the fragile Earth, and contribute to environmental degradation and planet-wrecking climate change? Will so many billions, jostling together cheek by jowl, go to war more frequently and deepen the bitter well of violence? These questions go to the core of the Malthusian worry that there are simply too many people – and the more people there will be in 2050, the worse off the world will become.

Yet, counter-intuitive though it may seem, these are not mainly demographic matters, and at a global level, trends in the overall size of the population will have variable effects. In some ways, Malthusian concerns are a distraction.

Consider the link between population and political violence. It seems intuitively plausible to think that the more people there are,

FIG 1.4 **A league of megacities**

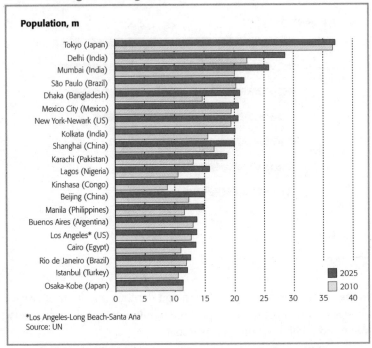

Population, m

Tokyo (Japan)
Delhi (India)
Mumbai (India)
São Paulo (Brazil)
Dhaka (Bangladesh)
Mexico City (Mexico)
New York-Newark (US)
Kolkata (India)
Shanghai (China)
Karachi (Pakistan)
Lagos (Nigeria)
Kinshasa (Congo)
Beijing (China)
Manila (Philippines)
Buenos Aires (Argentina)
Los Angeles* (US)
Cairo (Egypt)
Rio de Janeiro (Brazil)
Istanbul (Turkey)
Osaka-Kobe (Japan)

■ 2025
□ 2010

0   5   10   15   20   25   30   35   40

*Los Angeles-Long Beach-Santa Ana
Source: UN

the more likely they will be to come into conflict. This is especially true when the numbers of young men are growing, or when groups of people are competing for a fixed or scarce resource, such as water.

In some areas where population growth is exceptionally rapid, local conflicts do indeed seem likely. West Africa is one such. The Sahel and the waters of the Niger river are likely to come under extreme pressure. Pakistan and the Indus valley is another. Pakistan's population is likely to grow from 175m in 2010 to 275m by 2050 – and the water table in its main farming area, the Punjab, is disappearing rapidly. This could produce conflict directly, for control of scarce land or water, or indirectly, through migration and the spread of refugees. In 2008 there were just over 200m people living outside their place of birth, according to the International Organisation for Migration, making up 3% of the world's population. That number had doubled in the previous decade, and will rise further as people seek to leave poor, teeming countries for greener pastures.

But there is a difference between worrisome local conflicts and what is happening on a global scale. The world's population rose from 3 billion to 7 billion in the 50 years to 2010 (and the number of sovereign states increased almost as dramatically). But the number of wars between states fell during that period; the number of civil wars rose and then fell; and the number of deaths in battle fell from 20 per 100,000 people per year in the late 1940s to just 0.7 per 100,000 in the late 2000s, less than the homicide rate of the most peaceful societies.

This pattern of violence does not seem to have been influenced by the relentless pressure of population. Moreover, though the number of migrants rose in the first decade of the 21st century, the number of refugees or internally displaced people remained steady at around 10m. Indeed, the share of the migrant population which is most vulnerable to violence actually fell by half in 2000–10. What seems to have made a difference to levels of global violence is the decline in the number of post-colonial wars, the ending of cold-war conflicts and, possibly, the growth in the number and strength of international peacekeepers. If – obviously a big if – these trends were to continue, there seems no reason why a larger population in 2050 would necessarily be associated with greater levels of violence.

Something similar could be said about environmental damage. Almost all scientists accept that profound planet-wide changes have occurred: to the climate, to biodiversity, to levels of acidity in the oceans and to the nitrogen cycle (the process of converting nitrogen into its various forms). And human activity is overwhelmingly to blame. But it does not automatically follow that the more people there are, the worse all these forms of environmental damage will get. That depends on where and how people live.

In 2005 America and Australia each emitted almost 20 tonnes of carbon dioxide per person. In contrast, more than 60 countries – including the vast majority of African ones – emitted less than 1 tonne per person. The richest 7% of the world's population produce 50% of carbon emissions; the poorest 50% of the population produce 7% of the carbon. If these patterns remain unchanged, a doubling in the population of poorer countries would have a relatively minor impact on climate change, compared with the likely 30% rise in the population of the United States. To put it another way, stopping one American being born will have 20 times the environmental impact of stopping one birth in Africa.

Most of the world's population growth in the next 40 years will occur in countries that make the smallest contribution to greenhouse-gas emissions and will not automatically produce a big rise in carbon emissions or chemical pollution. It depends on how people live. If they become as energy-dependent as Americans or Australians, their growth will have huge environmental consequences. If not, the impact of growth will be smaller (though still large, given that poor countries have every intention of becoming richer and consuming more). Either way, how much fast-growing countries contribute to global warming will depend more on the pattern of economic growth than on patterns of population.

Population growth itself does make a bigger difference in a third area: food. Even people with the smallest carbon footprints have to eat. All things being equal, it will be harder to feed 9 billion than 8 billion. The extra numbers will create more competition for food and, all things again being equal, push prices up. Because there will be more people around in 2050, and because their appetite for meat will rise as they get richer and move to cities (ie, because meat becomes more affordable), the world will need to grow around 70% more food in the decades to 2050. Still, to put that into context, 70% is considerably less than the increase in global agricultural output that took place during the previous four decades, when cereal output went up 250%. The total amount of food needed by the growing population should, in theory, be a solvable problem.

Again, the more intractable constraints lie in other areas: slowdown of growth in agricultural yields after 1990 (yield has traditionally been seen as the main measure of success in farming); a scarcity of new farmland ready to be taken under the plough; chronic water shortages and the overuse of fertilisers; and climate change, which will tend to reduce yields almost everywhere, in many places by a third or more. All these mean there would be a problem feeding the world in 2050 anyway, even if the population were growing more slowly. The good news is that solutions exist (without draconian population controls): in more efficient use of water and other inputs; in better crop selection through genetic marking; in waste reduction; and so on. Such measures will have a bigger impact on feeding the world than moderating the growth in the world's population.

The implications of population size, then, are not as severe as Malthusians urge. But that does not mean population does not matter. It is relative changes – the growth of one section of the population compared with another, the average age and average family size – more than the absolute number of people that will make the difference.

Falling fertility

Of these relative changes, falling fertility is by far the most important. In 2050 the world's total fertility rate – roughly, the number of children a woman can expect to have during her childbearing years – will fall to 2.1. That is the "replacement rate" of fertility, at which a population exactly reproduces itself. The precise replacement rate varies somewhat from place to place, depending on infant mortality. It is somewhat higher in poor countries. But 2.1 is usually taken to be a magic number, the rate that causes a country's population to slow down and eventually to stabilise. This will probably be the first time in human history that the global rate is 2.1 or below. In all previous generations, when the population was stagnant or falling, the fertility rate was high, but balanced, or negated by, an even higher mortality rate.

A rate of 2.1 would represent a staggering fall. In 1970 the total fertility rate was 4.45 and the typical family in the world had four or five children. In 2010 the rate had plummeted to 2.45 (see Figure 1.5). Almost half the world's population – 3.2 billion out of 7 billion – were then living in countries where the rate was 2.1. By 2050 almost all nations outside Africa will be living at or below 2.1 and even many African ones will be around their replacement rates (which, because of infant mortality, may be higher than 2.1).

After 2050, the rate of population growth slows right down and begins to dwindle to zero. Even in 2010, the countries with below-replacement fertility included not just those well-known for low demographic growth, such as Japan and Russia, but those more usually associated with fast-rising populations, such as Brazil, Tunisia

FIG 1.5 **The family way**

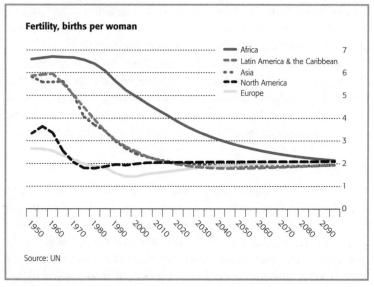

Fertility, births per woman

Source: UN

and Thailand. Some of the fertility declines have been staggering: Bangladesh's rate halved between 1980 and 2000; Iran's fell from 7 in 1984 to just 1.9 in 2006.

The fertility decline is likely to decelerate in future as it falls towards 2.1. In countries where it has long been below that – such as in northern Europe – fertility has already begun to bounce back; the rise will continue as people rediscover the joys of larger families. In parts of Africa, the fall in fertility has not been as marked as in other continents at comparable stages of wealth. But big declines will continue in other places: Brazil's fertility rate will dip to 1.7 in 2050; Ethiopia's, now 3.9, will fall to 1.9.

The fertility fall will release wave upon wave of demographic change. Most obviously, it will cause the world's population growth to slow right down. The rate of increase has been falling for a long time – peak growth was as far back as 1965–70, when it went slightly over 2% a year for the only time in modern history. But changes in the number of babies in one generation take another generation or more to show up in the overall numbers. The lag is about 20 years.

Because of this demographic inertia, the number of extra people in the world continued to rise for two decades after 1965–70, peaking in the late 1980s, when the overall population was rising each year by almost 90m people. The growth rate stayed relatively high after 1970, dropping sharply only in the 1990s as the impact of lower fertility began to be felt. So the number of extra people in the world will only now begin to slow down drastically. The annual increment, almost 78m in 2010–15, will fall to 52m in the late 2030s and to about 30m in the mid-2050s, only a third of what it was in the late 1980s. By that time, the rate of the world's annual population growth will be below 0.5% for the first time since about 1800. The huge and relentless increase in global numbers that began in Europe at the start of the Industrial Revolution and spread to every corner of the world will be over.

Cashing the demographic dividend

Lower fertility profoundly alters the balance between different age groups within a population. To simplify a good deal, a fall in fertility sends a generational bulge surging through a population, leaving a trail of changes in its wake. The generation in question is the one before declining fertility really begins to bite, which in Europe and America means what is commonly called the baby-boom generation, born between 1946 and 1964.

At the start, when the "bulge" generation is in its childhood, countries need to invest heavily in education and the other resources that children need. Typically, this is a period in a country's life with large families: lots of children scamper around but there are few grandparents (because they had been born at a time when life expectancy was lower). It is frequently – not always – a period when women stay at home to look after their family. That defines the situation in Europe in the 1950s, in East Asia in the 1970s and in Africa now.

But as the select generation grows up, it enters the labour force and, for about 40 years – an adult working life – a country benefits from a "demographic dividend". During this period there are relatively few children (because of the fall in fertility); relatively few older people (because of higher mortality earlier on); and lots of economically active adults (including, now, many women, who enter the labour force in large numbers). This is a period of smaller families, rising incomes and larger middle classes, of rapidly rising life expectancy and of big social change, including higher divorce rates, later marriage, more single-person households and (in some countries, at least) greater middle-class pressure on authoritarian rule. This was the situation in Europe in what the French term the "*trente glorieuses*" (1945-75) and in much of East Asia in 1980-2000.

After that, though, the golden generation turns silver and retires. Now, the dividend becomes a liability. There are disproportionately more old people needing the support of the smaller generation that is behind them. Moreover, if – as sometimes happens – the fertility rate has begun to rise again after a long period of below-replacement levels, the post-baby-boom generation faces a double burden: more pensioners to provide for and more grandchildren to raise and educate. This is a period in which populations start to fall, parts of a country are abandoned and the concerns of the aged grow in significance. This will be the situation in Europe and America in 2010-40, and in East Asia in 2030-50.

These generational shifts will have big economic consequences in the next four decades. Demography anyway has a large influence upon economic growth, because the presence of a large number of working-age adults increases the labour force, keeps wages relatively low, boosts savings and increases demand for new goods and services.

But this demographic dividend does not automatically generate growth. The question is whether the country can put a growing labour force to productive use. In the 1980s Latin America and East Asia had similar demographic patterns. East Asia enjoyed an economic miracle and Latin America experienced a "lost decade". But the dividend does make growth possible, and where a country or region can take advantage, contributes greatly to it. One study calculated that a third of East Asia's GDP growth in 1965-95 came from its favourable demography, notably the bulge in the labour force. And demographic contributions were not confined to East Asia. In the decade 2000-10, America's GDP rose about 3% a year, of which its increasing population contributed one percentage point.

Demography is likely to be a drag on growth in future, stronger in some places than in others. In East Asia, in 2010–20, demographic factors can be expected to contribute only about one percentage point to annual GDP growth, half the amount they contributed in 1995–2005, according to calculations by the Reserve Bank of Australia. In America, their annual contribution will be just 0.5 points of GDP (compared with 1.3 points before). In Japan they will be a drag on growth of about one point each year and in Germany the drag will be almost half a point (ie, because of demographic change, national output will be almost half a percentage point lower than it would otherwise have been).

This drag will get worse as time goes on. In the 40 years to 2010 the world as a whole reaped a demographic dividend thanks especially to developments in the rich world and East Asia. In 1970 there were 75 dependants (children and people over 65) for every 100 adults of working age in the world. In 2010 the number of dependants had dropped to 52 – a measure of the greater share of working people in the world and a primary source of growth. This helped boost economies, especially in China, where, under the influence of the one-child policy, the dependency ratio reached an unprecedentedly low level of 38 (in other words, the working-age population was not far short of double the size of the rest of the population). But by 2050 the world's "dependency rate" will have turned around and be back up to 58. This is not a huge reversal. The deterioration in 2010–50 will be only about a quarter of the improvement that took place in 1970–2010 (a six-point worsening compared with a 23-point gain). So the demographic "losses" over the next 40 years will be mild compared with the gains of the previous 40. Nevertheless, there will be losses for the first time. And in some countries and regions, the reversal will be dramatic.

Young, middle-aged and old

In the 40 years to 2010 every main region and country in the world except Japan saw an improvement in the ratio between working adults and the rest of the population. Some of the improvements were small, such as in Africa, where it was just six points, mainly

France v Germany

France's fear of its larger eastern neighbour has been one of the unspoken motivators of European politics for 100 years. When Napoleon dispatched his armies throughout the continent, France was Europe's most populous country, and able to recruit more young soldiers than anyone else. But German unification and declining French fertility in the 19th century changed that, so by 1918, at the Treaty of Versailles, the French prime minister, Georges Clemenceau, was worrying that "one can put all the clauses one wants in a treaty, one can take all the guns out of Germany, one can do whatever one likes, France will be lost because there will be no more Frenchmen." Between 1870 and 1945, France fought three wars to restrict German power and, after 1945, set up what became the European Union to contain the central European giant.

But over the next half-century, the balance will change, and France will become larger. As recently as 2000, Germany's population was 23m bigger than France's – 82m compared with 59m. Even now it is 20m larger. But with France's fertility rising and Germany's stuck at far below replacement levels, the French population is climbing, Germany's is falling, and the two will cross over just after 2050, according to the UN's projections. By 2060 the German population will have fallen to 72m, but France's will number 74m. By 2100 France will have 10m more people than its neighbour.

What the EU will look like then is anyone's guess. But if it is still driven by French fear of western Europe's most populous country, then the Anglo-French relationship will replace the Franco-German one as the thing to watch: in 2050 Britain's population will (briefly) overtake France's.

because of high fertility and so the large number of dependent children. Others were huge, such as in South-East Asia and North Africa, whose dependency ratios fell by 40 points. But even "ageing"

Europe and America ended the period with fewer people dependent on the working population.

That will change in 2010–50. Then, the world will become divided into three categories. The first will be the beneficiaries of continued demographic improvement: India, sub-Saharan Africa, and the Middle East and north Africa. Their dependency ratios will continue to fall, their median age, at less than 40 in 2050, will remain below the global average and they will have a large, cheap labour force.

In Africa and the Middle East, this will raise the stakes: more young workers will produce either more growth or – if they do not find work – more instability. Africa is already starting to show something like the demographic improvement that underpinned the economic transformation of East Asia in the 1980s and 1990s. Whether its public institutions are as competent and its policies as outward-looking as in East Asia remains to be seen.

The Middle East is slowly shaking off its youth bulge as the children of earlier periods of high fertility move into the workforce. The early stages of this process played an important role in the revolutionary tumult of the "Arab spring" of 2011. The process will continue in 2010–50 and prove a big challenge to the winners of the Arab spring, whether they be new regimes or old. Few economies with vast oil earnings have yet managed to generate large numbers of jobs. But Middle Eastern countries have certain advantages that East Asian ones did not have when they began their period of economic take-off. Educational levels in the Middle East are higher than they had been in Asia; elements of the middle class are already in place; and the educational gap between men and women is narrower. The emerging demographic dividend opens up the possibility – however unlikely it might seem today – that the Muslim Middle East will boom in the decades to 2050.

India should also see its growth continue. Its dependency ratio will continue to improve. It did not reap the same demographic dividend as China in 1970–2010 (it cut its total dependency ratio by 25 points compared with China's 39). But India's demographic patterns will be more favourable to growth than China's in the next four decades, when China's dependency rate will rise by 26 points and India's will fall by seven. This means the period of low-wage manufacturing and services will last much longer in India. In 2050 children and old people will still number less than half the working-age population, whereas in China they will be two-thirds of it. This does not necessarily mean India will outstrip China economically. India still has huge drawbacks: mass adult illiteracy (it is on its way to becoming the first society with equal numbers of university graduates and illiterate people); disproportionate numbers of young men (the result of a traditional preference for sons meeting a modern desire for small families and easily available sex-identification technology); and highly skewed demographic trends between north and south – the north being poor, illiterate and more populous, and the south richer, more entrepreneurial and with below-replacement fertility. Still, China's problems are even worse. In the perennial struggle between the two giants to outdo each other, demography seems to be on India's side.

The second group influenced by demographic change will consist of those countries that see only a modest deterioration in their dependency ratios (20 points or fewer) and a rise in the median age to between 40 and 48. These include the United States, Latin America and South-East Asia. America's demographic profile has long been more stable than Europe's, thanks to relatively higher fertility in the 1980s and 1990s (contributed to by, but not solely the result of, Latino immigrants). Its dependency rate was slightly higher than Europe's in 1970; in 2010 the two sides of the Atlantic had similar rates but, assuming American fertility remains relatively high, the United States will have a dependency nearly ten points lower (ie, better) than Europe's in 2050.

The big losers from the demographic patterns of 2010–50 will be Europe, Japan – and China. The share of the old-age population in Japan has long been the biggest in the world and it is getting bigger. Japan's dependency rate will deteriorate by a staggering 40 points in 2010–50. By 2050 the country will have almost as many dependants as working-age adults. No society has seen such a thing before. Japan will then be the oldest society ever known, with a median age of 52.3 (ie, half the population will be aged over 52). Europe's dependency will not rise as far but it will still be the next highest (and there will be little difference between western and eastern Europe).

It is far from clear how these countries will react. It seems plausible to think that, just as working-age adults tend to be associated with greater business risk, more innovation, more new-household formation and higher savings and equity ownership, so older societies will be more risk-averse in business and asset ownership (preferring government bonds to equities, for instance). But there is no certainty about that.

Nor is it clear how these countries will bear the burden of ageing. Even large and sustained increases in fertility would fail to reverse the ageing trends for at least two decades. Extremely large migration flows would help both by providing younger workers to look after pensioners and by increasing – for a while – the fertility rate (immigrants from countries with high fertility tend to have larger families for a while, but eventually, the immigrants' family patterns tend to match their host country's). This would require large and painful shifts in social attitudes. But at least these countries' level of income gives them some room for manoeuvre.

Far more constrained is China. With fertility artificially suppressed by the one-child policy, it is ageing at an unprecedented rate. China's median age rose from 22 years in 1980 (characteristic of a developing country) to 36 in 2010 (characteristic of a rich one). China will be older than America in 2020 and older than Europe in 2040. This will bring to an end its period of cheap-labour manufacturing. The Chinese are right to worry that they will get old before they get rich.

They also face massive problems of sexual imbalance because the one-child policy, a traditional preference for sons and sex-selective abortion have combined to produce a generation of what the Chinese call "bare branches": unattached young men. In 2025 there will be 97m men in their 20s (and therefore of marriageable age) but only 80m young women, a worse ratio even than India's. But scrapping the one-child policy may be ineffectual: social support for small families and low fertility have become entrenched and may persist. So China is likely to starting importing large numbers of young women as brides for its "bare branches" (as richer Asian countries have already done). Because China is so huge, the migration of young women would have to take place in huge numbers. This would be extremely disruptive to family life elsewhere – and even then could not plug the sexual gap caused by generations of gendercide. Demography itself has a good claim to being the biggest problem the Communist Party will face in the next 40 years.

Yet even this is not the biggest change that China, East Asia, the Middle East and much of the developing world will face because of demography. Emerging markets have benefited from the sort of dividend that changed Europe and America generations before. These countries have emulated – and will catch up with – the West in terms of income, family size, education and the formation of a middle class. Most of them say they want to keep their traditions of filial piety and family order unsullied by contact with Western values, Western mores and the trends that accompanied greater wealth in America and Europe, such as divorce, single-parent families and a greater stress on individual freedom of expression. Yet it is hard to see how they can stop these things from happening. In some of Asia's largest cities a quarter of women in their early 30s have never been married – an astonishing rejection of tradition in societies where the vast majority of adults always used to get married, often very young. Hundreds of millions of young Asians have migrated to cities or foreign countries, leaving their children to be brought up by grandparents, not within the confines of the immediate nuclear family as was always the case in the past. Such trends will probably accelerate in future.

If you look at the changing size of the world's population, then, the picture is one of growing stability and a return to the flat population growth of the 17th and 18th centuries. Below that statistical surface, though, tensions are growing, the traditions of family life and the balance between generations are shifting, and societies are being churned up in ways never seen in the more static pre-modern world. In the decades to 2050 these changing demographic patterns will, perhaps more than anything else, shape how the world changes – politically, economically and socially.

2 The health of nations

Charlotte Howard

Sickness and disease are part of the human condition. There will be stunning advances in health care in the coming decades – and many new challenges

IN 1980 NO ONE HAD HEARD of acquired immune deficiency syndrome. The term did not exist. But the virus that causes AIDS, having long festered in chimpanzees, had already jumped to humans. In June 1981 America's Centres for Disease Control and Prevention (CDC) sounded a muted alarm, using a few short paragraphs to describe a rare pneumonia in five gay men in Los Angeles. Some reporters warned of "gay cancer"; in 1982 the CDC coined the term AIDS. Cases were reported in Australia and Mexico, South Africa and China. By 1992 AIDS was the leading cause of death for American men aged 25–44. The 1990s brought fervent research, frustration and public campaigns. A quilt in memory of AIDS victims cloaked the National Mall in Washington, DC. In 2001 the world's leaders gathered at the United Nations, vowing to reverse the epidemic.

Happily, they have made progress. The number of new infections in 2009 was 19% lower than it was ten years earlier. Antiretroviral therapy (ART) has transformed the disease from an untreatable killer to a chronic condition, and with improved drugs the infection rate will continue to drop. Even more exciting would be the development of an HIV vaccine. More than 33m people were living with HIV in 2009 – but the burden is not shared evenly. Nearly 20% of South African adults are infected with HIV, compared with 0.6% of Americans and 0.2% of Britons. Too few patients receive treatment; and the rate of new infections is still too high. But in only a few decades, a deadly

FIG 2.1   **California living**

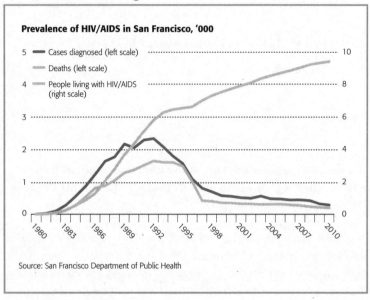

Prevalence of HIV/AIDS in San Francisco, '000

- Cases diagnosed (left scale)
- Deaths (left scale)
- People living with HIV/AIDS (right scale)

Source: San Francisco Department of Public Health

disease has followed an arc from terror and confusion to action and hope (see Figure 2.1 for this 30-year pattern in San Francisco). Think of the threats and discoveries that the next four decades will bring.

There remains the fear of the unknown – the next pandemic, say, or a superbug so powerful as to render our medicinal swords mere toothpicks. Trends that would seem to have nothing to do with health, such as climate change and urbanisation, may have a profound impact on it, particularly in the poor world. In the rich one, a difficult battle is being fought to curb obesity among children: if the battle is lost, a generation will be doomed to a life of chronic disease. And politicians meanwhile will argue bitterly over how to pay for the care of the old.

The flip side of this anxiety is excitement. Already, as the 21st century unfolds, the field of health is brimming with anticipation. Companies are working to develop new technologies that will make health care better, cheaper and more accessible. Scientists are trying to unlock the secrets in our genetic code. Over the next 40 years, an army of demons may assault mankind – but science and hard work may yet overcome them.

Out with the old

Of the many problems facing global health in the first half of the 21st century, one set is particularly ripe for action: the ailments that have been banished from the rich world but still plague the poor one. For these illnesses, a lack of science is not the problem. Simply deploying existing technologies, according to the Bill and Melinda Gates Foundation, could shrink the number of deaths of young children by half by 2025.

The most obvious targets are ailments for which there are vaccines. Some 2m children die each year from vaccine-preventable illnesses. History suggests that this might be stopped. After successful vaccine programmes, the World Health Organisation (WHO) in 1980 declared that smallpox had been eradicated (it exists now only in laboratories). Or take polio. In 1952 polio paralysed or killed more than 24,000 Americans a year. Today an iron lung, used to maintain breathing, seems as old-fashioned as a leech. Rich countries rid themselves of polio decades ago. This is not true of developing countries, but it should be well before 2050. The number of polio cases has shrunk by 99% over the past two decades, to fewer than 3,000 cases each year.

The tide of several other ailments should ebb as well. Pneumonia and diarrhoeal disease are the two biggest killers of children under five years old, responsible for 18% and 15% of their deaths in 2008, according to the WHO. Deploying vaccines broadly could have a profound effect. The challenge will be to get vaccines and treatments to those who need them, and to do so cheaply.

Technology will help. Scientists have so far struggled to produce vaccines that do not need to be refrigerated during transport. By 2050 such vaccines will be common. Companies will make vaccines simpler to administer: one patch, for example, might deliver many vaccines at once, eliminating the need for multiple trips to a health clinic. The cost of a drug will drop as the supply chain continues to be transformed, with research and production spreading to what is now the developing world.

FIG 2.2 **They will survive**

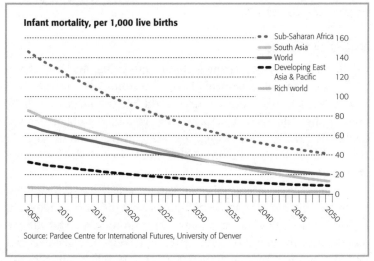

Source: Pardee Centre for International Futures, University of Denver

These developments will contribute to dramatic changes in health outcomes. Infant mortality in poor countries will fall further, and life expectancy will rise (see Figures 2.2 and 2.3).

For many diseases, the most effective battle plan will include both old and new weapons. Malaria has plagued humanity for millennia, with the offending parasite delivered by mosquitoes. Man has tried various ways to fend off these tiny attacks (because scientists in the 1930s discovered that British mosquitoes preferred hog blood rather than the human variety, they urged that pigs be placed under beds, according to Sonia Shah, author of *The Fever*). More recent tactics have included bed nets, walls treated with insecticide and malarial treatment drugs – with decent effect. The death toll from malaria dropped from 985,000 in 2000 to 781,000 in 2009. In 11 African countries malaria cases or deaths dropped by more than half over the same period. Eradicating the disease, a goal set by the Gates Foundation, now might be feasible: research on malaria vaccines, paid for in part by the foundation, is showing promise. Positive results could mark a turning-point in the fight against an ancient foe.

The battle against a newer enemy, AIDS, is more complex. The

FIG 2.3 **Many happy returns**

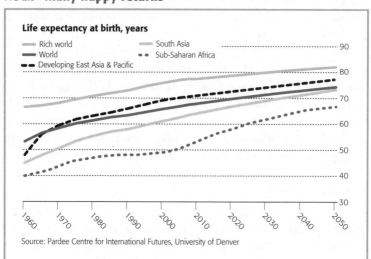

Life expectancy at birth, years

Source: Pardee Centre for International Futures, University of Denver

first challenge is to treat patients who already have HIV. Without any changes in treatment prices, caring for the 33m people with AIDS today will cost $40 billion each year for the rest of their lives, a financial burden that neither the rich nor the poor world will be ready to shoulder. The second challenge is to stop new infections. A variety of methods may help to suppress rates of transmission, including condoms, circumcision and a new microbicide in the form of vaginal gel.

But it may be that treatment will prove the best tool for prevention. At least one mode of transmission, from mother to child, should be all but eliminated by giving infected mothers ART. Treatment may also prevent sexually active adults from spreading the disease. In May 2011 America's National Institutes of Health announced a remarkable finding: HIV patients who received treatment soon after diagnosis were 96% less likely to pass on the virus to their sexual partners.

The most transformative discovery, however, would be a vaccine. Researchers from Kenya to Maryland are working feverishly to develop one.

Progress on these fronts will not be steady. The most trivial forces can knock advances off course. In 2003 Nigeria was gripped by a rumour that the West was using polio vaccines to sterilise Nigerian girls. Polio rates surged.

The biggest threat is that the world's commitment will waver. Economic problems in rich countries may sap their appetite for helping the poor. Money may be wasted on futile efforts. If the world spends its cash wisely, however, there is a good chance that technological advances will wipe out one or two diseases and shrivel the death toll for others. For these scourges, the next few decades will bring a reckoning. For others, they will be a golden era.

In with the new

Each epidemic is a product of its time, a theory that dates back to Plutarch in the second century AD. As Madeline Drexler describes in *Emerging Epidemics*, Mongol armies, with their attendant rodents, brought bubonic plague from Asia to Europe. The Spanish conquistadors unleashed smallpox on the New World. Tuberculosis, caused by bacteria happiest in filth, thrived in the Industrial Revolution. The first half of the 21st century may, in its turn, launch a host of maladies.

One reason will be continued urbanisation. In 2010 just over half of the world's population lived in cities; by 2050 some 70% will, mostly in the crowded metropolises of the developing world. Infection will travel rapidly through dense slums and inadequate sanitation will exacerbate the problem. So will climate change: rising temperatures will bring a longer breeding season for mosquitoes.

Napoleonic micro-organisms seeking global domination will be helped by an ever more connected world. An increasingly international food chain will bring pathogens from a foreign field to your local market. Airlines already carry more than 2 billion passengers each year, making the spread of a disease from one continent to another as simple as a mosquito hitching a ride on a Boeing 747 – which may have been how in 1999 West Nile virus arrived in New York.

Most worrying will be the maladies that do not yet exist. Since the 1970s new diseases have arrived at a rate of one or more each year, according to the WHO. The next epidemic may well be a virus that has its origins in the wild, and then hops gingerly from beast to man. SARS, HIV/AIDS, Ebola, West Nile – all began in wild animals.

Pandemic influenza remains the most daunting threat. Two main factors make influenza particularly dangerous. First, it is among the nimblest of viruses. One strain mutates and swaps genes with another, occasionally resulting in a strain against which humans have no defence. The second problem is that, once a strain exists, it can easily spread. Malaria needs a mosquito as its middleman. Influenza needs no such inefficiency, spreading from man to man on the wave of a sneeze. H1N1, otherwise known as swine flu, was identified in North America in April 2009. Within six weeks it had spread to 69 countries.

The question is not whether a new pandemic will emerge, but when and how the world will respond. In the long term, changes in technology will help: the old way of developing flu vaccines – over months, using lots and lots of chickens' eggs – will be replaced by nimbler methods that use plants or cell cultures. Most promisingly, scientists are working to develop a universal vaccine; one influenza vaccine, in future, might protect us for life.

In the meantime, the challenge will be to contain a virus before it spawns a pandemic. Google.org is already trawling internet-search data for early signs of an outbreak. Nathan Wolfe, founder of the Global Viral Forecasting Initiative, imagines a decentralised "immune system" gathering lab tests and other data to spot unusual sickness. Cheap DNA sequencing will help to identify dangerous new viruses quickly.

Just as frightening as a new virus is the threat that familiar foes will become invincible. The spectre of a superbug, impervious to man's scientific advances, is more than 60 years old. In 1945 Alexander Fleming, who had accidentally discovered penicillin in 1928 (mass production, thanks to the work of Howard Florey and Ernst Chain, began only in the second world war), gave warning that the misuse of antibiotics might speed the evolution of resistant microbes. Fleming's prophecy came true rather quickly. By 1946 a British hospital said that 14% of *Staphylococcus aureus* infections were resistant to penicillin. By the 1990s more than 80% were. In the 21st century vast factory farms have become evolutionary accelerators: farmers use antibiotics to fatten animals faster, providing a perfect environment for bacteria to mutate and swap genes – and creating the ability to fend off antibiotics.

Cassandras can imagine a dire future (though some biologists argue that, for a bug, developing resistance is costly, and therefore likely to be self-limiting). A skinned knee could become a grave medical problem. Surgeries now considered commonplace could become deadly. And it is not just bacteria that are developing resistance. Parasites and viruses are too – witness the new strains of malaria and HIV that are resistant to drugs developed to deal with them.

It is unclear how scientists will defuse this looming disaster. Better surveillance might catch a new strain early; officials could then provide guidelines to prevent misuse of a given antibiotic. Or pharmaceutical companies could create a new quiver of antibiotics to replace the old, useless ones. Unfortunately, companies do not seem likely to act. According to the WHO, eight of the 15 big drug companies that once invested in new antibiotics research have abandoned their programmes. Two other firms have shrunk them. Just over a decade into the 21st century, Big Pharma is more interested in treating the ailments that you do not catch.

I am 70, older and wider

The unknown, be it in the form of a superbug or pandemic influenza, is certainly ominous. No less intimidating, however, are two trends that are entirely predictable. First, the world will become much greyer. In 2050 the population aged 60 and over will reach 2 billion, three times larger than it was as the beginning of the millennium. Second, the world looks set to grow much fatter.

The rich world leads the poor in these two, unenviable respects. The median age in developed regions in 2000 was 37 years, compared with 24 in less developed ones. Similarly, adults in rich countries are more than twice as likely to be overweight (see Figure 2.4). These trends bring a mass of health problems. Obesity wreaks havoc in the form of diabetes and heart disease (see Figure 2.5). An ageing population must grapple with cancer and other ailments that plague a weakened body. Most challenging may be the illnesses of the mind.

FIG 2.4 **Bigger ...**

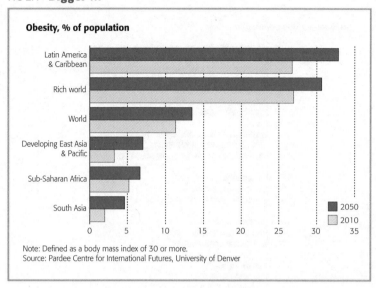

Obesity, % of population

Note: Defined as a body mass index of 30 or more.
Source: Pardee Centre for International Futures, University of Denver

FIG 2.5 **... but not better**

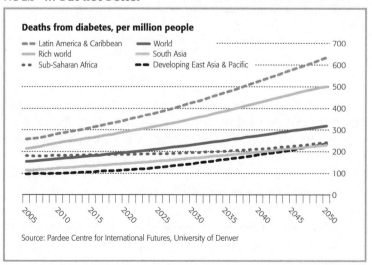

Deaths from diabetes, per million people

Source: Pardee Centre for International Futures, University of Denver

FIG 2.6 **Cause for thought**

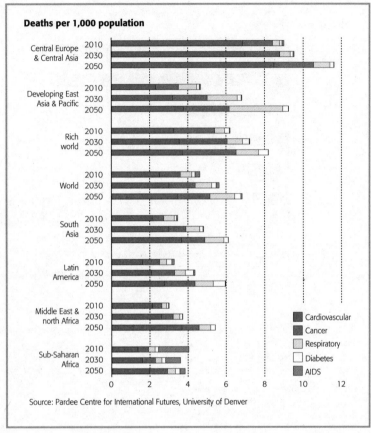

Deaths per 1,000 population

Legend:
- Cardiovascular
- Cancer
- Respiratory
- Diabetes
- AIDS

Source: Pardee Centre for International Futures, University of Denver

Today 5.4m Americans have Alzheimer's disease, according to the Alzheimer's Association, an advocacy group. By 2050 that number may mushroom to 16m. Other forms of dementia will similarly become more common as the population ages. The result will be financial pressure on governments – and a huge incentive for the pharmaceutical industry to develop palliatives, or even prophylactics and cures.

But it will not be the rich countries alone that struggle with these problems. Among the most striking developments of the 21st century will be the spread of chronic conditions from rich regions to poor (see Figure 2.6). By 2050 some 85% of those older than 60 will live in what are now poor countries. The incidence of cancer is expected to grow by 82% in poor countries by 2030, compared with a 40% increase in rich ones. Even in Africa, the WHO expects non-communicable diseases to become the most common cause of death by 2030.

In developing regions, urbanisation will increase the risk of chronic disease. New residents will be more sedentary than they were in rural areas. They will have better access to cigarettes, pollution and junk food. The accompanying – and inevitable – health woes may be exaggerated in urban slums. Already in wealthy countries, it is the poor neighbourhoods that foster chronic illness: in Spanish cities, for example, diabetes rates are nearly three times higher in poor areas than in rich ones. The enormous shanty towns of the developing world will doubtless follow a similar pattern.

These trends will place poor countries in a tough predicament: trying to fight chronic diseases while still battling infectious ones. Some cities are already struggling with this double burden. In the slums of Kolkata, infectious diseases are the leading cause of death for young children; for adults over 40, heart disease and cancer are the main culprits.

Today's health systems in the developing world are poorly equipped to respond. The rich world has ten times as many doctors per person as the poor world. Foreign donors often funnel their help through narrow programmes, such as one for HIV/AIDS, while broader health systems remain weak. In the absence of health insurance, many patients have to pay out of their own pockets for treatment, with a devastating effect on family finances.

To deal with the century's new challenges, health systems in both rich and poor countries must be strengthened and insurance expanded. Even then, however, tackling problems of ageing and chronic and infectious diseases will be difficult with today's technologies. Thankfully, by 2050 science will have transformed care itself.

Medicine on the march

The history of medicine is one of bumpy progress. The discovery of a smallpox vaccine in the 18th century led to the elimination of the disease two centuries later. Changes in sanitation in the 19th century helped to shrivel the threat of cholera in the rich world. Fleming's serendipitous discovery of penicillin transformed the treatment of infection. Today new threats may undermine progress, as in the case of superbugs. Some fear that bioterrorists may unleash the smallpox virus. But this chapter has already discussed ways in which technology will help to overcome new enemies: through Wolfe's immune system, for example, or through vaccines to prevent AIDS and malaria.

The most transformative developments, however, will fall into two categories. The first will be a revolution in the way that health care is delivered. In 2011 patients spend days in hospital after surgery. Nurses tend to the old at home. Mothers in developing countries travel for hours for simple health services. Diabetics grapple with finger pricks, insulin pumps and trips to the dialysis clinic. By 2050 such tools will seem impossibly clunky.

In developing countries, devices that are portable, inexpensive and simple to use will compensate for a shortage of health workers. A machine might test a patient for a variety of diseases, such as dengue fever, malaria and tuberculosis. Some devices will judge the symptoms themselves; others might connect the patient to a remote team of doctors for diagnosis. Variations in care, a problem in both rich and poor countries, will be dramatically reduced. Health workers will have easy, constant access to medical guidelines, updated continuously to reflect advances in knowledge.

The treatment of both acute and chronic conditions will involve much less work. Surgeries will become ever rarer, as tiny devices trawl our insides to remove a tumour, for example, or repair an organ. A diabetic might have an implanted pump that automatically releases insulin when needed. Those living alone in old age will be able to do so with dignity, with their health monitored in the same way as the temperature in our homes. Sensors will detect not only whether a patient has fallen, but also whether he or she has taken the right

New heart? No problem

The next 40 years will bring innovations unimaginable at present. But progress today does provide a hint of what may be to come.

No field of research is more exciting – or controversial – than that of stem cells. Embryonic stem cells have the intoxicating ability to replicate any type of tissue in the body. Coaxing stem cells into action will transform our bodies' ability to heal. Scientists are also testing ways to transform one kind of adult cell into another – such programming might, for example, help to mend a damaged heart.

Other technologies promise to repair ailing bodies in different ways. The nerves that once controlled real arms can already be rewired to control fake ones; in future amputees' control of their new limbs will become much more advanced and the technology itself more widespread, as will technology to help paraplegics regain movement of their own arms and legs. Those who need a new kidney will have a much easier time acquiring it, thanks to new manufacturing techniques involving 3D printers that lay thin cells on top of one another to create complex organs. Eventually, it may even become possible to "print" organs within the body.

A surge in vaccine research, meanwhile, holds new hope for illnesses that have long eluded researchers, such as cancer and addiction. Some ailments may prove more stubborn. Scientists have hoped they might fight Alzheimer's disease by targeting sticky plaques in the brains of those with dementia. Despite hundreds of millions of dollars-worth of research, treatment has been elusive. New tests to diagnose Alzheimer's earlier – and identify healthy people at risk of the disease – will surely help. Most promising, however, may be a step taken in 2010. The world's biggest drugmakers said they would share data from their failed trials, to better understand what went wrong. In learning from defeat they may, in time, find success.

pills or slept well. Simple tests will measure cognitive abilities. An implanted device might measure sugar levels and blood-cell counts. If any unusual data emerge, a signal will alert a nurse or doctor. Such systems will create a new paradigm. More people may be old and sick; new devices will ensure that they do not feel that way.

The second set of advances will have an even greater impact, as they will help us understand illness itself. Despite medicine's progress, many diseases remain a mystery, their root causes obscured. Genomics will change that.

In 2000 two sets of scientists announced that they had sequenced the human genome. The achievement laid bare our genetic code; reporters wrote that this would expose the secrets of disease and herald a new era of personalised medicine. Today that promise is still unfulfilled. Scientists know that the genome contains a trove of information. But, as David Altshuler, a director of America's Broad Institute, explains, "It's a book written in a language we don't know how to read."

Over time, however, scientists will become better translators. Altshuler's Broad Institute, a collaboration between Harvard University and the Massachusetts Institute of Technology, is one of the world's top genetics laboratories and work there and at other research centres is proceeding apace. Some sticky questions will arise from what they find in the genome's text. Expectant parents with rare genetic ailments can already test their embryos for the presence of disease. In future, parents will be able to test for a range of qualities. Which embryo might go on to develop an agile brain? Might their little one have a big nose? Parents may even be able to engineer certain traits to their liking.

These issues will prompt serious debate. But they will be dwarfed by genomics's main gift, the illumination of disease. A new generation of cancer drugs already attacks specific genetic mutations that drive specific cancers. This science will continue to advance, as will the understanding of many other diseases. Most illnesses are complex, caused by an intricate blend of factors. But in future, Altshuler predicts, having our genome sequenced will be as common as having a blood test or an x-ray. It will be a powerful tool to discover what ails us, and how we might get better.

It is easy to expect too much of genomics – or any scientific advance, for that matter. "There's always a hope," says Altshuler, "that the next technology will take the common scourges of man and turn them into very simple problems." This will not happen. We will continue to age. Viruses will continue to evolve. Diseases will continue to cripple people and states. But, faced with old and new maladies, man will have more ways to fight them than ever before.

3 Women's world

Barbara Beck

Women hold up half the sky, as Mao Zedong put it, but they will need time – especially in developing countries – to be equally rewarded

IN THE OLD TESTAMENT BOOK OF LEVITICUS, the Lord gives Moses guidance on the redemption tax payable to the priests by those who have devoted themselves to the service of God but wish to be released:

> Speak unto the children of Israel, and say unto them ... thy estimation shall be of the male from 20 years old even unto 60 years old, even thy estimation shall be 50 shekels of silver ... And if it be a female, then thy estimation shall be 30 shekels.

Throughout most of recorded time women have been valued less than men and have played only a shadowy part in the affairs of nations. The history of the world is the history of men. There was Eve, of course, and plenty of goddesses: half a pantheon of them in ancient Greece and Rome, but the boss was male. There were Amazons, a terrifying though mystical tribe of female warriors. There is even said to have been a female pope, Joan or John, perhaps in the 9th century, who pretended to be a man to get the job, but she, too, was probably the stuff of legend. And dotted throughout history there were some real queens without kings attached, from Cleopatra and Boudica to Elizabeth I and Victoria. But they were rare and invariably got there through family connections.

So will things be different by 2050? Will women finally attain equal value and status with men? And, if so, will their rise to equality be a universal phenomenon or one confined by geographical limits, with women in developing countries still undervalued in comparison with their rich-world sisters? Part of the answer will come from examining how far women have advanced to date, especially in the West.

Until relatively recently most women in most places were expected to stay behind the scenes and be wives and mothers. There have always been exceptions: artists, entertainers, writers, adventuresses who travelled to exotic places. But they needed to be remarkable individuals to succeed, and they were few and far between. For women as a whole, the push for equal rights did not start until the Enlightenment. When Mary Wollstonecraft, an early British feminist, published her treatise *A Vindication of the Rights of Woman* in 1792, women were still thought to be the weaker sex, both in body and in mind, in need of protection by fathers, brothers or husbands. The laws on inheritance usually disadvantaged them. On marriage they had to relinquish legal and property rights (if they had them in the first place). Remaining unmarried was no solution because they would have no social standing and no means of support.

The Victorian age with its rigid moral codes did women no favours, even though a female monarch sat on the British throne for most of the 19th century. John Stuart Mill, a philosopher, was still ahead of his time when making a strong case for sexual equality in his essay on "The Subjection of Women", published in 1869. Queen Victoria herself wrote in 1870:

> Let women be what God intended: a helpmate for man, but with totally different vocations and duties.

From the late 19th century the legal position of women gradually improved, but in some countries it was not until nearly a century later that they enjoyed full equality in civil law.

Aux armes, citoyennes

Political rights were just as slow in coming. The debate about universal suffrage in the 19th century was mainly about extending the franchise for men rather than giving it to women, although from the end of the 19th century the suffragettes started mounting the barricades. Most Western countries gave full voting rights to women only in the 20th century, many of them after the first world war in recognition of women's contribution to the war effort, but some much later. Switzerland got round to it only in 1971 and Portugal not until 1976 (see Table 3.1). Nor is the process yet complete: a number of countries, mainly in the Arab world, still do not allow women to vote, though change is coming there too: even Saudi Arabia has said it will allow women to vote (albeit only in municipal elections). Globally, fewer than 20% of seats in parliament are held by women (with America at a surprisingly low 17%, though the Nordic countries and the Netherlands have got close to half). Ministerial jobs go mainly to men, and female leaders such as Margaret Thatcher in Britain in the 1980s and now Angela Merkel in Germany and Dilma Rousseff in Brazil remain the exception.

TABLE 3.1 **Voting rights for women**

Country	Year achieved
Finland	1906
Norway	1913
Denmark	1915
Netherlands	1919
Germany	1919
US	1920
Canada	1920
Sweden	1921
UK	1928
Spain	1931
France	1944
Italy	1945
Greece	1952
Switzerland	1971
Portugal	1976

Source: Françoise Thébaud (ed.), *A History of Women in the West*, The Belknap Press of Harvard University Press, 1996

When societies were mainly agricultural, poorer women worked in farming as well as bringing up their families, and some kept shops or inns, but the range of occupations open to them was limited. It widened somewhat with the Industrial Revolution, when many of them moved into the textile mills and factories. In England a census in 1841 showed that 23% of women and girls were in employment, the vast majority of them concentrated in domestic service, textiles and farming. Opportunities were gradually increasing: that same census (the first to list women's jobs separately) also counted 469 female blacksmiths, 389 carpenters and joiners, and 125 chimney sweeps. Later in the 19th century women were increasingly able to take up clerical jobs too.

But it was the first world war that gave the women of the belligerent nations their big opportunity to move into previously male occupations. While the men were at the front, women were driving trams and working in offices, banks, shops and munitions factories – and being paid good money for their efforts. In Europe the proportion of women in the labour force rose significantly; in America, which entered the war late, the effect was slight. But the principle that women were perfectly capable of doing a wide range of jobs had been established, and the experience had a huge effect on their image of themselves. All the same, after the war most of the surviving men reclaimed their jobs and most of the women went back to the kitchen and the nursery. The usual pattern was for young females of modest means to work until they got married or, at the latest, when the first child appeared. The better-off still generally led lives of leisure.

Only a couple of decades later the second world war brought millions of women back into the labour force to replace the men sent into battle, and once again when the fighting was over they went home to bear lots of children to make up for the losses inflicted by the war. The result was a generation of baby-boomers – more numerous, better educated and more confident than its predecessors – that is only now beginning to retire.

The widespread adoption of labour-saving technology in the home from the start of the 1950s (refrigerators, cookers, washing machines) did not immediately lead more women to take paid jobs:

instead, it allowed them to turn their homes into gleaming temples to domesticity. As mobility increased, fewer people lived with their extended family, so the new model became the nuclear family with a breadwinner husband, a homemaker wife and several well-scrubbed children.

Well-schooled for a better future

But not for very long. From the 1970s women in rich countries started moving into the labour market in ever greater numbers. One big reason was that they now were much better educated. Once again, this took a while to come about. In America compulsory primary-school attendance for both sexes did not start until around 1830; some European countries got round to it earlier, some later. But education for girls gathered pace, and now mandatory schooling for both sexes for at least ten years from age five or six is universal in developed countries. Even in the developing world 78% of girls are now enrolled in primary schools, against 82% for boys (though women still account for two-thirds of the world's 770m illiterate adults).

Secondary and particularly tertiary education for women took even longer to spread. Harvard, Oxford and Cambridge opened their first women's colleges in the 1860s and 1870s, but Oxbridge did not confer degrees on female students until the 1920s, and it was not until after the second world war that women were treated as full equals by universities everywhere.

Happily, they have more than made up for it over the past few decades. In tertiary education they now outnumber men everywhere except in sub-Saharan Africa and southern and western Asia. In OECD countries an average of 33% of women aged 25–34 have had some form of tertiary education, compared with only 28% of men in the same age group. The greatest rises in the number of highly educated women have been in Japan, South Korea and Spain – evidence of big changes in traditional attitudes.

In rich countries girls now generally do better academically than boys (though in developing countries the reverse is still true). The OECD's Programme for International Student Assessment (PISA) shows that girls aged 15 in all member countries are markedly ahead of boys in reading, though boys in most countries score somewhat better in mathematics and science. But the degree subjects chosen by men and women are strikingly different. An average of 75% of degrees in mathematics and engineering are awarded to men and 71% of degrees in humanities and health go to women. At the postgraduate level the imbalance is even greater, with obvious implications for job choices. Women with humanities degrees overwhelmingly go into teaching, whereas a majority of male science graduates work as professionals in physics, mathematics and engineering.

With education as well as civil and political rights under their belts, women in their perfect post-war homes soon started to get fidgety. Running a household and rearing children no longer seemed enough. The feminist movement that took off in the 1960s gave voice to their aspirations. Betty Friedan, in her 1963 book, *The Feminine Mystique*, called for a re-evaluation of the role of women in industrial societies; they now wanted to be treated the same as men not just as citizens but in the workplace too. Slowly but surely, legislation in developed countries caught up. In America the Equal Pay Act of 1963 mandated the same pay for the same work for men and women; Title VII of the Civil Rights Act of 1964 prohibited sex discrimination in employment; and the Pregnancy Discrimination Act of 1978 made it illegal to fire a woman just because she was having a child. In Britain the Equal Pay Act of 1970 was followed in 1975 by the Sex Discrimination Act and the Employment Protection Act. Similar legislation was passed in most other developed countries.

Equal in law, not money

Nobody imagined that such measures would bring instant equality in the workplace, but they reflected important social trends that were already under way. "Traditional" families, in which only the husband had a paid job and the wife looked after the home and children, began to decline in number. In America in the early 1970s some 52% of all families with children were of that kind. By 1975 the share was already down to 45%; now it is a mere 21%. America does have a larger proportion of women at work than many other rich countries, but the same trend is evident everywhere. The share of working-age women

FIG 3.1 **Jobs for the girls**

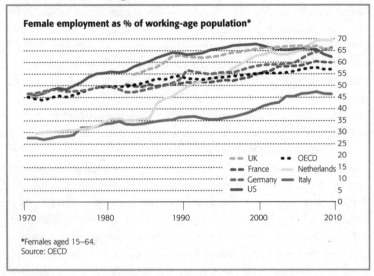

Female employment as % of working-age population*

Legend: UK · OECD · France · Netherlands · Germany · Italy · US

*Females aged 15–64.
Source: OECD

with jobs in the OECD as a whole went up from an average of 45% in 1970 to 58% in 2008 (see Figure 3.1). The Nordic countries have the highest scores, mostly well over 70%, only a few points below those for men. At the other end of the scale fewer than half of Italian and Greek women have paid jobs. The score in the Netherlands went from Italian levels to near-Nordic ones after the government changed the rules to make part-time work more attractive.

For all the huge numbers that have been moving into the labour market, and for all the equal-pay legislation, women on average still earn significantly less than men. The gap in median earnings for full-time employees has shrunk since the 1960s and 1970s, but it now seems to be stuck at an average of about 18% in the OECD. Again, it is smaller in most of the Nordic countries and much bigger in countries such as South Korea and Japan. The figures take no account of part-time workers, who make up a quarter of all employed females and are generally less well paid, so the real picture is somewhat worse. The pay gap is biggest at the highest pay levels, which suggests that many women still hit a "glass ceiling" on the way up.

Women are concentrated in a much narrower range of jobs than men, mainly teaching, nursing and personal care, and clerical work – none of which is generally a route to riches. But the continuing expansion of white-collar jobs (where hours and conditions are often convenient) has provided them with plenty of opportunities, at a time when manual jobs are in decline and male manual workers are becoming unemployed. Nearly a tenth of working women in rich countries are self-employed, which may be an indication that they cannot easily find jobs with hours and conditions that suit them. Even when they work full-time, their average hours are shorter than men's.

That is not because they are idle, but because they have other things to do. Women in almost all rich countries spend at least twice as much time as men on unpaid work, and in some countries a lot more, mainly looking after children, elderly relatives and the like. Men everywhere say they have more leisure time than women, none more so than Italians, who spend nearly 80 minutes a day longer than their womenfolk enjoying themselves. Norwegian men, by contrast, toil away around the house for almost as long as women.

But child care, at least in rich countries, is no longer the never-ending task it once was, not least because a woman's average fertility rate in the OECD has dropped to just 1.6 children, one child less than 40 years ago and well below the replacement rate of 2.1. That is partly thanks to the spread of the contraceptive pill in the 1960s, which for the first time in history allowed women to control reliably how many children to have, and when. Women now start families later, often after establishing their careers, and most keep them small. Birth rates in America, France and the Nordic countries are holding up better than in the Mediterranean countries and eastern Europe, which are getting perilously close to one child per woman. In recent years some countries, including Britain, have seen a slight recovery in numbers, but there is unlikely to be a return to the organ-pipe model of the family: a household full of children of assorted ages. Even single children, of course, still take time and money to look after, but less so than the large families that were the norm only a few generations ago, and the effort is spread over a shorter period, so women in general are far freer to pursue a career as well as having a family.

Over the past couple of hundred years, then, and particularly the

Skirting the issue in the c-suite

It is a fair bet that by 2050 women will be somewhat closer to half of company board members in most rich countries. Less clear is how that share will be reached: with the help of legal quotas, or without it.

The proportion of women at the top of the corporate world is still woefully low (see Figure 3.2): 15% of board members in big American companies and 10% in Europe. Several European governments are following Norway's example in legislating that listed companies reserve 40% of the seats on their boards for women. In America, such an idea might be ruled out on the ground that it discriminates against men, and critics of quotas say they force firms to pad their boards with token non-executive directors or to allocate real power on the basis of sex rather than merit. With or without quotas, in the decades to come the need for firms to attract the best talent in order to compete will surely help to push the share of women in the boardroom closer to that of men.

FIG 3.2 **Girl power**

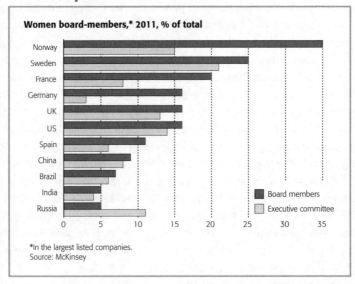

Women board-members,* 2011, % of total

*In the largest listed companies.
Source: McKinsey

past 50, women in rich countries have made tremendous strides. They have achieved full equality under the law and full voting rights, though female legislators are still very much in a minority. Not only do women enjoy equal access to education, but as a group they are also becoming more highly educated than men. They are able to control the size of their families, which have got smaller and more manageable. They have moved into the labour market in droves, so in a number of countries their participation rate is close to that of men; indeed in America they now hold down half of all jobs. The pay gap with men has narrowed, though by no means disappeared. Women in top management and in the senior ranks of the professions and the civil service are no longer a rarity, even though they are still greatly underrepresented. Some countries have introduced formal or informal quotas for female board members in order to hurry things along (see box).

Future perfect and imperfect

So where do women go from here? In the developed world they are spoilt for choice. Provided they can find a rich enough husband, they can marry, become a full-time homemaker and have as many children as they like; or they can embark on a high-flying career and forget about having children or even husbands. But the vast majority now aim somewhere in between, having a family but also holding down a job. How easy that will be depends on where they live. Some governments have adopted family-friendly policies, providing generous parental leave, tax breaks and child care; some have not. As the working population in many countries shrinks and qualified workers become scarcer, governments and employers will try harder to attract women into the labour force and keep them there. Certainly the advances women have made in all spheres of life will not be reversed. Some men grumble that in many ways women now get a better deal: they may not be able to have it all, but at least they can take their pick from a menu that is not available to men.

Some social, economic and technological trends over the next four decades will be helpful to women in rich countries and others will make their lives slightly harder and more uncertain, but none

Factors affecting women's lives

Barring catastrophes it is already clear that the following factors will have a big impact on women's lives in the next 40 years:

- **Demographic change.** Given the steep fall in birth rates in the past few decades and the steady increase in life expectancy, populations in most rich countries, and some emerging markets too, will become older. In many places the number of people of working age is shrinking. That in time will probably produce labour shortages, particularly in skilled and professional occupations, which will give women access to more and better jobs. But women will also have to work for longer as their earlier retirement ages are phased out and pension ages for everyone go up. An increase in the number of very old people will also mean more need for their care. Such duties are likely to involve women far more than men, and if they are also holding down jobs they will become busier. At the same time, birth rates in developed countries may recover slightly from their current low point, meaning that child care could become heavier just as care for the elderly does.

- **Social trends.** Since 1970 marriage rates in the OECD have roughly halved and divorce rates more or less doubled.

will bring about the sort of epic change that has marked the past century or so. Most of the big battles – equality before the law, equal educational opportunities, control of fertility and free access to the labour market – have already been won. The years to 2050 will see the consolidation of what women have already achieved and, as their labour becomes more highly prized in a market where skills are at a premium, there will be more measures to make it easier for women to combine career and family.

The outlook for women in emerging markets is very different. In many developing countries women still lack legal and political rights, and in some they still cannot vote. Even though 186 countries

Growing numbers of people now just cohabit and often drift apart again. Out-of-wedlock births in most OECD countries already range from around 30% to over 50% of the total. In future, even fewer people will get married and even more couples, whether married or cohabiting, will break up. This will result in more single-parent households, putting more pressure on women to go out to work while bringing up a family.

- **Education.** Most rich countries are still planning to increase the numbers of young people in higher education, sometimes aiming for up to half of the age group. Women already outnumber men in tertiary education, and in the "talent war" of the future labour market highly educated women will prosper.

- **Structural and technological change in the economy.** As the manufacturing sector shrinks, most jobs in modern economies will be in services. They will tend to suit women, but will often involve temporary contracts and part-time work, offering less security than the contracts for core workers. At the same time technology will make it much easier for many jobs to be done remotely, giving working mothers more flexibility.

have signed the UN Convention for the Elimination of All Forms of Discrimination against Women, 42 of them have imposed at least one reservation that limits the treaty's application in practice, mainly to do with equal rights in marriage and the family, nationality rights and compatibility with religious laws. In many countries women have no autonomy in the household, often suffer domestic violence and lack access to the justice system.

According to the UN, in 2010 the share of women with paid jobs was below 30% in northern Africa and western Asia, below 40% in southern Asia and below 50% in the Caribbean and Central America. Although the gap between the participation rates of men and women has narrowed a little in the past 20 years, it remains wide. And where women do have jobs, they are often precarious ones: as casual agricultural labourers, family workers or domestic servants, in factories and workshops, or running tiny businesses of their own. If they are lucky, they work as clerks or in service jobs. Few make it to the ranks of managers or senior officials, and almost all get paid much less than men.

The more advanced emerging markets, however, present a much more hopeful picture. This is where in all probability most of the economic growth between now and 2050 will be concentrated. China and India will become the world's largest and third-largest economies respectively, and there will also be rapid growth in countries such as Mexico, Turkey, Indonesia, Egypt, Malaysia, Thailand, Colombia and Venezuela. This fast growth will be particularly helpful to women. Experience in the West has shown that education is a crucial prerequisite for women's advancement, and as countries get richer they will spend more on education. World Bank figures show that in Brazil, Russia and China literacy among younger adults of both sexes is already almost universal, with women accounting for around half of those enrolled in higher education.

Rapid growth will also bring more competition for skilled and talented staff, which will open up many more opportunities for women. Across the BRIC (Brazil, Russia, India, China) countries 30–50% of women are already in the labour force, and many of them are highly ambitious and determined to work their way to the top. Although traditional attitudes towards women are generally hard to dislodge, there is so much change going on that entrenched prejudice may have become easier to combat. A study by the International Labour Organisation has shown that occupational segregation by sex (ie, men and women doing different jobs) is lower in countries like China and India than in the famously egalitarian Nordic countries. In China, in particular, there is now a growing number of women entrepreneurs with hugely successful businesses.

Another advantage that working women in the BRIC countries have over their counterparts in the West is that child care is much less likely to be a problem. There is more of an extended family to lean on, domestic help is inexpensive and easily available, and there is no cultural taboo on getting other people to look after your children. However, some of these advantages may diminish over the decades, and there is meanwhile a strong expectation that women will care for their parents and in-laws once they become infirm, adding the burden of extra duties later in their careers.

Emerged and emerging

The prospects for women over the next 40 years, then, are hard to sum up in a simple formula. In the rich world, where they have already achieved equality in principle, if not yet always in practice, there will be improvements at the margin: better institutional arrangements to make it possible for women to combine work and family, more effort on the part of companies to offer flexible employment conditions, perhaps a more overt acceptance that men, too, have families and need to play their part in caring for them. But further large-scale change is unlikely.

In the world's poorest countries, where women are generally disadvantaged in many ways, nothing much will change until education for both girls and boys improves, bringing more rapid development in its wake. Educating girls has enormous consequences for the social and economic well-being of a country (female illiteracy and the low status of women are big factors in the backwardness of Afghanistan, for example). Well-educated women have better prospects of getting well-paid employment, can choose to limit their families and are able to make decisions about bringing up their children that improve their chances in life. But in countries where inequality for women is anchored in religion or culture, progress is likely to be slower (ironically, economic development in India and China could surely have been still more impressive if their societies did not practise dismaying levels of "gendercide", with their preference for male children).

In the more advanced emerging markets, not only the BRICs but also many others, women will enjoy exceptional opportunities over the next few decades. In many of these countries women are already as well educated as men. Rapid change resulting from breakneck growth will allow them to overcome prejudice and embark on careers that a generation ago they could only have dreamt of. This will be good not just for them but also for the economies that benefit from their contribution.

But there will be a price to pay. Women in the developing world will have more choices, but face many more pressures too. As the West has already found, once women move out of the home and into the workplace, society changes irrevocably, in ways that profoundly affect not only women but men and children too. On balance, though, most people – and women in particular – would agree that it is a price worth paying.

4 Friends indeed

Martin Giles

Always connected and always online: welcome to the social supercloud

THE WORLD IS IN THE MIDDLE of an unprecedented collective experiment. By the time you read this, Facebook may well have become the first online social network to boast a billion members – which, were it a nation, would make it the third most populous on Earth after China and India. Of course, there is no guarantee that Facebook, which at the time of writing claims some 800m active users (see Figure 4.1), will get to the billion-member mark. But its success has already shown how the notion of friendship in the physical world can transfer successfully to a virtual one. And we are still in the early days of this social revolution in cyberspace – one which is going to play out in many different areas between now and 2050.

As well as online social networks, a plethora of other "social media" services is reinforcing links between people on the web and off it, as those who strike up friendships online subsequently meet face-to-face. These media include everything from blogs and "wikis" (sets of web pages that can be edited by anybody) to online-dating sites and services such as Foursquare that share a person's location with his or her friends.

Along with Facebook and its ilk, some of these services have provoked fierce debates about the future of privacy in an increasingly networked world. But there has evidently been a shift towards greater openness online, a trend that emerges clearly from an overview of the relatively short history of social media. The early part of this timeline can be thought of as the BFF period, running until the end of 2003.

FIG 4.1 **Facelift**

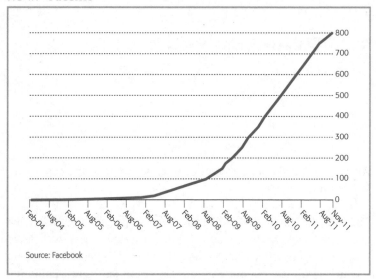

Source: Facebook

Often used by teenagers to designate their favourite buddies as "Best Friends Forever", the abbreviation is used here to denote the time "Before Facebook's Founding".

Genesis and evolution

At the beginning of this pre-Cambrian era of social media, online friendship and information-sharing was largely the preserve of tech-savvy types who hung out in online communities such as The Well or on bulletin-board systems, which allowed their users to post messages to one another and play online games. Although some people used their real names on the discussion boards and in the chat rooms that blossomed in the 1980s, many hid behind online aliases and took pleasure in taunting neophytes who tried to join their ranks.

During the next stage in the evolution of online social networking there was a gradual democratisation of the tools that allowed people to communicate with one another via the web. Firms such as CompuServe and America Online introduced e-mail, chat sites and discussion boards to many more people – though their membership never reached anything like the stratospheric levels of Facebook. Thanks to these commercial services, which offered relatively secure electronic "walled gardens" in which users could exchange information, people began to get more comfortable using their real identities in cyberspace.

Then, in the mid-1990s, the world wide web unleashed a torrent of innovation that ultimately brought social media to the masses. The number of blogs exploded. By July 2011 there were over 166m public ones in existence according to Nielsen, a research firm (see Table 4.1). Wikis multiplied too. Perhaps the best known of these, Wikipedia, which was set up in 2001, has since grown to become one of the most popular sites on the internet, boasting 20m articles on everything from obscure diseases to equally obscure actors. A triumph of online collaboration, Wikipedia benefits from the fact that hundreds of people edit its existing entries each day (for the most part, though not always, improving them) and add new ones to it.

TABLE 4.1 **Blogospheric**
Number of blogs tracked by Nielsen[a], m

2006	2007	2008	2009	2010	2011
29.4	49.2	78.7	110.3	126.9	162.7

a Data are for mid-June and come from BlogPulse, an automated trend-discovery system for blogs.
Source: Nielsen

But perhaps the most important development in the 1990s was the rise of social-networking services such as SixDegrees.com, which linked personal profiles with the ability to search for and contact other users. These paved the way for the likes of Friendster and Myspace, two social networks that attracted plenty of attention in the early part of this century. These sites, along with others such as CyWorld in South Korea, Skyrock in France and VKontakte in Russia, differed from most of their predecessors in two important respects. Instead of being structured according to topics or themes, they were unabashedly "egocentric", placing people at the centre of online communities. And their simple interfaces made it easy for non-techies to join and use them.

Yet the fortunes of both networks ultimately faded while those of Facebook, founded in 2004 by Mark Zuckerberg in his dorm room at Harvard University, began to soar. The Facebook era of social networking has seen the notion of formalising and nurturing friendships online shift from a minority pursuit to a mainstream activity around the world. And this is changing the notion of friendship and collaboration in several ways.

Social graph-iti

One of the biggest changes is to get people to use their real identities online and to make explicit their links to others. Facebook, for instance, encourages its users to reveal whether or not they are married, single or dating, as well as to signal whether any of their "friends" are family members too. The techie types who run social networks like to refer to the resulting electronic web of connections as a "social graph" that can be mined to better understand a person's relationship network and web of interests.

The Facebook era has also seen a significant increase in the amount of information that people are willing to share with their friends online. In part, this reflects a shift in societal norms towards greater openness, a trend that has also given rise to, say, reality television shows. But it also reflects the fact that online networks have created fine-grained privacy controls that give users a greater sense of security when sharing sensitive data, such as details of their latest purchases or the state of their health – though (see below) online privacy remains a big concern for many people. The rapid growth of Foursquare and Loopt, which also lets people signal their location to their friends, is another striking example of just how far attitudes have changed.

So, too, is the fact that social networking seems to be crossing the generational divide. Although youngsters are still much more likely to "poke" and "friend" one another online – and to post snaps of semi-clothed pals at parties – their grandparents are starting to sign up in droves too. A survey of over 2,000 adults conducted in 2010 by the Pew Internet and American Life Project, a non-profit research group, found that the number of Americans aged 65 or more using social networks doubled between April 2009 and May 2010, from 13% to 26%. That still pales in comparison with the 80% of 18–29 year-olds using such networks, but the gap will narrow over the coming decades as more and more "silver surfers" discover online sharing.

How have Facebook and other networks managed to get so many people to sign up? Part of the answer is what tech folk like to call a "network effect": if many of your pals have signed up to a site, you will want to be there too. Another part is that many sites have followed Facebook's example by creating "platforms" to allow other developers to launch software applications ("apps") on them for everything from games to charitable giving. This makes the sites more valuable to existing users and helps attract new ones.

Unlike their predecessors, the current generation of social networks has also benefited from developments in consumer electronics, such as digital cameras and smartphones, which have made it easy and cheap to produce mountains of digital media. One of the secrets to Facebook's stunning success is that it created a simple photo-sharing capability that allows users to share snaps with their friends. Each month its users share more than 30 billion pieces of content, including photos and blog posts, with one another. In response many other content-sharing sites, such as Flickr, a photo-sharing service, and YouTube, a video one, have added more social-networking capabilities.

Another defining characteristic of today's social-media landscape is that some sharing is now being done in real time, and not just by location-based services. Twitter, a micro-blogging service, has led the way, often spreading news before traditional media outlets. Celebrating its fifth birthday in July 2011, the company revealed that its users were producing some 200m "tweets" a day (compared with just 2m in January 2009); their contents, just 140 characters at a time, would fill 8,163 copies of Tolstoy's *War and Peace*.

Collaboration and its consequences

These changes have given rise to several trends that will become even more pronounced in coming decades. The first is the growing influence of friends on decisions. People have always consulted their pals for advice. But canvassing them via mass e-mails or multiple phone calls takes considerable time and effort.

Social networks make this process much simpler. For one thing, they enable users to post queries that can immediately be seen by all their online friends, who can then respond to them. For another, they have created "social plug-ins" on other websites that let their users interact with their pals there. Facebook alone now boasts links with more than 7m apps and sites. As a result, friends are becoming increasingly important social filters of content as more and more of the internet is colonised by social networks.

Another trend is the "crowdsourcing" of intelligence. Wikipedia is a prominent example. Another is Quora, an online question-and-answer engine with a social twist. The service, whose founders are former Facebook executives, gets its users to provide answers to queries posted by other members and to vote for the best responses, which are then given prominence on its pages. The best contributors see their online reputations enhanced, encouraging others to pay attention to their answers. In the years ahead there will be many more such collective online endeavours to advance human knowledge.

Blogs and social networks are also contributing to a third important phenomenon. By simplifying mass communication and information-sharing, they allow people to organise faster than ever before around particular causes or issues dear to them. And they make it possible for their users to publicise their grievances widely, without having to rely on mass media such as newspapers and television stations. The use of services such as Facebook and Twitter by protesters during the uprisings that occurred in north Africa and the Middle East in 2011 is a case in point. The role that social media played in the revolts has perhaps been exaggerated, but blogs and social networks undoubtedly helped amplify the grassroots discontent that swept the Arab world.

This groundswell effect is also starting to reshape politics in the rich world too. America's presidential election in 2008 highlighted the potential of social media to encourage political engagement, and since then they have grown in influence. According to another study by the Pew Institute, over a fifth of adults in America with access to the internet used Twitter or a social network such as Facebook to get information about political campaigns before and during the

2010 mid-term elections. In doing so some 7% of them had started or joined a political group.

Many of those using social networks to connect with political campaigns are young people who have not before been politically active. Moreover, it seems that the use of blogs and social networks for political goals is less influenced by a person's socioeconomic status, income and education than other forms of political activity. Both of these developments suggest profound changes in how people take part in politics and imply that social media will significantly alter long-standing patterns of political engagement in coming decades.

Blogs, social networks and other social media are already influencing other forms of civic activity, such as philanthropy. As well as helping to sensitise people to the impact of, say, tsunamis and other natural catastrophes, they are also encouraging mass giving. For instance, Causes, an online site devoted to philanthropy, helps people to set up platforms for particular charitable activities and to tap into their networks of friends to promote them.

Social workers and players

Social media increasingly influence not just people's personal lives but their professional ones, too. Many companies are setting up internal blogs, wikis and other tools in a bid to boost internal collaboration and speed up the circulation of new ideas. And software firms are touting Facebook-like corporate social-networking solutions with names like Yammer and Chatter – might Blather be next? – that companies can use within their digital firewalls. This phenomenon will gather speed as more and more firms realise that stimulating internal collaboration via technology is a source of competitive advantage.

Another trend that will become ever more important is professional social networking. Many social networks are used to forge links with close friends: the average user on Facebook, for instance, has 130 connections. But research has shown that it is actually professional contacts – and their contacts – that provide the best source of job leads. This explains the rapid growth of services such as LinkedIn and Viadeo, which allow people to create networks of business partners, suppliers and total strangers. Cultivating these networks will become vital for job-seekers as more recruiters use them to identify potential candidates.

Work is not the only thing becoming more social. So, too, is play. The stunning success of online games such as Mafia Wars and FarmVille that are built on social-networking platforms has shown how eager people are to interact with their pals as they tend their virtual vegetables (see Table 4.2). This has forced gaming firms to adapt gadgets such as Microsoft's Xbox 360 gaming console so that people can compete against or collaborate with their friends as they blast virtual baddies to smithereens. In future, most games will have social capabilities embedded in them. Internet-enabled televisions and other devices used for entertainment will also allow people to interact easily with their friends.

TABLE 4.2 **Playtime**
Top ten games on Facebook, July 2011

Name of game	Number of active users, m
CityVille	80
Empires & Allies	45
FarmVille	36
Texas HoldEm Poker	34
Gardens of Time	16
FrontierVille	12
Café World	11
Monster Galaxy	11
Bejeweled Blitz	11
Diamond Dash	10

Source: AppData.com

All these moves towards greater connectedness provide benefits. But a controversial trend of the Facebook era is the gradual erosion of online privacy. Attempts by Facebook and other networks to make information about users available by default to anyone on the web have led to repeated backlashes by people who fear they are losing control of their data. And there has been a general outcry over the way in which companies have been mining for commercial purposes some of the data that social networks produce.

These privacy issues will become even more fraught in coming decades as new technologies such as location-based social networking catch on. And the chances are that governments will respond by producing "digital bills of rights" which seek to define more clearly who owns a customer's data and in what circumstances they can be used by third parties. None of this will be easy, and given differing cultural views on privacy it will be especially tough to reach a global consensus on the best way forward.

Towards a socialised state

This continuing tension is nevertheless unlikely to halt the growing social interconnectivity of the planet. Social networks and other social media will follow the example of the internet before them and work themselves into many different parts of our lives. By 2050 we will all be living in what amounts to a socialised state, in which our online networks of friends are available to us wherever we are; notions such as collective intelligence will seem commonplace rather than novel.

There are already several early indications that social connectivity is well on its way to becoming ubiquitous. One is the fact that many people now access Facebook and other services via mobile phones rather than personal computers. This has a couple of important implications. First, mobile-phone users tend to be far more active on social networks than those who access them via PCs, so the amount of information-sharing is set to grow dramatically. Second, the spread of broadband wireless connectivity in emerging markets over coming decades will allow billions of new users to create new networks of friends and contacts via their phones – which are fast becoming the computing device of choice in the developing world. That will turn the social-media revolution into even more of a global phenomenon.

Another sign of the growing ubiquity is the move to embed social connectivity in all sorts of different devices. Toyota, for instance, has announced plans for a new social-networking service to be launched in 2012 called "Toyota Friend"; this will allow drivers to share real-time updates with other Toyota drivers and to connect to Toyota dealers.

A dominant player?

Will this socialised state still be dominated by a single company? The admittedly brief history of social media suggests that there has tended to be a single dominant player in the social-networking industry at any one time whose network effects are so strong that they make it irresistible as a destination. However, the fate of Myspace, which is now a shadow of its former self, also suggests that fickle users will not hesitate to abandon a service for a rival offering that seems more useful.

Facebook appears to be well aware of this and has worked hard to position itself as a social utility that is, in effect, the repository of people's digital identities on the internet. It has also created an "ecosystem" of third-party applications to make it attractive to users. But it is not unassailable. The initial success that Google has had in attracting people to its Google+ social network, which makes it easy to create sub-networks for different groups such as friends, co-workers and family members, is a sign that people still remain willing to experiment with ambitious new offerings.

If there is still a single, dominant social network around, it will almost certainly be the subject of tight regulations imposed by governments nervous of its influence. Already comparisons are being drawn between Facebook – which has its own currency in the form of Facebook credits and a thriving online economy – and a nation-state. If it gets much bigger, it is bound to attract the attention of policymakers worried about its influence over everything from grassroots political activism to online privacy. Any rival that overtakes it will likewise come under serious scrutiny.

Other carmakers are also looking at how to give drivers access to social networks on the road. By 2050 all cars will have the voice-activated means to connect people to their network friends while on the move. In future this online networking function will be found in many other devices, from cookers to checkouts in stores.

A third force for ubiquity is the growth of cloud computing, which involves storing large amounts of information on servers that can be accessed almost anywhere and via many different kinds of device. As further innovations drive down the cost of this computing power, they will make it even easier and cheaper to tap into social media on the move. Coupled with advances in areas such as artificial intelligence, this will help produce a kind of social supercloud by 2050 that automatically serves up the most relevant information and contacts from a person's social networks.

It is, however, possible that by 2050 the social-media landscape will end up looking very different. Growing tensions over privacy could cause people to abandon commercial behemoths and to place their digital identities with one of a series of non-profit repositories that work only on behalf of the customers whose information they hold. These would consolidate much of a person's data and release it to other sites only in accordance with his or her instructions.

Instead of being identified as Facebookers or Google+ members, people will then be free to take their own identities to whatever sites interest them and choose which friends they want to engage with. Technology will have also evolved to the point where it will send much more targeted information to people so they will no longer be swamped with irrelevant information and news forced upon them by a mega-network. These data will be delivered to them without them even having to request it, as ubiquitous connectivity and real-time sharing become the norm.

It is, of course, almost inevitable that some new and disruptive social technology will emerge from a garage in Silicon Valley or even a shack in Kenya in coming decades to change completely the nature of online social interactions. But whatever happens to the underlying infrastructure of sharing, it is clear that the drive towards an ever more interconnected world will only accelerate.

Some have even predicted that, thanks to advances in technology, we will all end up being able to manage far larger networks of close relationships. The average Facebook user's network today of around 130 friends is not far off the 148 (often rounded to 150) people that Robin Dunbar, an anthropologist, has claimed is the maximum number of stable relationships a human being can maintain. But Mark Pincus, the boss of Zynga, the online-gaming company behind Mafia Wars and FarmVille, has predicted that within a few decades this figure could hit 500.

Even if the actual number turns out to be more modest, there is little doubt that the changes outlined in this chapter are bringing the internet ever closer to the vision of its founding father, Sir Tim Berners-Lee. In his book, *Weaving the Web*, Sir Tim explained that the web was always meant to be more of a social creation than a technical one. By 2050 it will surely have become just that.

5 Cultural revolutions

Robert Lane Greene

**Globalisation and technology will have their cultural impact –
but the world's tastes will remain stubbornly local**

WRITING ABOUT "CULTURE" across a sweep of 40 years is even more
perilous than writing about more numerical areas like economics,
demography or climate change. Present trends may mean next to
nothing over such a long span. An incautious writer speculating in
1962 might well think that mop-topped foursomes in matching outfits
singing in harmony would have taken over the music world by 2012.
The next four years would prove him spectacularly right; the next 50,
wildly wrong.

Moreover, culture means so many things. To those intimidated by
the word, "culture" means things that rich people enjoy, like paintings
and opera. To anthropologists and sociologists, culture is everything
from language to cooking to folkways among even the most primitive
of societies. It can mean the sorts of things people do in their spare
time (see Figure 5.1). But whatever the difficulties with definitions, a
few broad themes stand out.

One is that affinity matters. Globalisation and technology are
often said to have meant the "death of distance". In physical terms
this is true; a Californian and a New Yorker can chat in real time
about their favorite bands in their common language through a range
of media (Twitter, Facebook and Skype are just three of the present
possibilities) that is sure to expand. What has not happened, however,
is the death of cultural distance. The new wealth of Chinese and Arab
art buyers has meant a boom in sales – but, in large part, of Chinese
and Islamic art. Communication technology has made it ever easier

FIG 5.1 **Leisure time**

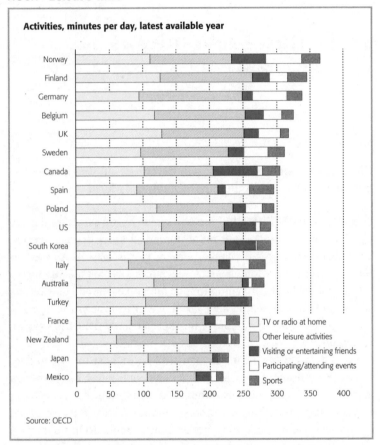

Activities, minutes per day, latest available year

Source: OECD

for people to be exposed to opinions around the world; especially opinions just like their own, which is what many people seem to want.

Second is that money moves trends, but it cannot move everything. The economic growth of China – the anchor of any "next 40 years" story – means that art is increasingly flowing in that direction. But it does not mean that Chinese will take the place of English around the world or that Chinese films will steal Hollywood's shine. Whereas financial capital can move in a hurry, human capital cannot. Languages are learned over years and used over a lifetime; the rapid growth of China will not mean the rapid growth of Chinese. And where technical skills cluster (like those required to produce a Hollywood blockbuster) they will not quickly cluster elsewhere.

Finally, gatekeepers still matter. Technology makes it easier for people to listen to any kind of music they like, but digital availability and ubiquity are steering them increasingly to the biggest hits, not the niches. Bloggers and podcasters and tweeters have shaken up purveyors of news, but not replaced them. Book publishers, art dealers and film producers will still play the biggest role in what gets bought, read, contemplated and listened to.

The dragon's share

Visual art provides perhaps the most striking evidence for a durable trend that is changing the world of culture. Its centre of gravity is moving eastwards. The rise of China's economy and the oil fortunes of the Middle East have caused a reversal of the flow of cultural treasures, now moving from West to East.

In 2010 China became the world's second-largest art market, surpassing Britain and taking second place behind America with a global share of 23%. This was a result of both short-term and long-term trends. The financial crisis that began in 2008 clobbered Western markets, and the rich people who spend money on art in them. This led to a 33% contraction in the global market for sales of art and antiques in 2008–09. China was relatively undamaged by the crisis.

But art is a volatile market that booms by 50% or more a year when people are flush, and crashes during bad years by as much as a third. The real story is the year-after-year growth of China, whose art-market turnover increased by a gaudy 530% between 2002 and 2010. Auction sales grew by nearly nine times in the six years to 2010. Classical Chinese paintings, calligraphy, porcelain and decorative objects made up many of the high-end sales. In America, average prices for fine art jumped up and down wildly with the economy. But Chinese prices kept on growing steadily (see Figure 5.2).

This rise in big Chinese sales accounts for China's growth. But the

FIG 5.2 **The tortoise and the hare**

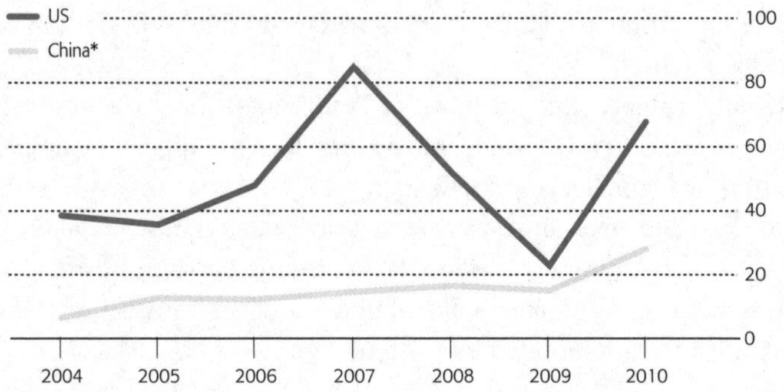

Average auction prices for fine art

*Includes Hong Kong, Macao and Taiwan.
Sources: European Fine Art Foundation

distribution of sales is indicative. In mature Western markets, there are many medium-sized transactions, whereas big-ticket ones drag the average sale price up. In 2010 the average British sale was worth €48,500, but the median was just €3,200.

Compare that with the new markets for art. In China the average auction price was €27,800, and the median was a striking €23,000. Similar to China were the figures in the United Arab Emirates, where the average price was a sky-high €56,300 and the median was a still impressive €20,500. Where the super-rich lead, will the slightly-less-rich follow?

Some like it local

In contrast to high art, for the cinema it is head count, not the number of highly rich people, that matters. For decades, filmmakers around the world have been making well-crafted and thoughtful movies that explore the human condition. The best of global cinema has always crossed borders. But, all things being equal, people like things produced near them, in a language they can understand. This is why cinema is growing in populous places: India's Bollywood is the world's largest centre of film production by volume. Russia has

New buyers, new curators

China and the Gulf are both building museums at a brisk pace. The policy of the oil-moneyed Gulf monarchies has been to convince Western museums like the Guggenheim and the Louvre to build offshoots in their deserts. The Al-Thani family that runs Qatar has been buying up as much of the best Islamic art as it can find on the market for the past 25 years. In 2008 a museum for Islamic art designed by I.M. Pei, a Chinese-American artist, opened in Doha, Qatar. In China, too, museums are spreading. Modern and contemporary art museums will spread beyond Hong Kong, Beijing and other coastal areas that have money today, and this will continue to drive art sales.

But there is a difference between the art-buying of East Asia and that of the Gulf. China can hope to be one of those countries like Britain or America with a growing upper-middle class to undergird big sales with a higher volume of smaller sales. The Gulf countries' economic future depends heavily on hydrocarbons, and how long their petrodollars can underwrite the fortunes of small cliques among the rich families. Though the wiser of the Gulf monarchies are already planning for a future after oil and natural gas, their continued fortunes are far from secure.

China is buying art because it is getting rich. The oil sheikhdoms are already rich; they are buying art in order to be a tourist attraction when the money runs out.

been on a cinema-building spree. America still easily leads the pack in ticket sales, and will for a long time (its take at the box office is some nine times China's; America has a quarter of the population but much pricier tickets).

Will other film centres rise to challenge Hollywood as major exporters? Perhaps not. Hollywood is superb at making visually extraordinary films that can sell anywhere. A blockbuster costs upwards of $200m to make (and marketing costs can easily add

FIG 5.3 **Movie madness**

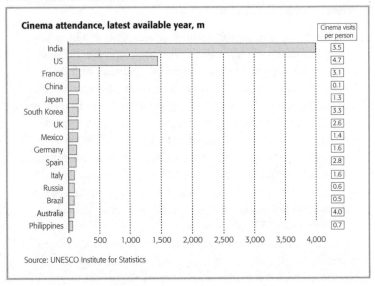

Cinema attendance, latest available year, m

Country		Cinema visits per person
India		3.5
US		4.7
France		3.1
China		0.1
Japan		1.3
South Korea		3.3
UK		2.6
Mexico		1.4
Germany		1.6
Spain		2.8
Italy		1.6
Russia		0.6
Brazil		0.5
Australia		4.0
Philippines		0.7

Source: UNESCO Institute for Statistics

another $100m); there is only one place in the world where that kind of money can find the talent to produce such a spectacle. From set builders to costume designers to computer animators to actors, in no place on Earth do talented people congregate as they do in Hollywood (though filmmakers chase subsidies in places like New York, Toronto and New Mexico to produce their movies).

This is not to say that other film-producing regions will not grow. The Asia-Pacific movie market is already worth about $3 billion a year, healthy in comparison to the world's biggest market, North America, at $5 billion. Given their cheaper ticket prices, Asians are clearly flocking to cinemas in their millions (see Figure 5.3). They like their own films, too: in early 2011, of the top 20 films in China, some 60% of revenues came from Chinese films – partly, it is true, because the market is rigged in their favour – and the top-grossing three were all Chinese films, despite the fact that studios in Hong Kong (the centre for Chinese filmmaking) lack the scale of India's. In India, the cinema-going experience will increasingly look like America's as that country adds to its middle class; a growing trend is the development of American-style multiplex theatres for the urban elite, showing films about middle-class life. Indeed, India's most luxurious multiplexes have separate, first-class-cabin-style seats and waiters bearing samosas; American and British cinema chains are looking to India for inspiration.

The fundamental trend – that, all things being equal, people like their own cultural productions, or extravagant ones – holds true in Africa, too. "Nollywood", Nigeria's film industry, churns out more movies (about 50 a week) than any place on Earth save Bollywood. They are popular throughout Africa, thanks to their depiction of local themes. Meanwhile, elite Africans from other countries spurn Nollywood as a cultural virus, much as French intellectuals disdain Hollywood. Production values may be rotten, but digital filming will allow Nigerians and the Africans imitating them to run quickly up the learning curve. And other centres, from Ghallywood (Ghana) to Lollywood (Liberia), have their aspirations.

On present trends, the old "big screen" and "small screen" look as though they will converge in many ways over the coming decades. As film-ticket prices rise, and on-demand movie-watching services improve, more and more people will enjoy films in their living rooms rather than at the cinema. Film studios, which in recent decades have relied on DVD sales to boost profits, will instead have to distribute their films cannily to pay-television and streaming services such as HBO and Netflix – or their successors in decades to come – to maximise their income. They may also increasingly seek to bypass the distributors and go direct to consumers.

With this change, it may be tempting to predict that the days of a television schedule are numbered: with the advent of on-demand everything, people will simply watch their favourite programmes when they feel like it. But this prediction will prove only partly true, and not for technical reasons. It fails to take into account the event-like nature of premieres of new shows: the new episode of a heavily plot-driven programme has become an event in itself, eagerly shared by viewers over social networks like Facebook and Twitter. The most diehard fans will no more wait a week to see a new episode than they will record a sports event to watch a week later. It is the same with reality TV: nobody wants to watch the X *Factor* a day after it airs. So

FIG 5.4 **Times a-changin'**

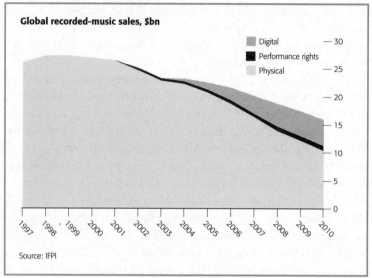

Global recorded-music sales, $bn

Source: IFPI

television producers will hype new series months in advance, much as they do new films now, hoping to maximise their control over when people watch them (and thus, again, how much money they can get from viewers and distributors).

In the meantime, television has become more cinematic. Long-running dramas feature some of the finest acting and writing in any moving pictures, a trend begun with HBO's award-winning shows and now successfully imitated by pay-television networks like Showtime and AMC. Hour-long shows with sex and swearing resemble short films more than they do the tame fare traditionally offered by America's broadcasters. And their success has been such that non-American pay-television companies will probably imitate their business models, while adapting the content to local tastes, of course.

Will music mimic film, in its preference for the local? America's biggest acts can be heard around the world, and there is no reason to think that this will not continue to be the case. The first decade of the millennium saw two revolutionary trends: the rise of broadband (including, later, mobile broadband) and the sharing of music over those broadband networks. In theory, nearly anyone in the world can listen to nearly any recorded music anywhere. As Stevie Wonder sang, "Music is a world within itself, with a language we all understand."

But he was wrong. People continue to prefer their local languages sung to local sounds. This is true whether or not a country's music is widely regarded internationally, and whether or not a country is "wired" to download music from the internet. Brazil is not particularly well-wired but makes music beloved around the world. Unsurprisingly, a majority of sales there (59%) are of Brazilian music. By contrast, South Korea is one of the most wired countries on Earth and – despite the influence of K-pop around Asia – is not known for universally beloved Korean tunes. Yet as with Brazil, 72% of South Korean sales are of Korean music. Neither globalisation nor technology will lead Lady Gaga or her successors to conquer the Earth.

Those revolutionary digits

That digital technology will remake the music industry is already a given (see Figure 5.4). America is well in the lead, with half of all sales being digital. But Europe has perhaps produced the beacon that will show the way forward for profitable digital music. Spotify, a service that streams millions of tracks instantly to customers at no cost on its basic model (save the occasional advert), is based on its Swedish founder's simple insight: legal listening must be not only cheap, but also more convenient than piracy. It can be best compared to pay (cable) television: if a service is good and convenient, including easy on-demand offerings, then people, at least in middle-income and rich countries, will pay a modest amount or put up with a few ads to save themselves the trouble of hunting for dodgy files on the internet.

The digital revolution will change the creation and curation of culture less than many might think. True, digital recording and image-making have transformed the ease of production. Every Apple computer comes with a free program called Garage Band, a recording suite with tools the best studios of 1960 could only have dreamt of. Digital photography has come so far, so fast that decent smartphones today produce images that are in most ways superior to the most expensive digital cameras of ten years ago.

All this has released a wellspring of talent. The time spent learning the craft of fine photography has been cut radically by immediately available digital images. Photography-sharing websites, notably Flickr, are communities where photographers can quickly learn what people like, share technical tips and tricks – and market themselves. People who started taking photos as a hobby are making successful late-20s and early-30s career shifts into portrait, wedding and even fine-art photography. Capable but uninspired photographers who once sat comfortably upon the rare knowledge of how to make a competent exposure will be driven from a newly energised and competitive business.

But a business it will be. The universal availability of high-quality cameras cannot eliminate the need for professionals to be in the right place, with the right image framed the right way, at the right time – a suite of skills that still requires both talent and practice. If you remain unconvinced, contemplate your wedding or your child being photographed by your uncle just because he blew his bonus on a fancy new camera. This goes doubly for filmmaking of any kind, with the vast array of factors that must come together for a good production.

Photography is one business that has allowed talent to bypass traditional distribution channels successfully. The talent, the portfolio (almost always a website) and networking with clients are all that is needed. But the digital revolution has not removed the gatekeepers of culture in other areas. It has simply changed the nature of their jobs.

Gatekeepers v media mayhem

Take the news business. It is a truism to note that blogging upended a complacent industry between 2000 and 2010. But another trend is less widely noted: the adaptation of media outlets to a bloggy world. Big-name political bloggers in America, the leader in the blogging trend, have been hired by traditional outlets in droves: Andrew Sullivan, Ezra Klein and Nate Silver were all pioneering bloggers; all now work for traditional media companies (the *Daily Beast*/*Newsweek*, the *Washington Post* and the *New York Times*, respectively), and they are far from alone.

Because high-quality content cannot simply be coughed up between other endeavours, content creators will still need to be paid, somehow, to do their best work. And digital communication has opened up the world to so many voices that consumers need a shortcut to find the ones worth listening to. Trusting established media companies is an easy solution.

The media companies also have another tool that would-be independent artists (whether authors, musicians or writers) cannot match: their marketing machines. Big artists have made their start online. Usher, an R&B star, discovered Justin Bieber on YouTube. Lenny Kravitz, another R&B singer, found Lissie, an alternative country and folk singer, on Myspace. But both stars are now on major labels: Island (Bieber) and Columbia (Lissie). Knowing that internet fame is evanescent, artists will continue to take the money and the sustained marketing push that a major corporate promoter can offer.

In publishing, too, e-books are transforming the industry, but not eliminating publishers. Amazon sold more e-books than hardcovers in 2010, and digital reading will make up a majority of book sales overall. Print copies will continue to exist, much as people still print out long-form articles published online, for ease of reading later. But they will eventually be an adjunct, often an on-demand product rather than the main offering from publishers.

At the same time, purely self-e-published works remain a niche phenomenon. Amanda Hocking is a rare success, having self-published and sold over 1m e-books (vampire novels and the like) via online booksellers such as Amazon and Barnes & Noble. But she, too, was quickly snapped up by a traditional publisher, St. Martin's Press. She explained that she did not want to answer e-mails, format covers and otherwise be her own publishing business.

So gatekeepers will remain. With the barrage of offerings, readers, music listeners and filmgoers like having someone to help them find the good stuff, and they often like consuming what others are consuming. This is a fact of human nature unlikely to change dramatically in the decades to come.

The declining tower of Babel

What about human culture more broadly? How will it change by 2050? Is it fated to become more homogenised with the death of distance, or will niche cultures live on in the "long tail" (to use another cliché)? The answer is inevitably a bit of both.

Take language, one of the best proxies for human culture. The 20th century may, in a few centuries' time, be noted for the meteoric rise of English as much as for many of the more explosive events of those 100 years. No language has ever had the global reach that English now enjoys. It has native speakers and official status on every continent; more than 2 billion people live in a country where English has official status (though not all of them speak English; half of these are in India.) It is the undisputed language of scientific publication. In 2001 it accounted for 90% of scientific papers, with no other language having a share bigger than 2%.

This kind of success has nothing to do with the internal characteristics of English, and everything to do with the global pre-eminence of first Britain and then America in the centuries that included the industrial and communications revolutions. That said, it is the kind of lock-in that is difficult to end. Much like the QWERTY keyboard, it has inefficiencies (no one would put the letter A on the left little finger if designing a keyboard today), but with the entire world knowing English, pulling off a switch would be nearly impossible.

What about Chinese? Mandarin – just one of many mutually incomprehensible "Chineses" – is gaining ground in the People's Republic, with official support. Protests in favour of Cantonese, to name one of the biggest alternatives, have been sporadic. Han Chinese settlers, most of them Mandarin-speaking, continue to move to the non-Han territories in China's west.

But Mandarin is not a language of wider communication in the world today, and it is unlikely to become one in the coming decades, regardless of China's rise. The language is simply not used by people of two different groups to communicate, except for the minority of people in the world doing direct business with China. This is largely because its character-based writing system involves the laborious memorisation of 3,000–4,000 characters for basic literacy, and more

Do you speak computer?

One thing threatens the dominance of English, and it is not Chinese. Computer scientists began trying in earnest as early as the 1950s to get computers to translate natural human language. Well into the first years of the 2000s, the results remained dismal. However, the nerds are now taking a different approach. Rather than trying to get computers to parse (and thereby "understand") language and then translate, computer scientists are assembling huge bodies of text translated by humans, and having the computers calculate by the brute force of statistics what is likely to translate into what. This is the approach of Google Translate, for example, which produces much better results than even the best "smart" program of ten years ago.

One scholar of the rise and fall of languages, Nicholas Ostler, argues that English will be "the last lingua franca". As translation technology improves, learning foreign languages will be an outdated skill like calligraphy. However, translating written prose and spoken language are two very different things, and so Ostler is placing a long bet that computers will be able to understand the halting, idiomatic mess that is most people's natural speech, not to mention translate it accurately and quickly. This may take more than the next four decades, at the rate that things have progressed in the past four.

In the absence of a universal translating device, what will happen to the world's 7,000 languages? Tragically, about half of them will die with their last speakers over the next 100 years, according to most linguists. Most will not be killed by English (though that is the case in places like northern Australia). Language-death hotspots include Amazonia and Indonesia; the languages killing them are thus Portuguese, Spanish and Bahasa Indonesia, all of which will grow in size as the states that use those languages integrate their territories more fully.

for advanced reading and writing. This requires many years of study for native Chinese, and few adult foreign learners of Chinese master the system to the extent that they would, say, be able to publish a scientific paper in it.

Moreover, China is wedded to the character system for cultural and historical reasons, and is unlikely to switch to the Roman alphabet. These factors all place a natural limit on the growth of Chinese. The language will surely become more popular, but it is simply not on a trajectory even to rival, much less replace, English. The more interesting question is whether English-speaking skills in China can improve quickly enough to boost China's rise. Despite the eye-popping numbers of Chinese learners of English (around 300m), the quality of instruction in the country remains poor, and few truly master English.

So the number of speakers of the world's languages are likely to bunch up near the biggest, with English remaining on top and with second-tier gainers being Chinese, Spanish, Portuguese and the like. Hindi will grow with India's population, but it is not even the lingua franca in India; Dravidian-language speakers in the south often resent it, and the elites prefer English. Russian's sphere of influence has receded with the end of the Soviet Union; the Central Asian and Caucasus countries are inching towards teaching English as a foreign language and romanising their own languages' writing systems. Arabic will remain fragmented; the millions living in Arabic-speaking countries share a literary written standard, but speak diverse dialects, often to their mutual incomprehension, and no body or state has the legitimacy to standardise them. A number of regional languages – such as Catalan and Welsh – will live on in a demi-monde, spoken by nationalists and supported by local-government policy, but constantly in the shadow of bigger neighbours.

In this way, language mimics art. Though globalisation and technology can in theory give anyone an audience, in fact not everyone will get one. Slow movers, unable to change, will leave the stage. But the influential and rich, whether media companies or entire countries, will find ways to use the new tools of technology to preserve their influence. The climb to the top was not easy, and they will not quickly be dislodged.

PART 2

Heaven and earth

The future of faith, the planet and government

6   Believe it or not

Anthony Gottlieb

The world will have more believers in 2050, but the secular will still eventually inherit the Earth

THERE IS PROBABLY ONLY ONE THING that could transform the fortunes of the world's religions between now and 2050, and that is the arrival of a messiah. Barring the return of Jesus, or the coming of Islam's Mahdi or the Moshiach of the Jews, we may reasonably expect today's patterns of religious belief to continue much as they are. This is because religion is largely inherited. In the normal course of events, you are more likely than not to share the religious outlook of your parents, at least approximately. So big changes in the world's religious map tend to take place only over the course of several generations.

For the purposes of this chapter, let us ignore the possibility of a supernatural cataclysm between now and 2050, and assume that the kingdom of God is still some way off. Even with this proviso, though, forecasting spiritual trends is tricky, because in religious matters it is often unclear what the present situation is, let alone what the future will be. Data about belief are notoriously unreliable, especially when based on polls and interviews, because people can be vague, confused and insincere about their spiritual lives. One man's God may be a being who answers prayers and judges souls, and another's may be a nebulous impersonal force. Finding out what proportion of a population say they believe in God is therefore sometimes not very informative. People may exaggerate or play down their degree of religious observance, in deference to social approval or disapproval. And in the case of supernatural beliefs, many respondents seem to treat questionnaires as a game, and will say the first thing that comes into their heads.

FIG 6.1 **Belief in numbers**

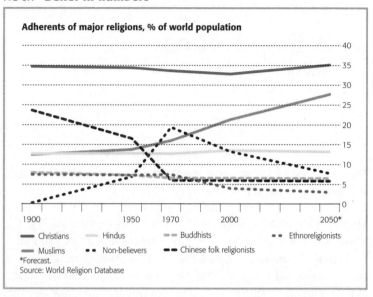

Adherents of major religions, % of world population

National census data, when they record broad religious affiliations, are subject to fewer problems than more detailed surveys of precise religious views. Yet even they are far from perfect: communist countries will undercount believers, and minority ethnic groups (Christians in Egypt, for example) may be similarly misreported by sensitive regimes. Also, many people will casually put down the religion they were raised in, even if they no longer practise it. Nevertheless, such official statistics, complemented by the research of major religious organisations, provide the best available information on large-scale trends. The most comprehensive compilation and analysis of this sort of data are the World Christian Database, produced by the Gordon-Conwell Theological Seminary in Massachusetts and its sister project, the World Religion Database (WRD).

Figure 6.1 uses WRD data to show what seems to have happened to the world's major religions in the course of the 20th century. There are reckoned to be about 10,000 distinct religions, 270 of them with more than 250,000 adherents in 2000. Figure 6.1 shows only those groups that have attracted more than 2% of the world's population, and it includes both agnostics and atheists combined into a single category of non-believers. It also projects the major groups' shares of world population to 2050, by extrapolating demographic trends to adjust for births minus deaths, and converts minus defectors, for each religious (and non-religious) group.

Two things stand out. First, although Christianity retained its comfortable lead as the world's most popular religion in the 20th century, Islam has grown considerably, from 12.3% of the world's population in 1900 to 21.1% a century later. This is almost entirely due to a population explosion in Muslim countries. Even though three people converted to Christianity for every one who converted to Islam in 1970–2000, Muslims have greatly increased their share of the world's believers, because Muslims have had many more children than Christians.

The second notable development is that, for the first time in recorded history, large numbers of people have abandoned belief in God. A conservative analysis by Phil Zuckerman of Pitzer College in Los Angeles suggests that the global total of unbelievers is 500m at the very least, which would make unbelief the fourth-largest religious category. Agnosticism and atheism are relatively new: they began to win adherents among a small number of the most highly educated Europeans in the late 18th century and gathered pace among the European elite in the late 19th century. In the 20th century, unbelief spread more broadly, rising from a mere 0.2% of world population at the beginning of the century to around 13% at its end. This rate of growth is enormously higher than that of any religion in the period.

After Marx and Mao

Most of the places with the highest levels of unbelief – such as France, Scandinavia and Japan, where nearly half or more of the population say they do not believe in God – are not communist or ex-communist states. But the rise and fall of communism in the former Soviet Union and eastern Europe greatly complicates the business of charting unbelief. So does China's communist revolution in 1949 and its government's increasing tolerance of some religions since Mao's death in 1976. It is a fair bet that many religious believers who lived under an authoritarian and officially atheist regime will not have had their religious beliefs recorded correctly. Similarly, it is only to be expected that many people who grew up with atheist secularism imposed on them will embrace religion once they are permitted to do so, especially if the secular regime was an unpopular one. That is why unbelief seems to have peaked in the 1970s (see Figure 6.1). According to Todd Johnson, a co-editor of the WRD, the global decline in recorded unbelief in the final four decades of the 20th century is explained by the collapse of communism in the former Soviet bloc. Because some of the people registered as unbelievers will not in fact have been any such thing, the fall in recorded unbelief is to some extent a correction of the figures rather than a reflection of any real change. It is also true, though, that religious belief seems to have genuinely increased in former communist countries.

Similarly, an expected decline in atheism and agnosticism in the coming decades (from 11.6% of the global population in 2010 to 7.6% in 2050) reflects a rising toleration of religion in China. Because China is home to about one in five of the human race, its religious trends will have an outsized effect on global ones for some time. Although the Chinese Communist Party continues to discourage religion among its members, it now officially tolerates (under fairly strict conditions) the practice of Buddhism, Taoism, Islam, Catholicism and Protestantism. Roughly two-thirds of the world's recorded unbelievers live in China, so as its citizens are allowed to rediscover religion, this is likely to swamp the effects of secularising trends in developed countries.

According to what is known as the secularisation thesis, societies tend – other things being equal – to become less religious as they become more economically developed. I shall defend a version of that idea later. For now, it is worth noting that the revival of religion in China, and in many former communist countries, does not really contradict this notion, even though those places are becoming richer. This is because the thesis aims to describe what happens in the normal course of economic and social development. It cannot be expected to apply when patterns of development are distorted by the rise and fall of authoritarian regimes that dictate what people should believe.

In addition to the dramatic natural increase in Muslim populations and the emergence of unbelief, the development of religion in the

20th century has been marked by two other global trends that are on course to continue, through probably at a slower pace. One is Christianity's shift towards the southern hemisphere: it has shrunk in its former strongholds of western Europe and North America, and grown in parts of Asia, sub-Saharan Africa and Latin America. The other trend is the globalisation of religion: traditional local beliefs have been losing out to the multinational faiths, mainly Christianity and Islam.

At the start of the 20th century over 20% of the world's population were classified as adherents of Chinese folk religions, which involve a mixture of local deities, ancestor veneration, elements of Buddhism, Confucian ethics, magic and Taoism. Chinese folk religionists are now reckoned to amount to less than 7%; this decline began only with the rise of communism, and has doubtless been exaggerated. More tellingly, ethnoreligionists – a polite term for what used to be called "heathens" – have also lost out, falling from 7.3% of the global population in 1900 to 3.8% in 2000. In the early 20th century, it was expected that these ethnic groups of polytheists, animists and shamanists would fall victim to the first proselytising religion that targeted them, and would disappear within a generation. In fact they have proved to be more resistant, and their decline has been much slower than predicted. According to an analysis by Johnson and his colleague David Barrett, there will probably still be more than 350m heathens in 2200.

The godly and fertile poor

In terms of crude global totals, the world is on course to become more religious, simply because of what is happening in China. But is it true, as it has been claimed, that there is also a resurgence of religion elsewhere? The alleged signs of this are many and various. Fundamentalist Islam, which began to revive in the 1970s, is on the rise, as every day's news seems to attest. Christianity is growing in several parts of Africa. Many citizens of the former Soviet Union are rediscovering their churches. Pentecostalism is swelling dramatically in Latin America – from 4.4% of the continent's population in 1970 to 27% in 1990, according to one estimate. And the growth of unbelief in the highly secular countries of north-western Europe seems to be slowing down. As for the United States, the country still displays the high levels of religiosity that are generally found only in much poorer nations.

What do these piecemeal observations add up to? Probably not much, because there are stories of religious decline to be told as well. Christianity's gains in Africa are offset by continuing losses in Europe. The rise of proselytising Protestant denominations in Latin America is balanced by the waning of its traditional sleepy Catholicism. The United States may be highly religious, but it is becoming steadily less so, according to the most objective data. Also, the slowing pace of secularisation in largely Protestant north-western Europe is counterbalanced by a still-accelerating drift away from religion in Catholic countries, such as Ireland and Italy, which started secularising relatively late.

In 2003, an analysis for Harvard University's Weatherhead Centre concluded that religious belief and practice were declining in most of the world's rich countries, but that the large and poor countries containing most of the world's population were in the midst of a religious resurgence. Demographic factors alone will ensure that the ranks of the religious will swell enormously. Suppose that the proportion of religious people in each relatively poor country stayed exactly the same for decades: the religious would still inherit the Earth, for quite a long while, because the populations of poor countries are growing much faster than the populations of rich ones. The believers are out-breeding the unbelievers. Figure 6.2 shows how much faster population growth is in religious countries than in less religious ones.

This effect is found within countries as well as in international comparisons: religious groups tend to have more children than their secular neighbours. In his book, *Shall The Religious Inherit The Earth? Demography and Politics in the 21st Century*, Eric Kaufmann, a professor at Birkbeck College in London, notes that the openly non-religious in developed countries "are displaying the lowest fertility rates ever recorded in human history".

Look inside any country, and the most striking changes in its religious make-up will often be the effect of variances in fertility. In

FIG 6.2 **Fertile with faith**

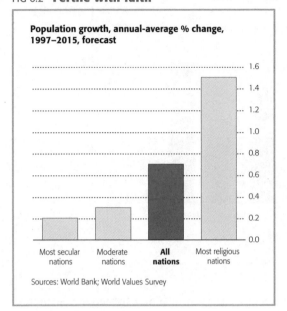

Population growth, annual-average % change, 1997–2015, forecast

Sources: World Bank; World Values Survey

Israel, for example, ultra-Orthodox families have three times more children than other Israelis; largely as a result of this, the ultra-Orthodox are on course to be in a majority in the second half of this century. Or consider Mormons, who not so long ago were a fringe group. Thanks to their large families, they are about to overtake Jews in America, or may already have done so. Kaufmann reckons that about three-quarters of the sharp rise in conservative evangelical Protestants in America between 1900 and 1975 was due simply to their high fertility, not to conversion. Like other demographers, he expects western Europe to become markedly more religious in the course of the 21st century, as a result of immigration from poor countries and the relatively low fertility of unbelievers.

So, other things being equal, will the world become steadily more religious forever? Probably not, because the high birth rates of the religious may be expected to fall as their incomes rise. Sooner or later, if the past is any guide, immigrant populations will come to resemble their hosts, and poor countries will become less religious

FIG 6.3 **God and development**

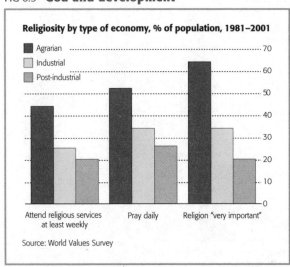

Religiosity by type of economy, % of population, 1981–2001

- ■ Agrarian
- □ Industrial
- ■ Post-industrial

Attend religious services at least weekly / Pray daily / Religion "very important"

Source: World Values Survey

and less fecund. There is a strong correlation between low economic development and religion, as Figure 6.3 illustrates.

Figure 6.3 pools data from 175 countries grouped according to their scores on the UN's human-development index, which measures GDP per person, life expectancy and education. The 97 ("agrarian") countries with the lowest levels of economic development are, by pretty much any measure, on average at least twice as religious as the 20 most affluent ("post-industrial") nations. And the 58 middle-ranking economies tend to be middle-ranking in religiosity too. (A strong correlation between poverty and religion also exists inside countries: the poorest citizens of each post-industrial country are on average almost twice as religious as their richest citizens.)

The American exception

According to the secularisation thesis, this trend will continue: religion will eventually weaken as countries develop. But in the past couple of decades, a minority of sociologists have begun to question this idea, mainly because of the apparently anomalous position of the United States, which seems to buck the trend by combining wealth and piety.

They argue that it is Europe, not America, which is the exception, and that the rest of the world will follow America's pattern, not Europe's. It is certainly true that economic development shows no sign of eradicating religion altogether, except perhaps in Scandinavia, where interest in religion is strikingly low. But it is not clear that any proponent of the secularisation thesis has ever believed that religion would disappear entirely. And it is bizarre to regard Europe rather than America as exceptional, because all the non-European rich countries except America – such as Canada, Japan and Australia and New Zealand – are secularising on the European pattern.

Let us therefore take a closer look at religion in America. This will give a clearer picture of the ways in which religion changes and declines in the face of economic development, and may help us to see what is in store for other countries as they develop.

First, though, what does it mean to say that religion is declining in a society? It cannot be just a matter of how many people attend religious services, or say they believe in God, or maintain that religion is important to them. We should also look at exactly what people believe, what their attitude is to the religious beliefs of others, and how their religious beliefs influence their moral and political ones. And we should look at the political power and cultural influence of religious institutions and groups.

Consider two imaginary societies, A and B. Suppose that in A, the established religion has the power to outlaw homosexuality and the teaching of evolution in schools. Suppose also that most people in A believe in the literal truth of their sacred texts and endorse supernatural beliefs, such as a belief in miracles. Again, suppose that most believers in A maintain that their own religion is the only valid one and that the adherents of other religions will suffer in the afterlife. Now imagine that none of these things is true in society B. The citizens of B, let us say, tend to believe that whenever sacred texts or religious traditions conflict with scientific evidence, science wins; that everyone finds their own path to God; that adherents of other religions will not necessarily suffer eternal torment; that God does not intervene in natural events or create natural disasters as a punishment; that morality is primarily a matter of personal fulfilment or social responsibility rather than of following God's orders; and that religious authorities should not have the power to dictate policy in education, sexual morality or family life.

In which of these two imaginary societies is religion stronger? We do not need to know whether it is A or B that has higher church or mosque attendance, or more people who say they believe in God, in order to know that it is A in which religion is the more powerful force. It is in B that the effects of education, individualism and other modernising forces have evidently done the most to erode the styles of religious belief that were more or less universal 500 years ago. That would remain true even if more people in B than in A attended some sort of church each week. As societies develop, according to the secularisation thesis, they become less like A and more like B. And, despite its relatively high levels of professed belief in God, and the large amount of media attention given to the views of fundamentalist and conservative Christian denominations, America turns out to be no exception to this rule.

In 1966 Bryan Wilson, a British sociologist of religion, observed that while Europeans had secularised by abandoning churches, Americans had instead secularised their churches. In other words, Americans continued to pay lip service to religion, but their religion became less religious. As Steve Bruce, another British sociologist, shows in his 2011 book, *Secularization*, the focus of American faith has "shifted from the next world to this one and from the glorification of God to the satisfaction of human needs". Bruce notes that there was a transformation in mainstream American Christianity from around the 1930s as religion began increasingly to be presented as a matter of personal growth. (One of the most influential pioneers of the modern American self-help movement, Norman Vincent Peale, was the minister of one of New York's biggest churches.)

Perhaps the most telling indication of this shift in American religion is to be found in the reasons people give for attending religious services. According to one study of an American city in the 1920s, the most popular reason given for going to church was that obedience to God required it; but when the study was repeated in 1977, the most popular reason was instead "pleasure". Another sign that American religion is becoming a lifestyle choice like any other can be found in the drastic decline of the idea that adherents of rival religions will be damned. By the 1970s, Americans were far less likely than they had been in the 1940s to say that Christianity was the one true religion and that everyone should adopt it. By 2008, about 70% of religious Americans agreed instead that "many religions can lead to eternal life". American beliefs have also become significantly less fundamentalist and more vague. The proportion of Americans who claim that the Bible is literally true has fallen dramatically, from 65% in 1964 to 26% in 2009. And in 2007, according to polls by the Pew Forum, nearly a third of American believers saw God as "an impersonal force", whatever that means, rather than as the traditional supreme personal being.

Non-believers and adherents of liberal denominations tend to be dismayed and baffled by the apparent strength of fundamentalist beliefs and the "religious right" in the United States. But the power of literalist and conservative denominations is exaggerated by what could be called the headline fallacy: fundamentalist groups are newsworthy precisely because their views are not the norm. And religious conservatives campaign noisily because they are losing all their battles ("Winners don't protest," as Bruce puts it). The "Moral Majority" movement was started by television evangelists in the late 1970s because conservative Christians felt, quite rightly, that a tide of secularism and liberal values had turned against them.

Since then, the religious right has failed to achieve any of its main aims: homosexuality and even homosexual marriage are more widely accepted, not less so; the criminalisation of sodomy is being swept away; abortion remains constitutional; more women with children work outside the home; more unmarried couples cohabit; creationism and "intelligent design" have not won equal billing with evolution in schools; America's strict barriers between church and state have not been eroded. The only battle in which the religious right has made any headway is the one over abortion, which is now harder to obtain in some places. But it is worth noting that this is one part of the religious right's agenda for which there is some support in the broader population.

So the apparent strength of old-time religion in the United States is not as great as it may appear to be. Furthermore, all broad measures of the country's religiosity are steadily declining. In 1948, just 2% of Americans said they had no religion, but by the end of the 1990s polls put the figure at 12–16%. Regular attendance at a church, synagogue or mosque was claimed by 41% of the population in 1971, but by just 31% in 2002, according to the National Opinion Research Centre. The future looks disappointing for American believers, because today's young are less religious than today's old, and degrees of religiosity tend not to change after early adulthood. In 2007, according to the Pew Forum, 57% of those aged 65 or older, but only 45% of those aged 29 or younger, were absolutely certain of the existence of a personal God. And each generation was less likely than its predecessor to claim a religious affiliation.

Nevertheless, the fact remains that Americans are, on average, significantly more religious than the inhabitants of other large, rich countries. Many explanations have been offered for this. One of the most plausible invokes the source of community that churches provide for an extremely mobile, ethnically diverse and immigrant population. Nearly 12% of people in the United States were born in another country – usually a poorer and more religious one than America – and the recently arrived turn for social support to churches used by other members of their ethnic group. More than two-thirds of these immigrants are from Christian countries, so they tend to strengthen the local religious institutions; in Europe, by contrast, most immigrants are Muslims or Hindus. Even native-born Americans are much more likely than people in other developed countries to live far from their families and friends: the average American moves home nearly 12 times in a lifetime, and America is a very large place. Churches provide an instant community for recent arrivals.

Aspects of poverty

No doubt several cultural, historical and demographic factors play a role in America's religious life. But from the point of view of the secularisation thesis, the most important fact about America is that, in many respects which are relevant to religion, it is more like a poor country than a rich one. Life is tougher in the United States than in any other developed nation.

Consider first the most basic measure of human welfare, which is life expectancy. America is not in the top ten countries ranked by this criterion; it is not even in the top 20 or the top 30. It ranks 34th out of the UN's member states. It is the only developed country without universal health care: well over 40m people have no health insurance, and illness often means financial ruin, even for the relatively well-off. Welfare safety nets are poor by European standards: lose your job, and you may well lose everything. Poverty and economic inequality are strikingly high. It is a violent country: the murder rate is by far the highest in the developed world – twice as high as in the next most murderous country – and a much larger proportion of Americans are incarcerated than in any other rich nation. In short, Americans live closer to disaster than the citizens of other rich countries. They are especially in need of God, because nobody else will help them.

According to a refined version of the secularisation thesis developed by Pippa Norris of Harvard University and Ronald Inglehart of the University of Michigan, "feelings of vulnerability ... drive religiosity", and it is a sense of security, economic and otherwise, that is strongly correlated with a secular outlook. This would explain why religion has a greater presence in America than in other rich countries: America's wealth has not generated the security that economic development usually brings. (It is notable that the poorer Americans are, the more likely they are to say that religion is important to them, and the more often they are likely to pray.)

So it seems that the secularisation thesis is broadly correct, in which case the world's developing nations can be expected eventually to follow the patterns of the past and, in the long run, grow less religious as they become richer and life becomes more secure. Of course, nobody knows how quickly poor countries will become richer, or which ones will eventually provide their citizens with the levels of security that seem to encourage a European style of secularisation rather than an American one. But to bet that religion will eventually weaken in the developing world is perhaps safer than betting on the arrival of a messiah.

7   Feeling the heat

Oliver Morton

Risks from a changing climate are unavoidable. The challenge – technological, ethical and political – will be to manage them

A HUNDRED YEARS AGO, pictures evoking the future showed skyscrapers and aeroplanes. Fifty years on there were spaceships and, for the more pessimistic, mushroom clouds. Now the focus has changed from things in the world, and out of this world, to the world itself. The most widespread pictures representing times to come, staring out from newspapers and computer screens and scientific journals, are maps tinted in various shades of alarm, their mottled yellows and deepening oranges and browns topped with ominously dark arctic red.

These maps, like the mushroom clouds of yore, are treated as warnings as much as they are predictions. In most parts of the world, most people who think about climate change agree with the broad scientific consensus, embodied in those horrid maps, that unchecked human activity will continue to warm the world. In this they are correct, though the absolute amount of warming is subject to quite large uncertainties.

The problem with seeing the maps as warnings, though, is that many who do so overestimate the degree to which such warnings can be heeded. They think there are courses of action within political reach that will simply avert the warming they fear. The world has, after all, managed for decades to avoid mushroom clouds rising over cities. With wisdom, diligence and luck it could continue that winning streak indefinitely. Warming is different; unlike war it has a momentum which makes it close to inevitable. The world is likely to be appreciably warmer in 2050 than it is today more or less whatever people do about it.

How much warmer is hard to say. The science of climate change is qualitatively fairly well understood – science can say why carbon dioxide and various other additions to the atmosphere warm or cool the world – but it is still quantitatively quite poor when it comes to predicting the amount of climate change produced by a specific alteration to the atmosphere. That provides one level of uncertainty. How the world will evolve in the coming decades in terms of energy use, fuel mix, forestry, farming and overall economic growth provides another level of uncertainty. And to add a further complication, what the climate does will influence what people do. A rapidly worsening future climate might spur more dramatic action than today's gently warming world has a stomach for. At the same time, the impacts of such warming might mean that the resources with which to act are stretched too thin for the job.

All this makes it hard to say where in the range of possibilities the climate will have reached in 2050. But, in part because of the momentum of both the climate system and the infrastructures that underpin humanity's interference in it, 2050 is not really the issue. While the state that the climate will have got to in 2050 is not known, it is also not easily altered to any radical extent. What the world has much more control over is the direction in which the climate is headed at that point. If the drivers of change are largely unabated, the world of 2050 is very likely to be one faced with serious risks on a planetary scale. If a more prudent course is followed, then the worst may have been averted, and a profound shift will have come about: humanity will have started to take responsibility for the future of the planet which it has long since come to dominate.

The rhetorical imperative

It is hard to accept the inertia inherent in climate change. Since the phenomenon is caused by human action – the emission of carbon dioxide, from fossil fuels and burning forests, along with other greenhouse gases emitted by industry and agriculture, and further pollutants with a mixed bag of influences – it is natural to think that it is a problem with a clear human solution, achievable promptly. Much of today's discussion of the issue is framed in a deeply unrealistic rhetoric of action (slash emissions now, ten years to save the planet, and so on) that ignores the factors which make such action so difficult. The drivers of climate change are built into today's infrastructure, making them extremely hard to influence in any dramatic way. The precise benefits of the shifts in infrastructure that decisive action would require are unknown. The costs and disruption they would impose, often on well-entrenched interests, are more easily seen. The benefits are also a long way in the future, and many of them may end up being felt by people whose polities did not pay the costs concerned. Given these constraints, it is hardly surprising that action on climate change cannot keep up with the rhetoric of simple solutions.

That rhetoric was at its peak in the months leading up to the Copenhagen conference in 2009. The reasons that the conference did not and could not live up to the hype still apply, and they explain why dramatic action is not to be expected in the short or medium term.

Before Copenhagen, there had been two key developments in the global response to climate change, both heralded, in their time, as successes. The first was the UN Framework Convention on Climate Change, created at the Rio Earth Summit of 1992, which committed its signatory nations – more or less everyone – to stopping dangerous climate change. The second was the Kyoto protocol to that convention, agreed upon in 1997, which committed rich countries to specific carbon-dioxide emission targets for 2012. The targets were not for the most part onerous, and the United States was not included because although it did much to shape the protocol it did not ratify it. Nevertheless, the protocol was deemed progress by its begetters. Copenhagen was to take things on by establishing more ambitious targets further in the future, and by creating commitments for all countries, not just rich ones. After a decade of increasing scientific agreement and public concern about climate change, politicians from various rich countries convinced themselves that this was the moment to "save the planet".

At the heart of the deal rich countries sought at Copenhagen was the idea that by 2050 the world should have reduced its annual emissions of greenhouse gases to half of today's level (see Figure 7.1).

FIG 7.1   **The Copenhagen ideal**

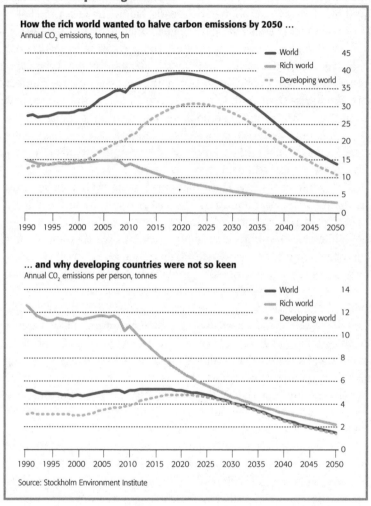

How the rich world wanted to halve carbon emissions by 2050 ...
Annual CO$_2$ emissions, tonnes, bn

Legend: World, Rich world, Developing world

... and why developing countries were not so keen
Annual CO$_2$ emissions per person, tonnes

Legend: World, Rich world, Developing world

Source: Stockholm Environment Institute

In the context of this halving the developed countries would commit themselves to a significantly more impressive 80% cut. Those deep cuts were portrayed as allowing the developing world room for manoeuvre: while developed-world emissions would reduce straight away, developing-world emissions (which in 2009 were more or less the same as those from the rich world) could continue to increase well into the 2020s, even the early 2030s, before they began to fall.

All manner of explanations have been offered for the Copenhagen summit's failure to bring this deal off: poor chairing by the Danes; cold weather at the conference; weak leadership by the Americans; resurgent climate scepticism stoked by the release of a large number of "climategate" e-mails from researchers at Britain's university of East Anglia; hopeless confusion among the Europeans; the impact of the recession; and the intransigence of the Chinese. But we don't really have to look much further than basic demographic trends to realise how hopeless the deal being proposed actually was.

The world of 2050 will have a population almost half as big again as that of 2009, and almost all the increase will be in developing countries. If rich countries did manage to cut emissions by 80% by 2050, the extra room for manoeuvre such cuts were meant to offer the developing countries would be entirely used up by their larger populations. To meet the 50% global-reduction target, developing countries would basically have to freeze their carbon emissions per person at today's level. This is not remotely plausible. There is currently no reliable and cheap alternative to fossil fuels for providing the bulk of the continuous baseload power needed by cities and industries; nor is there a readily deployable alternative to fossil fuels for moving people and transporting goods. There is no realistic way at present for developing countries to turn themselves into rich industrial and post-industrial economies without increasing their energy use per person a lot, and thus their carbon emissions per person a fair bit.

So the Copenhagen deal foundered. The consolation prize, fleshed out a year later at the climate conference in Cancún, Mexico, was an agreement that all nations would say what they intended to do about carbon-dioxide emissions – including those from deforestation – establishing non-binding targets against which they would be measured. China, for example, has said that it will reduce the carbon intensity of its economy by 40% to 45% by 2020, meaning that it will be emitting only a bit more than half as much carbon dioxide per unit of GDP then as it did in 2005. This is an impressive goal, and requires both large increases in efficiency and big changes in the way energy is generated. China is adding more wind capacity than

FIG 7.2 **The China syndrome**

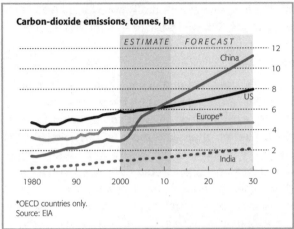

Carbon-dioxide emissions, tonnes, bn

ESTIMATE   FORECAST

China

US

Europe*

India

1980   90   2000   10   20   30

*OECD countries only.
Source: EIA

any other country at the moment, it is still building large dams, and it has ambitious plans for nuclear energy, even after the disaster at Fukushima in Japan. It is importing ever more natural gas, which emits less carbon than coal, while enthusiastically developing its own gas reserves. But almost all this clean and cleaner energy is addition, rather than replacement. China expects its GDP to increase at a considerably greater rate than that by which it will decarbonise, and so expects emissions to continue to grow into the 2020s at the very least (see Figure 7.2).

Broadly speaking, as China goes, so goes the world. Renewable-energy sources will probably make up more of the energy mix in 2050 than they do today, possibly quite a lot more, in countries that can afford the smarter and more capable grids these require. In developing countries solar off-grid solutions offer a promising growth area that could improve a lot of people's lives. Nuclear power may, eventually, increase its share of the mix, though at present it seems headed in the opposite direction. This will all be helped if rich economies improve the policies some have already implemented to put a price on carbon.

Quite possibly, then, the present rate of industrial emissions growth – 5.9% in 2010, an all-time high – may slacken. But as more and more developing economies grow quickly enough to improve the lot of their growing populations, global emissions are unlikely to fall for decades to come. The best we can realistically hope for is a plateauing of emissions in the 2030s, followed perhaps by a modest decline.

The fossil imperative

Inertia does not mean stasis. Oil production seems highly unlikely to keep up with the world's propensity for planes, trains and automobiles. As the extraction of oil from conventional reserves peaks and starts to decline, more and more will be needed from unconventional reserves, such as tar sands; and though these unconventional reserves exist, politics and difficult economics may mean that it is not possible to bring them on stream at a rate that will avoid episodes of tight supply and spiking prices. What is more, some alternatives to conventional oil, such as Canada's tar sands, produce a fair amount of extra carbon dioxide. In economies that put a price on carbon it might be possible to dispose of the carbon dioxide emitted in these processes underground, a technology that has been much discussed for power stations, too, but has so far notably failed to make progress.

Meanwhile, unconventional gas will take on a greater role. New technologies have already allowed America to get gas from shale formations that were previously unworkable, becoming self-sufficient and making gas a cheaper fuel than it was before. Other countries have similar bounties. This might at the same time be good news for the environment but not very good news for the climate.

When a coal-fired station is replaced by renewables there are two benefits: a long-term climate benefit and a short-term air-quality benefit. In many cases the second may be more politically and ethically pressing; smogs from coal kill tens of thousands in many countries, hundreds of thousands in China. But that second benefit is realised as well by switching to natural gas as by switching to renewables. If gas is a cheap, easy and plentiful alternative to coal, renewables and nuclear power become pure-climate plays, rather than climate-plus-clean-air-right-now plays, and will look less attractive as a result. The International Energy Agency's future scenarios featuring high levels of gas use also predict a less aggressive fielding of renewables and nuclear, leading to a climate outlook hardly any better than if the gas were not there at all.

To the extent that air pollution is driving renewables policy, gas clouds the climate issue. Coal, meanwhile, clouds the atmosphere, which leads to a striking irony. Smog particles produced by burning coal, in particular tiny sulphate particles, reflect sunlight away from the surface of the Earth, and thus cool it. If coal is replaced by gas (or for that matter renewables), that cooling goes away. It is possible that by removing this cooling effect, a major shift to gas would lead to a world in 2050 hotter than it would be if people had stuck with the more carbon-rich coal. That is not in itself a reason to avoid gas: the sulphates from coal cool things only while the coal is being burned, whereas the carbon dioxide emitted by that coal will warm the planet for centuries to come. But it all amounts to a potent reminder of the uncertainties, complexities and unintended consequences that abound when people try to manage the climate.

Doing the maths

The effects of sulphates bring us back to the scientific uncertainty around climate assessments. There are various reasons why calculating the warming effects of carbon dioxide from first principles is hard, regardless of the vast computing power that climate modellers now have at their disposal, and as a result such estimates tend to have an uncertainty of a factor of two or more. But given that people have been turning fossil fuels into carbon dioxide for more than a century – James Watt got things rolling in the 1770s – and taking the world's temperature with reasonable reliability over the same period, why is it not possible to come up with an empirical assessment on the matter? Some 1 trillion tonnes of carbon dioxide were emitted in the 20th century; the temperature rose by about 0.7°C. Surely we can just do the maths.

The effects of sulphate particles and other "aerosols", as tiny particles floating in the atmosphere are known, are one of the reasons this is not the case. Over the 20th century aerosols produced by people cooled various bits of the planet – some of them, it seems, quite a lot. This cooling masked some of the warming that the carbon dioxide was bringing about. Waxings and wanings in the warming trend may be a result of this balance seesawing back and forth. Warming was slow after the second world war, and then sped up in the 1970s and 1980s as clean-air legislation cut aerosol emissions from developed countries. It slowed down in the 2000s, as China's coal-burning went into overdrive. But the precise amount of cooling that aerosols have provided is impossible to quantify. If it was only a little, then the warming for a given amount of carbon dioxide is probably at the lower end of the range of estimates; if the cooling effect has been strong, then so has the warming effect, and the 21st century will get nastily hot.

Such uncertainties mean that for any given emission pathway there is a range of possible warming. The fact that the range of plausible pathways in the decades to come is relatively constrained (somewhere between today's growth trend continuing more or less unaltered and a distinct, but not dramatic, slowing down, with a peak no sooner than the 2030s if at all) means that as far as 2050 is concerned, the bigger uncertainty is in the science itself. A carbon-dioxide-induced warming of less than 1°C compared with the 1990s would surprise many climate scientists but is quite possible. A carbon-dioxide-induced warming of 2°C – perhaps unlikely by 2050, but again within the broad range of uncertainties – would be both damaging in itself and dire in its prognosis for the latter part of the century.

Either way, the level of the sea will rise, though by 2050 it is highly unlikely to have done so spectacularly: tens of centimetres or so, perhaps (see Figure 7.3). But because many coasts are subsiding, especially in the world's deltas, local sea-level rises may be larger than that. This could mean the relocation of millions of people and a lot of flood defences as well. Tropical cyclones, which account for much of the damage the sea does to the land, may become less frequent. But the number of the most destructive of such storms – category 4 and category 5 hurricanes – seems likely to increase. Bigger storms do disproportionately greater damage.

The rise of the oceans will come in part at the expense of the icy parts of the world, which will shrink. Arctic summer sea ice will mostly go, allowing more shipping and mining while removing a

FIG 7.3 **That sinking feeling**

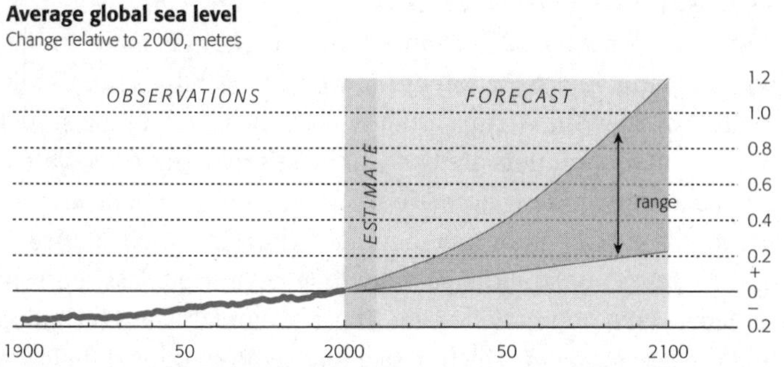

Average global sea level
Change relative to 2000, metres

OBSERVATIONS FORECAST

ESTIMATE

range

1.2
1.0
0.8
0.6
0.4
0.2
+
0
−
0.2

1900 50 2000 50 2100

Source: "Contemporary Sea Level Rise", by Anny Cazenave and William Llovel, *Annual Review of Marine Science*, 2010

landscape of which indigenous peoples were once an integral part (see box). Most mountain glaciers will diminish. Winter snows will increase in some places (warmer air can hold more moisture to fall as snow) but snowpacks will mostly melt more quickly, increasing the risks of spring floods and summer water shortages in the rivers they feed.

The probability of the summer of 2050 being warmer than the warmest recorded to date will be between 10% and 50% in much of the world, and higher than that in a few places (see Figure 7.4). People will also have to contend with shifts in weather patterns. Many models say the factors that give rise to the Indian monsoon are likely to weaken. The strength of the rainfall within it, though, is likely to rise, because of more water vapour in warmer air. How that will affect an Indian agricultural system that will have many more mouths to feed and has been depleting groundwater at a prodigious rate is hard to say; it may not be an unmitigated disaster, but expecting it not to be a problem seems pretty optimistic. As wet places, such as much of South-East Asia, get wetter, so increased evaporation will make dry places drier, an effect likely to be seen in southern Africa and the south-western United States.

This means the world will see more droughts, some of which

The Arctic: a new ocean

It will be the most visible change humanity has yet made to the way its planet looks: the top of the world will change from white to blue. In 2050 the Arctic Ocean will still be frozen in the sunless winter, but its summers are likely to be largely ice-free. Its waters will be a home to new ecosystems, a route for new trade and a site for the extraction of raw materials. There is a good chance that the region will be richer, more fully developed, less sparsely settled, even a booming frontier. There is more or less no chance that the landscape to which indigenous people adapted their way of life will not be changed past easy recognition.

Models – and recent experience – suggest that the Arctic will warm twice as fast as the world as a whole. The loss of ice will be the most obvious effect, but not the only one. Most of the high Arctic is currently a desert, mostly because there is so little evaporation from the ocean and thus so little precipitation. As ice recedes and temperatures rise that will change: there will be more snow and more rain, different patterns of erosion and vegetation. Forests will spread north over what is now taiga and tundra, adding warmth as they do so (dark firs, like dark water, absorb sunlight that snowy tundra and ice-covered oceans reflect away). Coastlines, especially in the deltas atop the Yukon, Mackenzie and Lena, will erode more swiftly as waves attack them for more of the year, and as permafrost within them melts. The summer warmth stored in the seas and released in the autumn will change wind and weather patterns, perhaps with impacts farther south.

The ocean will not just be warmer and sunnier; in many places it will also be enriched with new nutrients. Winds over open water help mix it up, drawing nutrients out of the depths. More plankton will attract new populations of fish, including immigrants from the Pacific and Atlantic. The resultant novel ecosytems offer the possibility of fisheries which, if well managed, could prove rich, if not vast. The retreat of the ice will also make it easier to extract the region's significant oil and gas resources, perhaps using production systems on the sea floor, as Statoil has done at its Snøhvit field in the Barents Sea. Such systems do not need to worry about the return of the ice in the winter.

If there are few rigs to be seen, though, there will still be a lot more ships dotting the opened seas. Some will be taking liquefied natural gas out of the Arctic (a trade that has already begun), some simply making use of the fact that, when ice-free, the ocean is a handy shortcut from Asia to Europe and parts of America. Shorter routes mean lower fuel use. Clean-fuel regulations that minimise the sootiness of a ship's exhaust will be crucial for such shipping to be an environmental, as well as an economic, success.

Indigenous factor

Managing the environmental impacts of new shipping, industry and fishing will be a challenge, but not an impossible one. And fears of escalating conflict over Arctic resources seem overblown. It is true that there are disputes over sea-floor resources between some of the eight Arctic nations. But diplomatic solutions are likely to be found. The eight meet regularly in an "Arctic Council" which, though founded to deal with environmental issues, increasingly concerns itself with other matters, too; in 2011 they signed the first binding agreement under its auspices, the Arctic Search and Rescue Agreement, which will help with development, and which neatly finessed territorial disputes.

A key to the future prospects of the Arctic Council is its decision to admit representatives of the Arctic's indigenous peoples as "permanent participants". Their lives were being deeply changed by development – by things like snowmobiles, alcohol and more fixed settlements – before climate change began to gear up. Further development will exacerbate some of these problems even as it improves things in other ways. Meanwhile, climate change will remove great swathes of the landscape within which those people have made their livings over generations. The Arctic is not a vast area (4% of the Earth's surface) or a highly populated one; but the scale of human change there over the next 40 years, as well as environmental change, may be unprecedented.

FIG 7.4 **A hotter home**

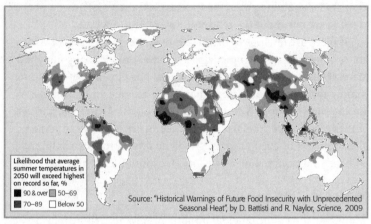

Likelihood that average summer temperatures in 2050 will exceed highest on record so far, %
- 90 & over
- 70–89
- 50–69
- Below 50

Source: "Historical Warnings of Future Food Insecurity with Unprecedented Seasonal Heat", by D. Battisti and R. Naylor, *Science*, 2009

may be catastrophic. The American dustbowl of the 1930s was not a purely climatic phenomenon, as new farming practices also played a big role in the destruction of the soil. You might imagine that modern agronomy would help avoid such synergies (though subsidy regimes can still encourage agricultural nonsense, as biofuel policies demonstrate, hurting food prices and encouraging peculiar crop choices for a climate benefit that is surely nugatory if not actually harmful). But even with smart farming, coping with droughts that could be significantly worse than that of the dustbowl will present challenges to the places they hit, which could include America and the Mediterranean.

In parts of Africa droughts have always been common – the tropics have larger and more co-ordinated shifts in climate than temperate regions, thanks in large part to the semi-regular oscillations of El Niño, a shuffling of warmth in the tropical Pacific. What happens to El Niño in terms of the frequency and magnitude of its primary Pacific manifestation is yet another of climate science's unknowns. But its effects in terms of droughts and flooding (the latter more associated with the other phase of the oscillation, La Niña) will probably get worse in a world characterised by higher temperature, higher evaporation and higher water-vapour capacity in the atmosphere.

Food for thought

Even without catastrophic droughts, people, regions and countries dependent on agriculture look vulnerable. No other basic human activity is so intimately bound up with the weather. Crops are sensitive to changes in patterns of rainfall and peak temperature, as well as to average temperature and precipitation; so are the pests and diseases that attack them, and the unfarmed ecosystems that provide water retention, soil quality and the other exogenous bounty on which much of agriculture depends. In high latitudes and some mid-latitudes warming should lengthen growing seasons, which is good up to a point. But hotter summers could affect the benefits of longer springs; even without droughts, very hot days, especially at some points in the season, can do disproportionate damage to crops such as maize. The warming climate is estimated to have reduced yields of wheat and maize by 4–5% over the past 30 years.

While the food-price rises from lowered yields and disrupted harvests would help some producers, they would hurt the poor, especially the rural poor, whose food is less likely to be subsidised and whose opportunities for employment fall in line with lower farm outputs. If volatile oil prices lead in turn to spiking prices for agricultural inputs, problems with food prices will be amplified, as they were in 2008.

Bad news for the rural poor will add to the growth of cities. Although this in itself is no bad thing – cities are good for low-carbon growth – it may be less beneficial than might be hoped. The transition to a richer, more urban economy normally follows or goes hand in hand with increases in agricultural productivity. Take away the latter, and the former may not do much, or any, good. There is tentative econometric evidence that a deteriorating climate may have contributed to excessive urbanisation in Africa: slowing, rather than aiding, development. If this is indeed the case, it could be undermining societies' ability to respond to climate change.

In all this gloom there are two reasons for some countervailing optimism. One is carbon-dioxide fertilisation. Higher carbon-dioxide levels make photosynthesis easier for most plants. In temperate climates this effect may outstrip that of climate change for the warming expected by 2050, increasing net yields. It should help in tropical countries, too, though few expect it fully to offset the effects of temperature and more extreme fluctuations in climate across growing seasons. The other reason for optimism is the ability farmers and their supporting industries have shown to adapt. Despite many warnings of doom, yields of arable crops have grown remarkably in the past half-century. They may well be able to grow further in the decades to come.

If they do not, wildlife, already stressed by the rigours of climate change, will bear the brunt. In a world with a growing population the alternative to more intensive farming on existing farmland is more farmland. Converting forests, as would often be the case, to farms would harm biodiversity, reduce ecosystem services such as the regulation of rain and flooding, and increase carbon-dioxide emissions. One of the reasons that decreases in deforestation look quite plausible – more so than decreases in industrial emissions – is that increasing yields in crops such as soy, where genetic modification is now near universal, mean there is no overwhelming pressure for more farmland. Decreasing yields would change that: instead, there would be a new wave of extinctions as habitat is destroyed and as the climate changes. Damaged ecosystems may worsen the fundamental problem, too. At the moment roughly half the carbon dioxide emitted from fossil fuels is soaked up again by plants and by the oceans. There is good reason to think that this kind service will be increasingly withdrawn as the world warms up, and it is a fair bet that the more denuded the ecosystems involved, the faster and more traumatic that withdrawal will be.

Manage the risks

It may be that the worst will not come to pass. A low sensitivity, bringing significantly less than 1°C of warming by 2050 even if nothing is done about emissions, remains a possibility. Some – they call themselves "lukewarmers" – argue that elements of groupthink in climate science are leading to a consistent underappreciation of that possibility. That said, others argue that an unwillingness to seem too shocking leads scientists to avoid talking about the highest sensitivities, too, underplaying apocalyptic developments which, while unlikely, cannot be ruled out.

The counsel of the lukewarmers is to wait and see how bad it gets and not take expensive actions until they seem more clearly warranted. But this ignores the inertia in the system, which means that the effects of today's actions on emissions will not be felt for decades to come, and that strong action in decades to come is unlikely to be possible from a standing start. And it falls to some extent into the same trap that the pre-Copenhagen boosters of radical action fell into: the idea that the changing climate is a specific problem (a pressing one, to Copenhagenites; one not yet proven, to lukewarmers) of the sort that might have a straightforward solution.

With its broad base, endless ramifications, constrained space for response and political intractability, climate change is really not that sort of problem at all. It is more like a context, or a landscape: a way of seeing the fundamental planetary terms of trade. It is the as yet imperfectly perceived geophysical and geopolitical basis of 21st-century civilisation. The challenge is not to solve a problem, but to manage a panoply of risks at every level from that of the farm and city, up through the state and region to the globe itself.

This risk-management approach is not yet mainstream, in part because the political forces that were aligned behind the "big problem-big solution" approach have not yet taken on board the degree to which their approach is failing. In practice, risk management may not look that contrasting in its ambitions. Emissions should still be reduced. But the reasons are subtly different. In the Copenhagen mindset, the idea was to try to make sure warming stayed below 2°C. A risk-management approach sees more benefit in the change that lower emissions would make to the long tail of unlikely but deeply damaging possibilities. Emission reductions that only diminish the likely warming a little can do a lot more to rein in these extreme possibilities. And they avoid the problem of treating all reductions below the utterly heroic as failures, turning them instead into foundations for future effort. A risk-management approach also puts considerably more stress on reducing the vulnerability of countries, economies and people to climate change, and on helping them with adaptation. Seeing a lasting solution entirely in terms of emissions reduction has persistently marginalised the need to invest in adaptation, too often taken to be an admission of defeat, or even a counsel of despair.

Another risk-management strategy is to look at the other things that humans are doing to the climate. Methane (natural gas) leaking from pipes and landfills and bubbling out of rice paddies, nitrous oxide, which comes from farmlands, particularly overfertilised ones, and ozone produced in smog are all greenhouse gases much more powerful in the short to medium term than carbon dioxide is. Measures to limit their emission can offer some quick progress that also provides other benefits; less ozone, for example, means better air quality and more productive crops. The same is true of "black carbon", sooty stuff produced by kilns, cooking fires, poorly designed stoves and diesel engines, as well as by forest and peatland fires. Black carbon can have strong local warming effects, and measures to control its emission have benefits beyond those on climate (reducing, for example, the indoor air pollution from poor cooking stoves that kills many mothers and children in India and elsewhere). Some estimates suggest that action on the black carbon from shipping and fires could set back the melting of Arctic sea-ice by a decade or more.

Radical ideas in the air

Without continuing action on carbon dioxide such measures will never be enough to decisively change the climate's overall trajectory, but they can help, perhaps buying time for better renewable and other zero-carbon technologies to emerge. Today's policies tend to involve spending a lot of money fielding current renewables that are not always suitable (solar cells are not a good way of powering cloudy, northerly Germany). A greater stress on advanced research into renewables could provide much better options later on.

There are also ways of intervening in the climate to cool it down, rather than just to slow its warming. Various technologies might be used to remove carbon dioxide from the air, though they seem at the moment either to be fundamentally limited in their capacity or far too expensive and technologically immature to employ on a planetary scale. Such technologies offer little benefit as emissions continue to rise. Once emissions fall quite low, though, things look different. Once it is up, the carbon-dioxide level is likely, if left to itself, to stay up for a long time even if emissions are reduced to zero. The only way to bring it down would be to actively remove some of the carbon dioxide. Like emission cuts, measures to draw down carbon dioxide directly would change the climate only over decades, or even centuries. But some climate impacts are similarly slow or slower – such as the breakdown of major ice sheets. If intervening to pull down the carbon-dioxide level allowed us to keep the Greenland and West Antarctic ice sheets from breaking down, it would be well worthwhile.

More dramatic are technologies that would cool the climate immediately by reducing the amount of sunlight that the Earth absorbs. There are various ideas about how to do this, but perhaps the most straightforward is to thicken the thin layer of sulphate aerosols in the stratosphere. Like the sulphates released by coal and oil into the lower atmosphere, sulphate aerosols in the stratosphere also cool the Earth; the effect is made plain when gases from a major volcanic eruption thicken the stratosphere's sulphate layer and temperatures drop. Stratospheric aerosols are much more efficient than those in the lower atmosphere, because there is no rain in the stratosphere to wash them away, and so they can stay up for a year or so, rather than just a few days. As a result a continuous injection of sulphur into the stratosphere could cool the world appreciably without the damage to health that sulphates cause in the lower atmosphere.

Such an injection would probably be technically easy. But it would be politically, ethically and climatologically fraught. Stratospheric sulphates would not cancel out greenhouse warming by carbon dioxide in an exact way and would probably leave some places drier than they are today, though not necessarily drier than they would be under unabated climate change. Cooling undertaken deliberately would trigger a different set of ethical issues from those raised by climate change as an inadvertent side-effect of other processes, and would arouse worries of a Faustian conceit or the prospect of a Frankenplanet. Politically, because a nation or set of nations would be seeking to control the climate of others, it might seem a hostile act. For all these reasons it is an unlikely path, one that a risk-management approach would seem to recommend only if the risks of the status quo rose quickly and demonstrably.

Filling the stratosphere with sulphate is thus not a solution to the problem of global warming. But then nor is anything else. Climate change is not a specific problem with an answer. It is not, like a skyscraper or a spaceship, one era's symbol of the future, rendered oddly quaint or utterly ordinary by the time the future actually comes around. It is more like something that contains the future than something that sits within it. This does not make it intractable. It does not mean there are not degrees of climate change between which people should distinguish, or that there are not better trajectories and worse ones, better ways to deal with the risks and worse. There clearly are. But climate change will be something that shapes the century's development, not something the century can avoid.

8 The future of war: the weak become strong

Matthew Symonds

Western military primacy will diminish – just as new threats join old ones

DEFENCE PLANNERS INVARIABLY SAY that their goal is to create forces that are flexible and adaptable. That is because they know how hard it is to predict what the next war or wars will be like – and therefore precisely the kind of fighting forces that will be needed. They have to try to guess, but if they bet too heavily on a guess that turns out to be wrong, the result may be national catastrophe. When it comes to warfare, it is difficult predicting even a decade ahead, let alone several.

Britain's 2010 strategic defence and security review (SDSR) shows how quickly experts can be proved wrong. As part of its effort to put the defence budget on a more sustainable footing, David Cameron's government decided that it could risk doing without any carrier strike capability for a decade. Yet with the ink hardly dry on the SDSR, Cameron committed Britain to saving the lives of Libyan rebels and (in effect) toppling Muammar Qaddafi, the dictator who threatened them. Unfortunately, the asset that would have been able to make the biggest contribution to the Libyan campaign, the aircraft carrier *HMS Ark Royal* and its Harrier jump jets, had just been consigned to the scrapyard.

If Britain's SDSR was quickly found wanting, it was mostly because it was driven by the need to save money. The same could not be said of Donald Rumsfeld in early 2001. On becoming America's defence secretary for a second time, Rumsfeld set about implementing far-reaching reforms at the Pentagon. He reckoned that the military brass was nostalgically trying to cling to the capabilities it had needed to face down the threat from the Soviet Union. The "visionary" Rumsfeld wanted to get away from doctrines that required massive deployments of ground troops and the heavy metal that went with them – the thousands of tanks, artillery and fighter jets and their endless logistical tail – in favour of lighter, more flexible forces that could be sent quickly to wherever they were needed and could leverage all the latest communications technology to achieve rapid dominance on the battlefield. Rumsfeld's evangelising zeal was one of the main reasons the aftermath of the Iraq war went so badly wrong. In his worst nightmares, the defence secretary might have imagined an event like September 11th 2001. But if you had told him that over the next ten years America would spend getting on for $1.3 trillion dollars fighting two industrial-scale "boots on the ground" counter-insurgency campaigns, he would have thought you mad.

For now, the pendulum has swung back the other way. Afghanistan and similar "wars among the people", entailing complex counter-insurgency operations accompanied by the training of local forces and various forms of civic capacity-building, appear to some American and British military planners – especially senior army officers – to be the only kind of large-scale campaigns they need to prepare for. Yet this cannot be true. Although the problems of weak or failing states and jihadist terrorism are likely to be with us for a very long time, the astronomical cost and ambiguous (so far) results of the interventions in Iraq and Afghanistan make it almost certain that Western political leaders (for which read American presidents) will try extremely hard not to do the same thing again for a very long time. In other words, we can be fairly confident that the future will be different from the present. We just do not know in what way.

Through a glass, darkly

The good news for the West's military strategists peering out 40 years ahead is that, compared with their 20th-century counterparts, they are not faced with any single existential threat. The extreme lethality of the two world wars and the ending of the enormously dangerous nuclear stalemate between America and the former Soviet

FIG 8.1 **Less deadly**

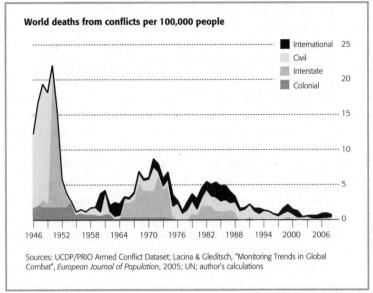

World deaths from conflicts per 100,000 people

Legend:
- International 25
- Civil
- Interstate 20
- Colonial

Sources: UCDP/PRIO Armed Conflict Dataset; Lacina & Gleditsch, "Monitoring Trends in Global Combat", *European Journal of Population*, 2005; UN; author's calculations

Union have made the likelihood of unconstrained war between great powers less likely (though not inconceivable) than at any time since the birth of the modern nation-state. Indeed, the rate of battle deaths in wars of all sorts has fallen dramatically over the past half-century (see Figure 8.1).

The bad news is that there is much greater uncertainty about the kinds of conflicts the defence planners must prepare for, where the threats will come from and what rapidly changing technology will mean for both friends and foes. And despite that unpredictability – something could happen next month that throws out every preconception in the way that September 11th 2001 did – they must still make decisions that could have a major bearing on how the wars of the next four decades will be fought. That is so because of both the time it takes to develop new weapons systems and the length of time they will need to stay in service.

Take the F-35 Joint Strike Fighter, the costliest defence-industrial programme in history with a projected through-life price tag, according to the Pentagon, of $1.3 trillion. The F-35 is intended to be the backbone of American and Western air forces from around 2020 until at least 2065. Although few doubt it will be the best of its breed with incredibly sophisticated software and sensors allowing it to carry out all kinds of tasks, critics point to its huge and growing expense (it was meant to be fairly cheap) and its limited combat range of about 600 miles (which puts its bases, especially carriers, at growing risk of attack). They argue that there is a more urgent need for a genuinely long-range strike aircraft, while most other missions in the medium to long term are more likely to be undertaken by different types of unmanned aerial vehicles (UAVs) or "drones". Buying big numbers of F-35s – and the Pentagon is still expecting to acquire over 2,400 of them – could be either very sensible or very stupid. With sufficient money you would want all of the above. But with budgets shrinking, military crystal-ball gazers will have little scope for hedging their bets.

Figuring out the potential flashpoints for tomorrow's wars is probably the easy part. People will go on fighting over the things that they have always fought over: resources, territory, tribe, religion, ideology and all the other tensions and misjudgments caused by rivalries between states. But the way in which all these may toxically combine will be different. Over the next 40 years, as the world's population heads for more than 9 billion (from its current 7 billion) and as the effects of global warming become more pronounced, the competition for resources and the social destabilisation it causes seem certain to intensify. Forecasts of the world reaching "peak oil" in the next few years have been called into question by the discovery of new reserves, deepwater drilling and the commercialisation of techniques for extracting oil (and gas) from shale. But the volatile politics of many oil-producing countries (not just in the Middle East), the vulnerability of the Gulf to disruption by either state or non-state actors and the potential for acrimonious international disputes over the riches beneath a melting Arctic have not gone away.

Oil, however, may not be the biggest source of commodity-related conflict in the years leading up to 2050. Given time and ingenuity, there are plenty of alternatives to oil. Water is another matter. It remains the essential ingredient for life. Climate change, intensive farming techniques and sheer population pressure are taking their toll. Yemen, already a tribal powder-keg and base for al-Qaeda, may be the first country to run out of water, perhaps by 2015. In nuclear-armed, terrorist-torn, over-populated, chronically unstable Pakistan, the once-mighty Indus, source of irrigation for the country's cotton and rice crops, has been reduced to a pathetic trickle as it reaches the sea. Water is one of the biggest obstacles in the path of a peace settlement in the Middle East: without the West Bank's underground aquifer and access to the headwaters of the River Jordan, Israeli lifestyles would have to change. Water issues could yet derail China's meteoric growth, triggering internal strains that could tempt a future government to find distraction in a more aggressive and adventurist foreign policy. Water shortages and climate are also likely to be the cause of major migration movements, any of which could lead to armed conflict between those wanting to get into more favoured countries and those wanting to stop them.

Territorial disputes may rarely produce major wars, but they still provoke plenty of small wars. As the Falklands war in 1982 between Argentina and Britain showed, old resentments married to military recklessness and opportunism (or desperation) can surface in the most unexpected ways in the most unexpected places. Kashmir and Israel's occupied territories will surely remain among the most dangerous flashpoints in the 21st century, but Taiwan is steadily rising up the list of American military planners' concerns as China becomes more assertive and as its growing military capability increases the risks for America of confronting bullying or worse from China. There are also tensions aplenty between China and its neighbours over islands (and the natural resources around them) in the western Pacific. These could turn nasty at any time.

The wars of religion

Perhaps the most surprising thing about this century compared with the last is that even as ideology as a source of confrontation has subsided (state capitalism along Chinese lines may offer an alternative model to Western liberalism, but it is neither as proselytising nor as imperialistic as Soviet communism), so religion has rediscovered all its old ferocious talent for dividing people and drawing them into war. Despite the hopes raised by the "Arab spring" of 2011, extreme Islamism, whether in the form of jihadist terrorist groups or the states that sponsor them, will continue its long struggle against Western values – undermining wherever possible the interests of America and its allies and in the process absorbing large amounts of military time and money. With the West unwilling to repeat the experience of Afghanistan and liberal interventionism being deemed unaffordable in all but the most clear-cut cases, failing or fragile states will grow in number, increasing the options available for terrorist networks. If Muslim Pakistan and largely Hindu India cannot find a way to settle their differences over Kashmir (a religious as well as territorial dispute), sporadic but spectacular terrorist attacks on increasingly prosperous mainly Hindu India will continue and may eventually become unbearable. The result could be the world's first war between two nuclear powers and possibly its first nuclear exchange.

Tensions will also continue to rise between Shia and Sunni Muslims in the Middle East, unless Iran's theocratic and expansionist regime is either overthrown or chastened in its ambitions. Iran's proxies, particularly Hizbullah in Lebanon and Hamas in Gaza, will remain more of a threat to Israel than to Iran's Arab neighbours. But when – rather than if – Iran becomes capable of producing nuclear weapons (whether or not it crosses the threshold of actually creating such weapons), the Arab states will not want to rely on the protection of an America that is already seen as an unreliable ally and a waning power within the region. In the resulting scramble to acquire nuclear weapons, Saudi Arabia and Egypt could well be joined by Iraq and Syria, both of which have tried to go down this route in the past. It is just conceivable that a stable deterrence will operate between the fractious and religiously divided countries of the Middle East as it did between America and Russia during the cold war, but that is a bold assumption.

While many of the potential causes of conflict will retain their potency throughout the first half of the 21st century, warfare itself and the technologies harnessed to wage war will change at bewildering speed. Moreover, the proliferation of many of those technologies will be deeply troubling to the West in general and to America in particular. At the same time, long-run geopolitical developments will also potentially threaten incumbent powers. In a 2011 study, the RAND Corporation, an American think-tank, identified the major military trends that look like accelerating in the decades leading up to 2050. It concluded that America's armed forces are facing a crisis of looming obsolescence.

Uneven balance

The first of these trends is that technological changes and the way in which they are being distributed are tending to undermine the previously unchallenged military dominance of the West by making future adversaries relatively better-armed or able to pursue effective asymmetric tactics.

For as long as most people can remember, America has enjoyed overwhelming technological "overmatch" in all four of the military domains (land, sea, air and space) in which it has operated. That may not be true for much longer. Off-the-shelf internet-based communications and encryption software, cheap battlefield precision-guided missiles and mortars, advanced mobile and man-portable air defences, anti-satellite systems, anti-ship missiles and highly accurate long-range ballistic missiles capable of carrying nuclear warheads are all revolutionising the capabilities of potential foes. These range all the way from an emerging "near peer" rival, such as China, that has all of the above capabilities and is adding others, to a non-state player, such as Hizbullah, that has only some but has demonstrated (in the 2006 Lebanon war) how they can be used with deadly effect against even well-equipped and well-trained conventional forces.

In addition, there is now a fifth domain: cyberspace. Cyber-warfare inherently bestows disproportionate power on technically adept but militarily weaker states (and even previously insignificant non-state actors). Complicating things further, unless it becomes feasible to identify with reasonable certainty where cyber-attacks have come from, it will be extremely difficult either to calibrate an appropriate response or to deter future attacks.

The second trend is a mix of (for the West) largely unfavourable geostrategic developments that demonstrate the range and complexity of the threats that 21st-century military planners have to wrestle with. One such threat is the spread of nuclear weapons to more countries in unstable regions, unless concerted international action, led by the

FIG 8.2 **China arms up**

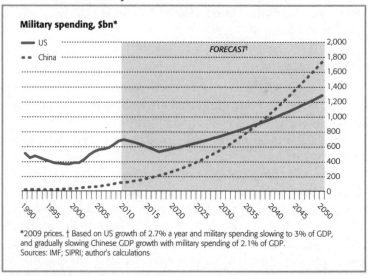

Military spending, $bn*

*2009 prices. † Based on US growth of 2.7% a year and military spending slowing to 3% of GDP, and gradually slowing Chinese GDP growth with military spending of 2.1% of GDP.
Sources: IMF; SIPRI; author's calculations

"permanent five" nuclear powers on the Security Council, is taken to get rid of all such devices. Another is jihadist-inspired terrorism at a time when America and its allies, scarred by their experiences in the first decade of the century, are no longer willing to conduct open-ended counter-insurgency operations or attempt nation-building in remote and hostile environments. A third is the growing ability of new powers to threaten the military space-based systems that America has enjoyed a near-monopoly of. Then there is the emergence of cyberspace as not only the fifth domain or theatre of operations, but one in which even relatively weak, albeit technically proficient, players can menace the military and civil infrastructure of much more powerful adversaries. The final threatening development is the rise of China as a military power with the ability to challenge America's security guarantees to East Asian allies that include Japan, South Korea and, most obviously, Taiwan (see Figure 8.2).

All this means a mounting array of challenges to the armed forces that have given America uncontested military primacy over at least the past 20 years (Figure 8.3 illustrates America's current dominance).

FIG 8.3 **Today's only military superpower**

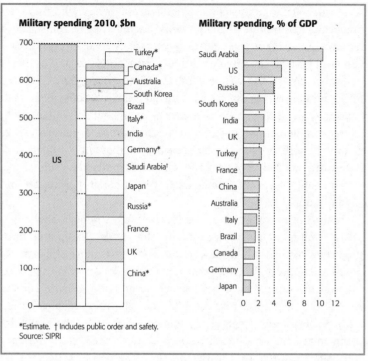

Military spending 2010, $bn

700
Turkey*
Canada*
600
Australia
South Korea
Brazil
500
Italy*
India
Germany*
400
US
Saudi Arabia†
Japan
300
Russia*
France
200
UK
China*
100

0

Military spending, % of GDP

Saudi Arabia
US
Russia
South Korea
India
UK
Turkey
France
China
Australia
Italy
Brazil
Canada
Germany
Japan

0 2 4 6 8 10 12

*Estimate. † Includes public order and safety.
Source: SIPRI

Their biggest concern is that many of the technical developments in progress lend themselves to asymmetric approaches to warfare in which the strength of a high-end military power can be eroded or even nullified by relatively low-end means. At its most extreme, it may be the difficulty that superbly equipped and highly professional Western soldiers have experienced in dealing with improvised explosive devices triggered by mobile phones in Iraq and Afghanistan. A little higher up the scale, Iranian-supplied missiles, sometimes costing only a few hundred dollars, are forcing Israel to spend hundreds of millions of dollars on advanced defensive systems to protect its armed forces. And a lot higher up are the capabilities China is acquiring to push American aircraft carriers farther and farther away into the Pacific.

The carrier problem is a particularly acute manifestation of this wider trend. America has long relied on carrier strike groups to project power wherever and whenever needed. Until recently, American carrier groups could operate more or less with impunity quite close to the shore of any potential enemy. They not only carry a massive punch themselves, but they can rapidly create the conditions, above all local air supremacy, to allow ground forces to land relatively unscathed. As highly visible symbols of American global military might, nothing comes close to its 11 carrier groups. Yet over the next 30 years they are likely to become increasingly vulnerable to attack. With its full complement of aircraft and missiles, a new Ford-class carrier is a $15 billion-20 billion target even before allowing for the cost of the escorts needed to protect and support it (probably a submarine, a couple of cruisers, up to three destroyers, a handful of frigates and a supply ship).

Both the number and the variety of strategic challenges are alarming: trends in technology that make traditional force projection for incumbent powers too risky or expensive; networks of international terrorism; recurring humanitarian crises in states that fail because of poor governance, population growth, climate change or water insecurity; unstable or aggressive regimes armed with nuclear weapons; and the tensions caused by the rapid rise of an increasingly assertive, resource-hungry "near peer" military competitor to America. Clearly, therefore, the period between now and 2050 will require big changes both in the way wars are fought and in how they may be prevented. Moreover, the proportion of their wealth that America and the rich West are prepared to spend to make those changes will diminish as defence takes an ever-declining share of national budgets under strain from ageing populations, shrinking workforces (unless supplemented by immigrants) and soaring health-care costs.

The capabilities that America will have to acquire in the decades ahead, if its military primacy is not to be gradually eroded, is daunting. It includes the defence of its bases and forces in the field against guided weapons, from precision mortars to long-range ballistic missiles; intelligence, surveillance and reconnaissance (ISR) systems that can remain operational under attack; comprehensive suppression of enemy defensive systems (from submarines to surface-to-air missiles); long-range strike aircraft; munitions that can destroy deeply buried targets, such as nuclear-weapons facilities; maritime bases that can survive attack; and the means to carry out counter-terrorism and counter-insurgency operations with lighter forces and well-trained and equipped local partners.

Most of these requirements will be technically difficult and costly. Using different types of interceptor missiles with different ranges, for example, to create a layered defence for ground or sea-based forces is feasible, but hugely expensive, while hopes that airborne laser-based weapons will prove effective have yet to bear fruit. Given the vulnerability of the low-Earth orbit satellites that the military relies upon for much of its near-real-time ISR, other platforms will be needed to ensure reasonable resilience.

A critical issue will be the ability of short-range tactical aircraft, such as the F-35, to operate from forward bases or carriers. Aerial refuelling by "buddy" planes of the same type will allow them to fly from more remote bases. But their very existence may be seen as an invitation to pre-emptive attack. High on the list of the American air force's priorities will be a long-range successor to the B-52 bomber, which could still be flying nearly a century after it was conceived in 1946.

War of the robots

The demand for increasingly sophisticated UAVs to act as "eyes and ears" and to seize fleeting opportunities to attack targets will grow to such an extent that by 2050 they will have replaced manned aircraft for the majority of missions. This reliance on drones is part of a wider trend towards robotised warfare conducted by technicians far removed from the theatre of conflict. Inevitably, this has raised ethical and legal issues that are unlikely to go away.

Whether there is any technological fix for fighting counter-insurgency campaigns with fewer resources will probably be a point of controversy for many years to come. The model, which is ironically not dissimilar to that envisaged by Rumsfeld, is likely to be highly networked special forces supported by armed UAVs and trainers to develop the capabilities of local security forces. If this model fails, as experience suggests it may, the hard choice will be whether to accept the need for an army large enough to do it the old way or to conclude

The China challenge

In 1996, when China tested ballistic missiles near Taiwanese ports, America did not hesitate to send two carrier groups to the Taiwan Strait as a warning to the Chinese not to overstep the mark. Should a crisis develop between America and China over Taiwan in 20 or even ten years' time it is unlikely that a future American president would feel confident enough to order a similar show of force. China's ambitious military modernisation programme is not aimed at matching American power, something that not even the most bellicose People's Liberation Army (PLA) general thinks is conceivable or even desirable. It is, however, intended to make it far more difficult and dangerous for American air and maritime forces to project power into East Asia. The goal of Chinese strategy is to stop American forces from entering the theatre of operations and to prevent them from operating without unacceptable losses within the area controlled by Chinese forces.

To that end, the Chinese are concentrating on the means to counter America's bases in the region, its surface ships (especially carriers) and the satellites and data networks that American forces depend upon for what is known as C4ISR (command, control, communications, computers, intelligence, surveillance and reconnaissance). The Centre for Strategic and Budgetary Assessments, a Washington-based think-tank that has analysed the rise of China's military power and its implications for America, lists what it believes will be the essential "components" of China's strategy by 2020: radar, satellites and UAVs for maritime

that such manpower-intensive missions should be undertaken only under the most extreme requirements of national security.

If unambiguous American military primacy has ceased to be a viable option before 2050, in large part because of the rise of China's regional dominance, American strategists will want to replicate the system of formal alliances that characterised the period of rough military parity with the Soviet Union that existed for most of the and aerospace surveillance; thousands of surface-to-surface missiles with a mix of warheads; thousands of land-attack and anti-ship cruise missiles; dozens of anti-ship ballistic missiles with manoeuvrable warheads; a layered and fully integrated air-defence system; large numbers of "fourth generation" air-superiority fighters; a powerful submarine fleet, including at least six nuclear attack submarines armed with cruise missiles and wake-homing torpedoes; directed- and kinetic-energy anti-satellite weapons; and, finally, sophisticated cyber-warfare capabilities.

With these forces, China is hoping that if a crisis were to arise, it would be able to deter American carriers and aircraft flying out of bases in the western Pacific from operating within what is known as the "first island chain", roughly a defensive perimeter running from the Aleutians in the north through Japan's archipelago to Taiwan, the Philippines and Borneo. Chinese strategists would like to be able to extend that perimeter out to the "second island chain" (from the Bonin Islands, moving southwards through the Marianas, Guam and the Caroline Islands) by 2050. There is no inevitability about China's relations with its near neighbours or with America deteriorating into the kind of "cool war" in which the risk of confrontation could become quite high. But America's influence will fall as China's rises unless it can reassure its allies that it retains the ability to project power in the region and defend them should growing Chinese assertiveness become something more threatening.

cold war. However, the alliances that will be most important in 2050 will be found from the Indian Ocean to the western Pacific rather than in Europe. Whether these will resemble NATO, which may well have ceased to exist as a coherent defensive coalition, will depend on how China chooses to manage its relationships with both its neighbours and America – whether it continues on its present course of economic co-operative competition ("co-opetition", as the neologism has it), played largely within the rules-based international system, or whether rising domestic tensions make it a more awkward and potentially belligerent rival.

The new nuclear threat

Despite the (understandable) obsession of American defence planners with China and the current panic over the threat to civilisation as we know it from cyber-warfare (carefully stoked by the ever-resourceful information-technology industry), the greatest danger that mankind faces in the first half of the 21st century is the same as in most of the second half of the last century: the use of nuclear weapons. Over the many years of the cold war, America and the former Soviet Union learned how to calibrate their adversarial relationship. Although they came uncomfortably close to war more than once, they learned how to maintain the balance of terror, while gradually ensuring that the use of nuclear weapons by design or accident was relegated to the remotest possibility.

New nuclear states do not have that kind of experience, nor do many of them have the kind of "strategic space" enjoyed by Russia and America (thanks to geography) or the assured second-strike capability that came with huge arsenals and low-vulnerability launch platforms, such as submarines. Countries with relatively small stockpiles of nuclear weapons and unpredictable or untrustworthy neighbours are in a far less favourable position to get through the next 50 years without using their nuclear weapons than were America and Russia in the past 50 years. The dangers of a superpower nuclear exchange that would destroy the planet have receded, but the possibility of a regional nuclear war that would still kill many millions of people and have devastating medium-term environmental and economic effects far beyond the theatre of conflict will grow exponentially unless proliferation can be slowed, halted and then reversed. And with the spread of nuclear weapons and fissile materials to unstable regimes in failing countries has come the associated menace of terrorist groups determined to steal, build or buy a nuclear device or devices.

The next 40 years will determine whether the world is prepared to live with a growing risk that nuclear weapons will one day almost certainly be used, or whether the danger will be seen as sufficiently intolerable that something will be done to eliminate the threat. There are some hopeful straws in the wind. In 2007, four veteran American cold warriors – George Shultz, Henry Kissinger, Bill Perry and Sam Nunn – co-authored what became a seminal piece in the *Wall Street Journal*. In it, the "four horsemen of the apocalypse", as they were quickly dubbed, argued that unless countries, led by America and Russia, which still account for 95% of the world's 20,500 nuclear weapons, were ready to begin multilateral negotiations to eliminate all nuclear weapons, a catastrophe would be almost unavoidable. Since then, both Barack Obama and Russia's Dmitry Medvedev have committed themselves to the cause of ridding the world of nuclear weapons, while an organisation called Global Zero, supported by more than 300 of the world's political, military, academic and business leaders, has emerged as a campaigning force. Very different from the old, pacifist-leaning "ban the bomb" crowd, it has called for a practical four-phase multilateral action plan, backed up at every stage by intrusive verification. This would start with America and Russia cutting their nuclear stockpiles down to 1,000 weapons apiece and would end with a treaty signed by all nuclear-weapons states to destroy their arsenals.

Global Zero's plan faces formidable obstacles – not least the difficulty of drawing the most dangerous countries into such a carefully choreographed process when little may have happened to persuade them that nuclear weapons are not intrinsic to their security. President Obama has said that while he would work for the goal of zero, he might not see it in his lifetime. By 2050, he will be 89. Even if by then the destination is not within sight, as long as the journey has started, the world will be a slightly safer place than seems likely today.

9   Freedom's ragged march

Edward Lucas

What the world's politics will need is an abundance of public-spiritedness – "democracy" alone is not enough

FORGET DEMOCRACY. Worry about freedom and justice instead. If you're lucky, by 2050 you will be in an e-government paradise where the state looks after your wishes as neatly as Amazon cares about your literary preferences. If you're unlucky, you will end up with something between Silvio Berlusconi's Italy and Vladimir Putin's Russia, ruled by cynical insiders skilled at manipulating public opinion and buying off their critics.

Technology and public-spiritedness will decide which outcome wins but in any case, start by ditching the term "democracy". It was the flavour of the month each year and decade after 1989, as people-power breached the Berlin Wall, capsized communist rule in the then Czechoslovakia and spread south and east until the end of history seemed in sight. It went hand in hand with a general rise in freedom (see Figure 9.1). It has triumphed in Latin America, where military juntas were once the default setting of all but a handful of political systems; now only Cuba remains a bastion of one-party rule. Even Hugo Chávez of Venezuela does not explicitly reject a multiparty system. Contested elections in Africa used to be a rarity; now they are commonplace. The "Arab spring" of 2011 has brought the prospect of political pluralism to countries from the Atlantic Ocean to the Gulf.

But in the years to 2050 the story of democracy will be a paradoxical mixture. Those that do not have it will gain more of it. Those that do have it will see it shrink. It will advance in authoritarian countries but retreat in free ones. In a rigid political system such as

FIG 9.1 **Degrees of freedom**

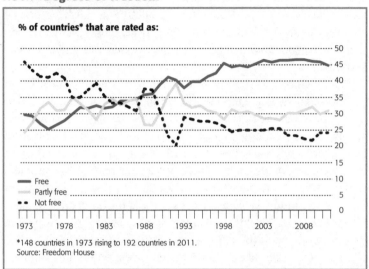

% of countries* that are rated as:

— Free
  Partly free
•• Not free

1973   1978   1983   1988   1993   1998   2003   2008

*148 countries in 1973 rising to 192 countries in 2011.
Source: Freedom House

China's, rulers remain vulnerable to the hunger for open political competition and free information. They will find it hard to justify the idea that they know best. As consumers exercise choice in their spending, and workers exercise choice in their migration within and across borders, the idea that a nation-state can determine what its inhabitants see, hear or read will be hard to sustain.

But the victory of democracy disguises its vulnerability. It is easy to idolise something you don't have. Campaigning for democracy is easier than exercising it. In practice, democracy is vulnerable: to manipulation by insiders, to the corrosive power of money, to voter apathy, to the frustrating constraints of real life, and to the inherent weaknesses of the whole idea – barnacled decision-making and the triumph of special interests. In the world's two most populous countries, the years to 2050 will bring both good news and bad. China will have to deal with the inherent weaknesses of a one-party state; India will struggle with the frustrations and shortcomings of a multiparty one.

As a result, in 2050 democracy will have a quaint and unfamiliar taste. Like the once-popular foods of past decades (anyone remember

Spam and salad-cream sandwiches, washed down with orange squash for the kids and Camp Coffee for the adults?) it will have proved an incomplete diet – easily but often misleadingly marketed, too frequently padded with substandard ingredients and unwholesome additives.

"Democracy" is handy shorthand for those opposing an authoritarian regime. Opponents of capitalism a generation earlier used "socialism" as a similarly potent label: in place of oppression would come freedom; in place of shortage, plenty; in place of exploitation, self-realisation. "To each according to his need, from each according to his ability" was a bewitching mantra. The problem came in trying to implement it. Marx offered a powerful critique of 19th-century industrial capitalism, but he and the other great thinkers of the left were sketchy in defining how a socialist society would actually work. In practice, the results were disappointing. Fear-fuelled planned economies like the Soviet Union were one result. Modified capitalist societies such as the European welfare states were another. A third was the doomed, debt-driven shambles of countries such as Yugoslavia.

Democracy has similar problems. Its historical roots are if anything more tangled than those of socialism. In the 19th century it had connotations of mob rule. And 50 years ago it was part of the communist lexicon. The Soviet zone of Germany declared itself the "German *Democratic* Republic" (GDR) in opposition to the "*Federal* Republic of Germany" that arose out of the American, French and British zones. For good measure "Democratic" was often prefixed with "People's". Algeria, Laos and North Korea are examples. A handy rule of thumb, now and probably for the future, is that any country using "Democratic" in its formal title is run by a self-perpetuating clique of insiders.

Only recently has democracy become generally accepted as a synonym for contested elections and (rather loosely defined) political freedom. These are fine things: in the conditions of eastern Europe in late 1989, it made sense to focus demands narrowly on free elections, just as in 2011 in the countries of the Arab spring. Free elections are a necessary condition for change – just not a sufficient one. They can be a priority when everything else that makes up a responsive, efficient modern state is lacking (a shortlist would include anti-monopoly agencies, financial regulators, consumer-protection bodies, the oversight of a country's security services and, most obviously, the rule of law). Free elections may create the conditions in which these can be built; but they do not guarantee it.

Be careful what you wish for

"Democracy" is not just a misleading and vague term. It easily becomes a fig leaf for misgovernment. Rulers can distract attention from their shortcomings by highlighting the electoral circus and then claiming a "democratic" endorsement. Democracy all too easily includes only one ingredient – electoral contestability – of the diet necessary for honest and open political life, and even that can lose much of its value. If things are going well, free and fair elections will be part of it. If they are going badly, these elections will probably be cosmetic. It would be better to use the more precise term "political freedom", in the explicit understanding that this is a narrow goal not a broad one.

Democracy has two Achilles heels. Both are on display now, and they will remain so in the decades ahead. One is money. Political-party financing plagues not only American politics, but many other countries too, perhaps most spectacularly India. For businesses, it makes sense to buy politicians, political parties, media, think-tanks and other bits of the political spectrum. A "prisoner's dilemma" is at work. Even businesses that would like to shun politics find they cannot afford to: if you don't play the dirty game, your competitors will – and to your disadvantage. Firms such as Microsoft and Google that once prided themselves on steering clear of Washington, DC, have found it necessary to open lobbying offices there. Companies that do business in the European Union have found they ignore at their peril the European Parliament, perhaps the ultimate lobbyists' trough. Tweaking a clause in European legislation – for example, by changing a product-safety rule – can mean a bonanza for one company and bankruptcy for another.

The mechanics of such influence-peddling are the same as in trade protectionism. The concentrated interests of a well-organised lobby are easily expressed and realised. The diffuse interests of wider society are harder to mobilise and defend. The blunt instrument of a five-yearly election has little chance of balancing the daily, insidious pressure of lobbyists for cartels and special interests. The feeling that decisions are taken by well-connected insiders at the expense of the majority stokes apathy and alienation.

How will this change in the years to 2050? On the plus side, information technology brings greater scrutiny. Why does 1km of road cost around five times as much to build in Russia as it does in Finland? The climatic and geological conditions are similar. Finnish wages, land prices and energy costs are higher. The reason that the Russian road is costlier is simple: corruption – which has never been easier to measure. With just a few mouse-clicks a concerned citizen can download a plethora of World Bank and OECD studies on public-sector efficiency. TED Talks online (created to disseminate "ideas worth spreading") make the views of the most insightful commentators on issues such as health, education and transport available to everyone, everywhere, free of charge. An informed citizenry, one supposes, is an empowered electorate.

But sadly democracy's second big weakness kicks in here: the vulnerability to manipulation. What happens between elections matters as much as the physical acts of casting and counting votes. The most articulate and best-informed campaigners for good government struggle to achieve critical mass in a system such as Russia's, designed to dissipate its critics' energies: far too often rulers who once feared elections now love them.

For a start, elections are easy to win if you have the media on your side. Public-sector advertising is a powerful tool for wooing editors and proprietors. Political parties, supposedly idealistic clubs of like-minded activists, have become quasi-commercial institutions with strong patronage networks. Gerrymandered constituencies create sinecures for the insiders and reduce the danger of upsets from those pesky voters.

Marks after Marx

The lessons of the former communist world, such as they are, suggest a few useful tweaks that may forestall some of the worst developments.

Parliamentary systems work better than presidential ones: they avoid the cult of personality, real or imagined; they encourage compromise over absolutism; and the need to build coalitions discourages a winner-takes-all approach that can lead to a politicised civil service. Keeping barriers to entry low for new political parties increases competitive pressure.

But in the former communist countries outside the European Union, the lessons are of gloom not improvement. Rulers can count on what are euphemistically called "administrative resources": anything from using the votes of public-sector employees, prisoners, students and other malleable groups, to falsifying the electoral list.

The result is still a system that claims to be democratic. The people vote, with at least some kind of choice. The votes are counted. The winners rule and business continues as usual. True, the risk of eviction at the polls may encourage politicians to govern well and wisely (or at least not conspicuously badly and stupidly). But it also encourages the use of dark arts, from spin to ballot-rigging.

On this front the story to 2050 risks being gloomy too. It is true that activist tactics are evolving fast. Twitter and Facebook are fine tools for outwitting a lumbering authoritarian bureaucracy. They are good for spreading news and focusing outrage. They increase the tempo of public life, in tandem with the growth of 24-hour news coverage. For the politically motivated, it has never been easier to campaign, whether by spreading news of a demonstration, launching an e-petition, scrutinising politicians' speeches or monitoring the integrity of an election.

But the political insiders are gaining ground faster. They have the panoply of commercial marketing tools: an election campaign is a product launch, followed by an attempt to gain market share. The most sophisticated demographic research enables the swing voters in swing constituencies to be targeted as never before. That can be by images, words and jingles, or by more cynical means such as the targeted distribution of public goods or outright bribery. Here the odds are stacked against the outsiders. The rewards of incumbency will grow faster in the years to 2050 than the capabilities of those wishing to challenge it.

Blogs and lobbies

Technology has reduced the barriers to entry into the media, so that the humblest blogger or tweeter can gain a national or international audience. But this is an asymmetric success. An individual can reach the masses, but not consistently or widely enough to shape their views. The media that most people read, watch and listen to do a poor job in holding politicians and public institutions to account. This is particularly true in poorer countries. In most of "old Europe" and the Anglosphere, it is still possible for an editor to pay good salaries for good reporting, because advertising, circulation and (in the case of public broadcasting) the taxpayer provide the necessary editorial budget. In most of the former communist world, and in poor countries, those budgets are not there.

The result is something like the coffee-house culture of 18th-century Britain. Gossip is risk-free. Agitation on a small scale is easy and fun. Like-minded people have never found it easier to fume together, even if they cannot smoke. This is an important element in civic dignity: the chance to complain publicly rather than grumble privately. But the blogs so far have had scant success in holding powerful officials and politicians to account.

A lobbying-driven, insider-run political system can still call itself a democracy. It still has a degree of competition: if Wall Street backs the Democrats and Big Oil backs the Republicans, one will end up on top. It is a contest of a sort, if not the kind that America's Founding Fathers had in mind. Elections still take place. But they are not a nutritious diet for the long term. Indeed, they are an ersatz rather than a genuine political choice. Without other conditions (of which more in a moment) they simply act as rigged referendums in which one or more cliques of cronies secure their hold on power.

Despite some elements of competition, that is the story of the past 20 years in the former communist world between the Baltic and Black Seas, and in other parts of the world where democracy is also supposed to have triumphed. It is the development at worst of power monopolies, at best of political and economic cartels: comfortable for insiders, tough for everyone else. To be fair, that is true of some "old democracies" too. The "Berlusconification" of Italy, involving the fusion of media, political and commercial power, the abuse of state institutions and the spread of a corrosive cynicism, was a process that in the former communist world would have had outsiders tut-tutting sadly about backward mentality and distance from "mainstream European values".

A better model

The big question in the decades to 2050 is whether the ideal's new custodians can make more of democracy than their predecessors did. In a properly functioning political system, elections are just one of the checks and balances that constrain greed and ambition and protect the rights of the citizen. Put together with electoral contestability, these elements – chiefly the rule of law, free media and public-spiritedness – make up the kind of political system that has made the countries of the so-called West (the term includes countries such as Australia and Japan) the best places in the world to live. But to label this mixture merely "democracy" is to sell it short. Many of the most important features of public and political life are not easily crammed under the "democratic" label.

The most important of these is the rule of law. Without independent, effective and speedy courts, with honest judges and uncowed lawyers, the electoral process is unlikely to reflect the popular will before, during and after the poll. This is partly true in a narrow mechanical sense. If parties cannot contest in court unfair rules and arbitrary rulings by electoral officials, they become dependent on the volatile and unpredictable last resort of mass public protest. That can work very well – as seen during the "Orange Revolution" in Ukraine in the winter of 2004–05. But it will not make officials honest or effective or facilitate effective modern government. In Ukraine the "democrats" won the election, and proved anything but democratic afterwards.

But the rule of law is not in itself a sufficient condition for democracy. Hong Kong under British rule had an elaborate and honest legal system, with free speech, the enforcement of contracts and plenty of official accountability. But the people of Hong Kong did not elect their governor: he was chosen by the queen (in theory; in practice by her government) in Britain. The future of the rule of law deserves a book on its own. But it can be neatly encapsulated in the idea that a citizen (or business) with a good case can sue the state and win an effective remedy. At a small-scale level, that guarantees the dignity of the citizen in the face of the official – no matter how imposing the uniform, or how big the gun.

Bear in mind, though, that the rule of law is not just about having the right legislation, or even having the right institutions. Legality exists primarily as a state of mind: chiefly the belief that bribing a judge, ignoring a court order, or betraying the principles and procedures of the system will be not only futile but also wrong. The European courts in Strasbourg (European Court of Human Rights) and Luxembourg (Court of Justice of the European Union) provide an important corrective to any weakness of national courts. But they cannot be a substitute for them. A confident citizenry needs the assurance that its rights are protected under the law, just as it needs to know that it can throw the rascals out at the ballot box if necessary, and *in extremis* take to the streets in peaceful protest without being shot by the police.

The rule of law is enjoyed by the powerful, as much as by the weak. Big business may believe that almost everything has its price. But even the most cynical and ruthless tycoon does not want a system in which judges' verdicts go to the highest bidder. It is better to have an honest system in which you lose sometimes than a dishonest one where you can be outbid by your foes. Russian oligarchs like the political system at home, where they can capture natural-resource and other rents by adept manipulation and influence-peddling. But they invariably choose to settle their legal disputes in the commercial courts of London, or in the Stockholm arbitration tribunals.

In the decades to 2050, a crucial question will be whether the rule of law spreads and deepens. Does the predictability and transparency of a law-based system provide long-term benefits that ultimately trump the short-term advantage of being able to rig a political decision? If we end up with a political system in which the humble can sue the powerful and win, then the shortcomings of the electoral system will be a secondary consideration.

That's the spirit

The other pillar of political life that far outstrips elections in its importance is sometimes called "civil society", although I prefer the less jargony and more accurate "public-spiritedness". When elections are pointless, when courts are expensive, slow and biased, and when the media either do not bark or cannot bite, then it is public-spiritedness that will motivate people to fight what may strike outsiders as hopeless battles. This may involve busybodies and do-gooders getting together, forming pressure groups and charities. It may involve just a lone, stubborn individual whose self-respect does not permit him to give up (such people largely comprised the dissident movement in the communist era).

Public-spirited people are unable to withdraw into the private realm of family, friends and hobbies. They mind that speeding cars endanger their children (or other people's), that pollution spoils their favourite landscape (or someone else's), or that politicians are stealing public money (even if they are not big taxpayers themselves) – and they do something about it. Sometimes it involves acting as if official channels for grievances were real, and relentlessly using them until the authorities' willpower gives way. Or it may involve civil disobedience. Or both. The cost in health and nerves can be heavy. But without public-spiritedness, democracy, as well as the rule of law and ethical journalism, is doomed.

The struggle between public-spiritedness and what one might call "economism" will determine what kind of political system we have in 2050. The economistic viewpoint counts well-being solely in rational and material terms. It distrusts altruism, principle and collective action. The job of companies is to make money for their shareholders, "within the law". The laws are made by politicians who are trying to maximise their own welfare by getting elected, which means raising money, building an image and making the rules as favourable as possible. The job of media outlets is to maximise their readership and audience, by providing media products that are as attractive as possible. Judges are in essence just another lot of providers of "legal services"; if they are honest, it is not because of the vague obligations of abstract morality but to preserve their competitive advantage against other jurisdictions (and perhaps because the penalties of getting caught are so severe).

From this economism viewpoint, competition between nations will raise standards of governance, just as competition between companies leads to innovation and more added value. The result may be labelled "democracy" but it is much closer to a well-run business, in which the enlightened self-interest of all concerned leads to a generally satisfactory result.

The reality, however, is that economism as a political philosophy does not stand up to much scrutiny: its seeming practical success obscures its weaknesses. A good example is Dubai, a successful trading entrepôt run, in essence, on commercial lines. The overwhelming majority of its inhabitants come from other countries, working in conditions ranging from luxury to misery. If you don't like Dubai, you don't lobby – you leave.

I doubt that it is possible to run anything big on these lines with Dubai's degree of success. The likely result is not a giant emirate, but a system like Russia's, also run as a business by a ruling syndicate – this time of ex-KGB men and their cronies. In this system public positions below the very top of the pyramid are bought and sold, with their value depending on the rents that the incumbent can extract from public transactions (such as traffic fines), from businesses (tax payments), or from the natural resources (radio spectrum, minerals) that the post controls. This does not involve the creation of an authoritarian monolith: Russia has a degree of political competition within the ruling elite. But the competition is managed – and on important occasions staged – in order to give the appearance of choice, and so provide safety valves for public discontent.

Scared – or complacent?

For much of the past two decades, market pressure looked the best counterweight to these tendencies. Surely the fear of bad rankings in good-governance indices, or a bad reputation among foreign investors, would keep political systems clean. Sadly, not so far. A bad international reputation does not seem to translate into effective political pressure at home, though success may help incumbents.

Countries that do well preen themselves. Rulers in countries that fare poorly simply shrug off the low rankings, or play the xenophobia card, blaming the ill will and ignorance of foreigners. A guaranteed big slice of a small cake, for many such politicians, is a better bet than the risky chance of a small slice of a big one.

Cultivating public-spiritedness is difficult. The places that need it most badly are *ipso facto* those that have the least of it. It flourishes in stable, unhierarchical societies with long traditions of political stability and freedom. In an English village or small-town America it can be almost stifling. In places where the price of not keeping your head down is that it gets chopped off, civil courage becomes rare.

So what next? The political systems of the West have not only failed to spread sustainably to the east and south. They are also at risk at home, from two great dangers: panic and complacency. Panic makes people timid. They yearn for strong leaders and short-cuts. They worry about the present not the future, and care more for private interests than public. With the right leadership, national danger can bring astonishing public-spiritedness (those of a certain age in Britain still remember the "Dunkirk spirit" when national obliteration loomed in 1940). The spirit of Egypt's Tahrir Square, with non-violent protesters conscientiously picking up their litter under the guns of the authorities' goon squads, was impressive too. But over time, uncertainty and upheaval have a corrosive effect, making people concentrate on their nearest and dearest. The panic can come from war, terrorism, or any manner of natural or economic catastrophe. But it will expose the weaknesses of a political system far more severely than it bolsters its strengths.

Complacency is if anything even more dangerous. Just as a biological immune system weakens when it is not tested, so the political system becomes flabby and vulnerable when it perceives no threat. Civic activism fades into the minutiae of local politics, while national politics are too dull to attract big thinkers. The idealistic turn their energies to culture, education and religion or to causes abroad. Those that are left in the democratic West haggle endlessly over nuances of procedure, or the division of taxpayers' money favouring one set of clients over another. That is no model for the billions in the rest of world yearning for real, more or better democracy.

10 Taming Leviathan: the state of the state

Paul Wallace

The state cannot afford the promises it has made to its citizens on pensions and health care. Something will have to give

THE STATE HAS PUT ON WEIGHT since – and because of – the financial crisis that struck in 2007 and the great recession that ensued. Spending has swollen while taxes have shrunk, leading to record budget deficits and a surge in public debt. This could be a mere foretaste of what is to come as populations age. One nightmarish vision of the state in 2050 is that of a Leviathan felled by its own weight as it struggles with the rising social burden of an older society.

An alternative vision sees a fitter state thanks to farsighted reforms – in particular those that will limit tax bills for pensions and health care, the two areas where ageing most threatens the public finances. But as government sheds some of its responsibilities in these areas it will need to assume more in other domains, notably in promoting a knowledge economy and in sustaining longer working lives. The state of 2050 will be smarter as well as fitter.

Which of these visions materialises will depend not just on politics but also on economics. Some argue that the necessary reforms will be blocked by older voters, selfishly guarding their own interests. But an overburdened state would imperil the economy and that would be in no one's interest. This suggests that the nightmare will remain just that – though with more than a few scares along the way.

The shock of the old

What is beyond doubt is that without some kind of government action demographic change will wreak havoc in the public finances.

There are two sources for this ageing process: first, the continuing rise in longevity; and second, the delayed impact of the post-war boom-and-bust fertility cycle, which is swelling the number of older people in the population while shrinking the share of younger adults. The fear is that as the baby-boomers retire they will relentlessly push up spending on pensions, care and health, and there will be relatively fewer workers to pay for the extra costs.

The potential fiscal fallout is daunting. From a budgetary perspective America's demographic prospects compare favourably with those for many other advanced countries, particularly hyper-ageing Japan and Italy. Yet the Congressional Budget Office (CBO) set out a bleak projection in 2010. On plausible assumptions about likely policies in coming years, which included revenues staying around their long-term average as a share of GDP, it predicted that by as early as 2035 America's federal debt will soar from around 60% of GDP in 2010 (already the highest since shortly after the second world war) to an unsustainable 185%. The worsening outlook is driven mainly by surging spending on health care through the two main programmes, Medicare for the old and Medicaid for the poor. Higher outlays on pensions (Social Security) are less prominent.

Projections through to 2050 for some 30 advanced countries from Standard & Poor's (S&P), a credit-rating agency, are just as dismal (see Figure 10.1). These show pressures on budgets from ageing intensifying from 2020. For a typical advanced country, age-related public spending will rise by around 10% of GDP between 2010 and 2050. As in America, pensions will play second fiddle, contributing three of those ten percentage points. Health will be the biggest culprit, making up half of the increase, with the cost of long-term care adding a further 1.3%. Assuming that taxes stay unchanged, big deficits become entrenched and net government debt (ie, gross debt less liquid financial assets) balloons, from 65% of GDP in 2010 to 329% by 2050, relegating a typical sovereign bond to junk status.

S&P's horror story is not confined to developed economies. Among the four BRIC emerging economies (Brazil, Russia, India, China), two countries will be unscathed. Age-related spending will barely rise at all in India, while in China the increase will be contained to 2.5% of

FIG 10.1 **Older and costlier**

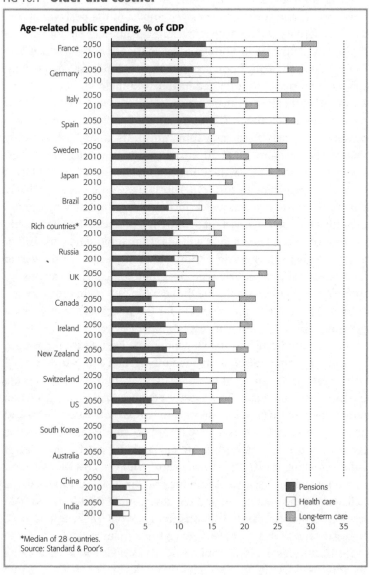

Age-related public spending, % of GDP

*Median of 28 countries.
Source: Standard & Poor's

GDP. By contrast, in Brazil and Russia age-related spending will shoot up by 12.5% of GDP.

With its population ageing fast, the projection for China may prove too sanguine. In 2000 the median age in China was 29.7, more than five years lower than America's 35.3. But as early as 2020, a typical Chinese will be older than a typical American, and by 2050 the Chinese median age will reach 48.7 compared with 40 in America. China may have been growing at breakneck speed but its living standards still trail those in the West – hence the risk that it, and other developing countries whose fertility has collapsed, will grow old before they grow rich.

When there is a shortfall between rising spending and less buoyant revenues – the essence of the fiscal damage from ageing – the danger is that the state starts to neglect some of its core functions, such as national security, as health and welfare gobble up more of the cake. This has been happening even before the age shift really gets under way. In Britain, for example, public spending on defence was close to that on health as recently as the late 1980s, at 4.3% and 4.6% of GDP respectively. Two decades later, the National Health Service (NHS) accounted for 8.5% of GDP whereas defence had shrunk to 2.5%. As Tony Travers, a specialist on public spending at the London School of Economics, puts it: "The NHS ate defence and looks set to devour much of the rest of the budget." The CBO projection for America would be even more alarming but for its assumption of a steep fall in all government spending other than Social Security, health care and interest payments, from 12.5% of GDP in 2010 to 9.3% by 2035.

At the extreme, states that are too greedy topple over: they undermine their fiscal capacity by overextending it. As impositions on taxpayers become ever more oppressive, business weakens, private capital takes flight, foreign confidence ebbs and the state fails along with the economy. In *This Time Is Different*, chronicling financial folly since medieval times, Carmen Reinhart and Kenneth Rogoff say:

> *Although private debt certainly plays a key role in many crises, government debt is far more often the unifying problem across the wide range of financial crises we examine.*

The case against fiscal fatalism

Do the public finances really have to reach such a pass? When looking forward it helps to look back as well. Compare government spending today as a share of GDP with where it stood a century ago and you might conclude that it is on an inexorable upward trajectory. But that comparison between the two points in time frightens to deceive. In between, governments have shown that they can get a grip on spending when it threatens to get out of control (see box and Figure 10.2).

Projections of an ever more bloated state broadly assume that things carry on as before even if they are unaffordable. But there are no tablets of stone decreeing that people can draw state pensions at a fixed age, typically 65, as they live longer and longer; nor is it a constitutional right for pensioners to rely on taxpayers to provide much more than a basic pension. States can redefine their duties and restrain future outlays. They will do this either through pre-emptive reforms or under duress. One way or another, a new contract will be written to limit the requirement on taxpayers to bankroll pensions and health care.

Reforms forced through during sovereign-debt crises, which have typically occurred in youthful developing countries but more recently have afflicted some of the older nations of the euro area, show what can be done when times are desperate. Greece illustrates just how much flab can accumulate in a pension system – and be excised. Projections by the OECD had shown its pension burden doubling from an already high 11.6% of GDP in 2010 to 24% by 2050. Emergency surgery following the country's bail-out in 2010 will strip out most of the increase, containing the rise to an extra 2.5 percentage points.

The excesses of the Greek pension system were extreme. Other countries have long been trying to curb future costs in their pay-as-you-go pension systems (in which today's taxpayers finance today's pensions). A first wave of reforms switched the indexation of benefits from wages to prices, which rise more slowly. A second has linked benefits to life expectancy at retirement, reducing the generosity of the pension in line with increased life expectancy (as is the case with private annuities).

History's hopeful lesson

In the late 1970s a simple extrapolation of welfare spending based on the preceding post-war decades pointed to much earlier fiscal ruin in the rich world, especially in Europe. The position was particularly dire in Denmark, where social spending, broadly defined, had risen from 9% of GDP in 1950 to 20% in 1971 and 33% in 1980. But the unsustainable trend was reversed: by 1986 social expenditure had fallen to 26% of GDP as Denmark pushed through one of the biggest fiscal consolidations on record. More generally, the late 1970s proved the high-water mark for welfare spending in the rich world.

Or go back to 1995 and revisit the agonies of Finland and Sweden, whose debt had surged in the early 1990s as their economies were felled by home-grown banking collapses. Who would have expected then that they would emerge from the 2007–09 financial crisis with debt so low? According to IMF projections their debt was set to reach 50% and 33% of GDP respectively in 2012 even though both economies had been hit hard by the great recession: Finland's GDP shrank by 8% in 2009, Sweden's by 5%.

The general thrust of reforms is to stop contribution rates from rising by clamping down on benefits as ageing pushes up the ratio of pensioners to workers. The state in 2050 will concentrate on ensuring minimum benefits to prevent poverty in old age. The better-off will be expected to provide more for themselves through private nest-eggs. Australia has already moved a long way in this direction. Its tax-financed pension is "affluence-tested", excluding roughly the top 20% of the population, while private retirement saving is mandatory. In other countries, like Germany, tax incentives are being used to encourage voluntary saving accounts to compensate for the declining generosity of its pay-as-you-go system.

A third wave of reforms is now starting but has yet to gather force. Working lives are being extended in order to slow the rise in

FIG 10.2 **Hooked on spending**

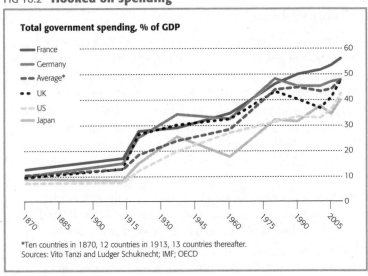

Total government spending, % of GDP

- France
- Germany
- Average*
- UK
- US
- Japan

*Ten countries in 1870, 12 countries in 1913, 13 countries thereafter.
Sources: Vito Tanzi and Ludger Schuknecht; IMF; OECD

the ratio of pensioners to workers. But getting people to work longer requires changes both by employers and managers, who must shed ageist attitudes, and by employees, who must improve their skills. Governments for their part are starting to raise the state-pension age (SPA), which sends both a social signal and a financial incentive to carry on working. In Britain, for example, it is increasing for women from 60 in 2010 to 65 – the current age for men – by 2018. It will then rise to 66 by 2020 for both men and women, and to 67 by 2028. An alternative policy especially in the longer term is to link the SPA with life expectancy. Denmark will do this after raising its pension age from 65 to 67 in the 2020s.

These new schemes will make pensions for baby-boomers less generous than those their parents enjoyed – which will mitigate the one-off bulge effect as the big generation retires. Time spent in retirement will no longer be an ever-rising proportion of adult lives. Overall, the reforms have not yet gone far enough, but they are moving in the right direction.

Doctor, can you spare a dime?

But even if pension costs can be controlled by the state of 2050, the task of taming health-care budgets looks more intractable as populations age. Average spending on over-65s is 3–4 times higher than that on younger adults; in Britain someone over 85 costs the NHS six times as much as a 16–44 year-old. As the share of older people in the population rises, spending seems bound to surge. This prediction is made so often that it has become conventional wisdom, but the gloomy syllogism on which it is based is suspect.

Treating the elderly costs a lot, not so much because they are old but because they are more likely to die. A closer look at lifetime medical costs shows that a big chunk of them is incurred in the year or so before death, regardless of age. In fact, among the very old, the bills tend to be, if anything, less than for youngsters or the middle-aged. As people live longer, these end-of-life expenses are in effect being deferred.

What this analysis of health spending suggests is that the patients of 2050 will not cripple the state of 2050. Medical spending will certainly rise over the next couple of decades as the baby-boomers eventually die. But this surge should in theory then subside as the boomers are replaced by a smaller cohort of pensioners.

In practice, ageing may drive up health budgets more than the "years-to-death" model implies since baby-boomers are likely to be pushier than their parents in demanding the best medical care. But that pressure will be only one among many influences that will continue to force up costs. The mid-21st-century state will have to solve the problem vexing the early 21st-century state: the inexorable increase in health spending, regardless of ageing populations, that has resulted from technological advances and inefficient medical markets.

One way forward will be for individuals to contribute more private funding through co-payments. Such a reform will have to be devised with care, with exemptions for the poor and chronically ill. But the priority is to enhance choice and competition in health care. An IMF study finds that strengthening market mechanisms is the single most important means of restraining excessive growth in health spending.

The Netherlands offers one template for pursuing this policy within a budget mainly (80%) financed from public funds. An innovative reform in 2006 has created a framework for "managed competition" in health care.

In an unfettered market, medical insurers will select the young and healthy and exclude the old and chronically ill. The Dutch solve this problem by requiring them to take all-comers regardless of their age, gender or health status, with their funding coming from budgets that are adjusted for the riskiness of their patients. The insurers negotiate on price and quality with hospitals and general practitioners working in primary care. Patients can switch between insurers and choose their provider when they need care. The government remains responsible for its quality and for ensuring that it is accessible and affordable. In particular, everyone pays a flat-rate premium to purchase basic health-care insurance, with the state picking up the bill for children and assisting poorer people.

Imitation is the sincerest form of flattery. Tellingly, in its effort to modernise its health system, cash-strapped Ireland is looking to what Fine Gael, the main ruling party elected in 2011, calls the "very efficient Dutch model".

As market pressures are brought to bear on health care, they should unleash big efficiency gains from the use of information technology. The medical sector has lagged far behind other industries in adopting IT. Study after study has concluded that waste and inefficiency in health care, including America's Medicare, are so widespread that striking improvements in care can be achieved even without extra resources. Peter Orszag, a former head of President Barack Obama's Office of Management and Budget, believes that technological innovation will help to promote big cost savings in the American programme for old people.

Smarter as well as fitter

In both pensions and health, such reforms will amount to a new form of private-public partnership (PPP), but between the state and its citizens rather than the state and companies. The underlying rationale will also differ. Too often PPPs were a way of subverting sound public finance by getting the private sector to bear the initial cost of investments in the public realm, like new hospitals and roads, which would then have to be repaid over decades by taxpayers. The joint undertakings in pensions and health will instead aim to limit financial overstretch on the part of the government.

The state in advanced countries can thus save itself and the people it serves through a new contract that caps public bills. Developing economies for their part can fend off some of their worries about growing old before they grow rich by leapfrogging to this new contract. In pensions, for example, once a pay-as-you-go scheme has been running for some time it is difficult to switch to one that is privately financed: the problem is the "double burden" created as the payroll revenues used to pay for today's pensioners are diverted into workers' saving accounts. But developing countries, especially in Latin America, have been able to make that move much more easily.

As part of this new partnership between state and citizen, the state itself will need a drastic overhaul. First, it must stop overpaying its employees. Overpayment is often through lavish pensions rather than excessive earnings. There is no reason why the public sector should not include good pensions as part of its employees' remuneration packages, but these must be properly accounted for so that the full costs are recognised.

Raising efficiency will be crucial. In contrast to industry, where technical advances and economies of scale can lead to continuing gains in productivity, the scope for raising the efficiency of labour-intensive services, especially in the public sector, has long appeared limited. In what is called "Baumol's cost disease", after the economist who spotted it, this raises unit labour costs relative to those in the private sector as public salaries rise broadly in line with economy-wide wages. It still takes five musicians to perform a Mozart string quintet, in the same amount of time, he and William Bowen noted, but their wages have shot up since the late 18th century.

But since William Baumol made his original diagnosis in the mid-1960s, a lot has changed. As Victor Fuchs, an economist at Stanford University, points out, the classical musicians' productivity has received a helping hand from recordings that make their performance available to millions around the world. In the public sector, advances in information technology have great potential to raise the efficiency of many aspects of public administration, from tax accounts to pension payments. New incentive schemes involving private providers, such as payments for outcomes, can also assist – for example, by rewarding contractors for programmes that move people from welfare to work or that reduce re-offending by criminals.

As well as becoming more efficient, the state of the future will need to promote growth in order to gain higher revenues. One way to do that will be to move away from incentive-curbing taxes on work and towards green taxes, levies on property and widely based consumption taxes. Another will be to reduce regulatory burdens. Regulation is often indispensable, as in finance or food standards. But it is also in effect a hidden tax, raising costs for businesses, and it needs to be constantly pruned.

The state of 2050 will invest in the things that enhance growth but are underprovided by the private sector. Backing pure science is uncontroversial, but there is also a case for supporting applied research and development. Governments could also invest in private venture-capital funds to support high-tech start-ups.

As populations age there will be a political bias to favour spending on the old rather than the young – but a smart state will do the opposite, because that will actually be the best way to support everyone. Growth will come above all from having a more skilled working population. The foundation of that human capital must be education, with the state shouldering the costs for schoolchildren, sharing them with university students and helping poorer adults to develop new skills.

Like a good general the smart state of the future will be better prepared for budgetary emergencies. One of the prime lessons of the 2008 financial crisis was the need to hold a strategic fiscal reserve, keeping debt low in order to allow a sudden surge in government borrowing. Future calls on the public purse could spring from many other sources, such as disasters caused by extreme-weather events as the climate changes. Fiscal rules are not enough to ensure that the public finances are being managed prudently. A better way will be to create independent official watchdogs such as Sweden's fiscal-policy council established in 2007 or Britain's Office for Budget Responsibility introduced in 2010.

The shape of the state in 2050 will be determined by the politics of the preceding decades. The gloomy view is that older voters will use their growing clout to get their way. If that is the case, the nightmare vision will be realised. But voting is not all about self-interest, and older people will always care about their children and the future. If politicians can explain why reforms are necessary, the state of 2050 will be smarter and fitter.

PART 3

Economy and business

The patterns of growth, innovation and markets

11 The age of emerging markets

Simon Cox

By 2050 the big economies will no longer be emerging, and the emerging economies will no longer be very big

FORTY YEARS AGO, "emerging markets" did not exist. The phrase, now ubiquitous, did not appear until 1981. It was coined by Antoine van Agtmael, an official at the International Finance Corporation, a division of the World Bank. He was looking for a more enticing title for his Third World Equity Fund, a name, he said, that evoked images of "flimsy polyester, cheap toys, rampant corruption, Soviet-style tractors and flooded rice paddies". Such images were not easy to dislodge from the minds of Western investors, whose horizons once extended little beyond their own shores. In his earlier job at Bankers Trust Company in the 1970s, van Agtmael recalls, his boss told him, "There are no markets outside the United States!"

His boss was wrong, of course, but not that wrong. In 1970 Deng Xiaoping, the champion of China's economic reforms, was still in exile. India's prime minister, Indira Gandhi, had turned to high socialism a few years before (nationalising the banks and throttling big business) and would turn away from democracy a few years later. Vietnam was still at war. The "Chicago Boys", liberalising technocrats schooled by Chicago economists like Arnold Harberger and Milton Friedman, had yet to gain influence in Chile, which had just elected a socialist president, Salvador Allende, who believed the economy could be centrally planned with the help of a Burroughs 3500 computer.

If Western investors were sceptical about the "third world", it was also suspicious of them. In the 1970s developing countries equated capitalism with exploitation and dependency. They lamented the declining price of their commodity exports and the lingering influence of foreign multinationals, which they regarded as relics of colonialism. At the United Nations Conference on Trade and Development (UNCTAD) in Geneva, they demanded a "new international economic order" that would better serve their interests.

Forty years later, a new order has taken shape, but one very different from that espoused in the 1970s. Developing countries have made their peace with capitalism. They now seek to attract foreign investment, not to expropriate it, and to entice Western consumers with competitive manufactured goods, not to squeeze Western importers with commodity cartels. Their policymakers promote their interests not at the left-leaning UNCTAD in Geneva, but 1,200 metres higher up in Davos, a Swiss ski resort where the World Economic Forum holds its annual capitalist jamboree of the great and the good in business, politics and the media.

Over the past 40 years, "emerging markets" (EMs) have entered the language and the portfolios of world investors. They are likely to attract over $1 trillion of private capital from abroad in 2011, according to the Institute of International Finance, which represents international bankers. Emerging and developing economies accounted for a third of world GDP in 2010, measured at market exchange rates, and almost a half when rates are adjusted for national differences in purchasing power. They contributed an even bigger share – two-thirds – of the growth of global GDP that year.

Blue-skies thinking

Looking back 40 years can induce vertigo, like looking down from a 40-storey building. So much seems compressed into such a short frame. Looking ahead 40 years produces a different kind of giddiness. It is more like gazing up into the blue yonder: the view is open, almost limitless, but also featureless. There is little to latch on to.

Some bold economists have tried to fill in the picture, producing long-range projections of emerging-market growth. In 1997 the World Bank's research department projected the long-run growth of what it called the Big Five emerging economies: China, India, Brazil, Russia and Indonesia. It calculated that their share of world GDP would double from 1992 to 2020. In fact, it doubled ten years earlier.

In 2001 Jim O'Neill of Goldman Sachs looked at four big emerging economies reshaping the world order. His list was limited to Brazil, Russia, India and China, which he dubbed the BRICs. Indonesia did not make the cut. If it had not been for the Asian financial crisis, it might have been impossible to drop. It was richer than India, more populous than Russia or Brazil and had grown faster than all three in the years before 1997. But the crisis threw Indonesia into disarray and spared the BRICs an extra vowel. The acronym was an immediate hit, inspiring investment funds, a new geopolitical club, a thousand puns and a small industry of long-range GDP projections.

Goldman Sachs's own projections first appeared in 2003. These scenarios did not represent a forecast of the future, it said, so much as a "dream" towards which the four countries could aspire. "We are sufficiently humble to realise that this scenario may not play out," it commented in a later paper.

Its humility proved amply justified. By 2008, its projections were already off track – though not in the way the Goldman Sachs forecasters had feared. They had predicted that China's GDP would be almost $2.8 trillion by the end of 2008. In fact it was over $4.3 trillion. Russia's economy in 2008 was more than twice the size Goldman had projected five years before; Brazil's was 2.3 times bigger.

Long-range forecasting is not, then, all that successful. Economics has many strengths. Unfortunately, predicting growth 40 years into the future is not one of them. Larry Summers, who would later serve as President Barack Obama's top economic adviser, and three co-authors once showed that there is precious little correlation between a country's growth over one five-year stretch and another.

These projections are, however, interesting, even if they are not always convincing. Even a "bad" number is often better than no number at all. If nothing else, these exercises serve as stark illustrations of the power of compound growth, a power that is often hard for people to appreciate. People often assume that something growing by 10% a year will be 100% bigger after ten years, for example. In fact, it takes only seven years, three months and ten days.

FIG 11.1 **The essential exponential**

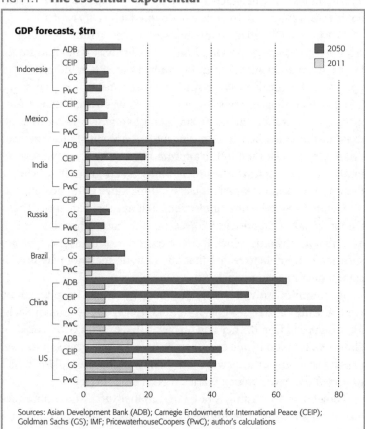

GDP forecasts, $trn

■ 2050
□ 2011

Sources: Asian Development Bank (ADB); Carnegie Endowment for International Peace (CEIP); Goldman Sachs (GS); IMF; PricewaterhouseCoopers (PwC); author's calculations

This is because economic growth is exponential. The amount an economy expands is proportional to its size, but its size is also a result of its growth. The economy therefore benefits from growth upon growth. For example, China's economy expanded by about 29% in dollar terms in both 2007 and 2008 (thanks to both rapid growth and a strengthening yuan). In each year it added to its size 29% of whatever its size was in the previous year. In 2007, that 29% growth added about $780 billion to China's GDP. In 2008, the same 29% growth added over $1 trillion. Growth adds to growth. "The greatest shortcoming of the human race", said Al Bartlett, a physicist, "is our inability to understand the exponential function."

Bartlett called it "the essential exponential". To illustrate its effects, Figure 11.1 reports the results of several recent projections by Goldman Sachs (GS), the Carnegie Endowment for International Peace (CEIP), the Asian Development Bank (ADB) and PwC, a consultancy. (In the next chapter, Laza Kekic provides some similar projections based on calculations by the Economist Intelligence Unit.)

The results are eye-popping. By 2050, according to Goldman Sachs, China's GDP will top $70 trillion; 80% more than America's. By this reckoning, the United States will be the only member of the current G7 that still qualifies as one of the seven biggest economies in the world. The other members will be surpassed not just by China but also by India, Brazil, Russia, Indonesia and Mexico. We will then truly be living in an age of emerging markets.

Apart from the exponential function, what else drives these startling results? Despite all the frills and trills that now accompany these exercises, they are at heart quite simple, even crude. Their results reflect three trends: the size of the EMs' workforces, the convergence of their productivity with that of America and the strengthening of their exchange rates.

Workers of the world

The world's workforce (people aged 20–64) may rise from 3.9 billion in 2010 to almost 5.3 billion in 2050, according to a mid-range scenario calculated by the UN. Of those 5.3 billion workers, almost 70% will live in what might today be considered emerging economies, on an expansive definition of the term. (This definition includes the less, but not the least, developed countries according to the UN's terminology.)

Interestingly, a slightly higher percentage of the world's workers live in those countries today. One reason for this stagnation in the EMs' share of the world's workforce is China. Over the next 40 years its population will shrink and age, diminishing its workforce by 15%. India's toiling masses, by contrast, will grow from 670m to 1.03 billion, from 77% of China's workforce to 141%.

Also notable is the rising population of the least developed

FIG 11.2 **Where to find the staff**

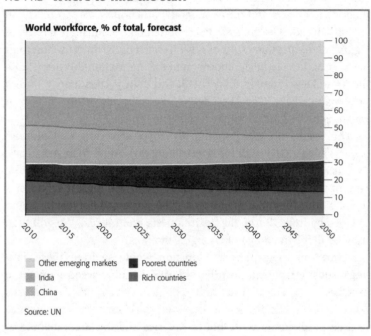

World workforce, % of total, forecast

Legend:
- Other emerging markets
- India
- China
- Poorest countries
- Rich countries

Source: UN

countries: desperately poor nations, mostly in Africa, that are not now generally classified as emerging economies. Today these 48 nations have a combined workforce of around 380m, which will more than double to almost 950m by 2050. Unfancied economies like Tanzania and Ethiopia will each have populations of over 130m by the middle of this century, bigger than today's Japan.

Tardy but speedy

This expanding workforce will contribute some of the emerging markets' growth. Some will also stem from additional investment in their stock of physical capital, such as machines and buildings. But that still leaves a lot of growth unexplained. This "residual", one economist says, is "a measure of our ignorance".

This unexplained growth is often put down to technological progress. In any prospering economy, firms introduce novel products, adopt innovative techniques and remould themselves into new shapes and sizes. Economic progress entails qualitative as well as quantitative change. It is an expansion of scope as well as size, variety as well as volume. Economic growth is more like the efflorescence of a forest than the growth of a tree.

Economists have labelled this residual "total factor productivity" or TFP. Whenever an economy gets some additional output for no discernible input, it is ascribed to growth in TFP. The concept has many profound flaws. Jesus Felipe, an economist at the Asian Development Bank, thinks it is largely a statistical artefact. But all long-run projections of economic growth rely heavily upon it – including those of the ADB. Over the long run, it is the growth of TFP in emerging economies, not the growth of their workforce or the accumulation of their capital stock, that will chiefly govern their fortunes.

But if TFP will determine the EMs' fortunes, what will determine TFP? In emerging economies the pace of productivity growth depends first and foremost on their "backwardness" – their distance from leading economies, such as America, which work at the cutting-edge of economic efficiency. The farther behind they find themselves, the faster EMs can travel down the path the United States has trodden before them. Backward countries with very low levels of productivity have vast scope for improvement and lots of low-hanging fruit to pick. As they graduate to more sophisticated techniques, productivity gains become harder to find, and growth slows.

The idea is often attributed to Alexander Gerschenkron, a great economic historian, who explained how Germany, Russia and other late industrialisers in Europe caught up with Britain, the leading economy of the time. Latecomers were willing to commit to recent technologies that early industrialisers were reluctant to adopt since it would entail scrapping their existing capital stock. Germany's blast furnaces, for example, swiftly surpassed the older vintages still used in Britain. Then Russia's even newer furnaces surpassed Germany's. Sometimes starting out is easier than starting over.

All the best-known 2050 projections rely heavily on this idea. The ADB gives the example of a hypothetical country that starts out only 20% as productive as America. This country's productivity grows at a

The emerging smartest

The workforce of the emerging world will be smarter as well as bigger in the decades ahead. The International Institute for Applied Systems Analysis in Austria (IIASA) has published projections of education levels in 120 countries over the next four decades. Samir K.C. and his colleagues divide the population into four broad educational categories (roughly corresponding to primary, secondary and higher education, as well as the unschooled). Based on these categories, we can calculate a single number – average years of schooling – to describe the education level of the workforce. It is an imperfect measure because the quality of schooling varies so much. But the projections are nonetheless intriguing.

Figure 11.3 shows the results for 12 prominent emerging economies in 2010 and in 2050. The countries all improve, and the gap between them narrows markedly. Countries like Bangladesh, Pakistan, India and Nigeria are projected to raise the average years of schooling of their workforce by about 3.5 years or more over the next four decades, while well-educated workforces, such as Russia's, barely improve.

This convergence is due to two factors. First, it is easier to raise the rate of school enrolment from, say, 40% to 50% than from 80%

steadily diminishing rate as it gets closer to the technological frontier. The frontier itself is assumed to advance each year at 1.3%, the average TFP gain for America over the past century or so. It would take this country until 2104 to become 60% as productive as America, and a further 66 years to reach 80% of the American productivity level.

The later a country industrialises, the faster it does so. But if backwardness or lateness were the only determinants of productivity growth, then all economies would be catching up with the leader. In fact, some economies are stagnating; others are even falling farther behind.

All the futurologists therefore fiddle with their basic convergence equation in an attempt to capture the difference that good institutions to 90%. Second, raising the enrolment rate has a bigger effect in youthful countries. In such countries, children are large in number relative to the size of the working-age population. So educating these children better has a bigger impact on the educational mix of the workforce as a whole.

FIG 11.3 **Making more time for education**

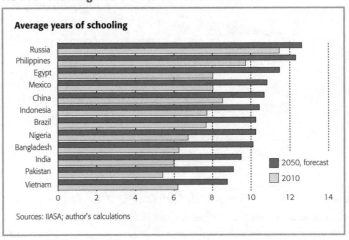

Average years of schooling

Sources: IIASA; author's calculations

and policies can make. Goldman Sachs, for example, identifies no fewer than 13 variables (from life expectancy to inflation) that may influence the speed of convergence.

Of this laundry list of factors, the one that has attracted the most attention from growth scholars is education. In a 1966 paper, Richard Nelson and Edmund Phelps, a Nobel prize-winning economist, argued that productivity-improving tricks and techniques spread faster in countries that have better-educated workforces. In America, for example, more-educated farmers adopted innovations faster than less-educated farmers, because they better appreciated the information passed on by farm journals, the radio, seed companies

FIG 11.4 **Teach yourself productivity**

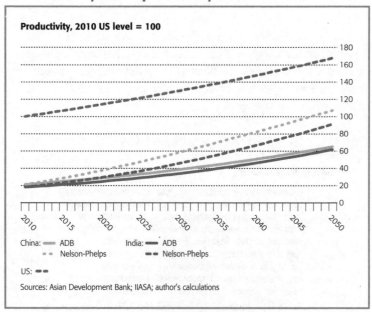

Productivity, 2010 US level = 100

China: ━━ ADB   India: ━━ ADB
    •• Nelson-Phelps   ━━ Nelson-Phelps

US: ━━

Sources: Asian Development Bank; IIASA; author's calculations

and even the Department of Agriculture. "Education speeds the process of technological diffusion," as Nelson and Phelps put it.

If they are right, the implications of extra years of schooling on emerging markets could be profound. Figure 11.4 shows this author's calculations of the effect they may have on productivity catch-up in China and India. (The calculations use plausible estimates of the contribution of extra human capital to the speed of technological diffusion, drawn from work by Jesus Crespo Cuaresma of the IIASA.) For comparison, Figure 11.4 also shows the (slower) convergence envisaged by the Asian Development Bank in its Asia 2050 report.

Yuan rising

Catch-up growth gets the emerging economies part of the way to the eye-popping GDPs projected for 2050 by Goldman Sachs and others. Exchange-rate appreciation takes care of the rest.

Poor countries tend to have "cheap" currencies. Dollars seem to stretch much further in developing economies, as American backpackers discover to their delight. Take India: in mid-2011 $1 bought about Rs44 on the foreign-exchange market; but Rs44 in India stretched about as far as $3 in America.

This is because locally produced goods and services, such as restaurant meals and haircuts, tend to be far cheaper than their counterparts in the rich world. As countries grow richer this gap narrows, or even reverses. Americans who visited Europe or Japan in the 1960s would marvel about how cheap things seemed. They do not do that any more.

In the Goldman Sachs model, if an EM's output per worker grows 1% faster than America's, then its real exchange rate appreciates by 0.5% against the dollar. This appreciation can take a variety of forms: either the EM's currency rises, or its domestic prices rise relative to America's, or a bit of both. These appreciations make a big difference to the dollar GDPs of all the BRICs, except Brazil. Figure 11.5 shows how much of the BRICs' rise is due to the growth of their real GDP and how much is due to changes in their real exchange rate.

Without exchange-rate appreciation, the future GDP of the BRICs seems far less impressive. Does that mean the BRICs' dream is partly a monetary illusion? The lower GDP number is indeed better for some purposes. It shows how the volume of goods and services will grow in each economy. The bigger figure, in contrast, also captures how the value of that output will change. It reveals a mighty swing in the price of BRIC goods and services relative to those in America. If you want to know how many more haircuts and restaurant meals China will be serving in 2050, use the smaller number. If you want to know how many American haircuts and meals the Chinese will be able to afford, use the bigger one.

A world of services

As economies grow in size, they also change in shape, undergoing what economists call a "structural transformation". Agriculture recedes in importance, while industry and then services grow. Economic activity migrates from the field to the factory and then to the cubicle and the retail outlet. Workers go from tilling the field to manning the till.

FIG 11.5 **Backpackers beware**

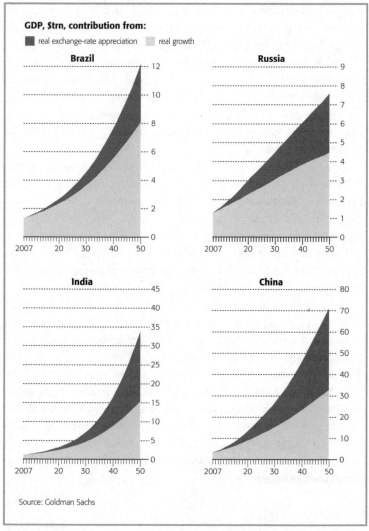

GDP, $trn, contribution from:
■ real exchange-rate appreciation ▢ real growth

Source: Goldman Sachs

Crudely speaking, poor countries are mostly agricultural; middle-income countries are heavily industrial; and rich countries are dominated by services. By 2050, however, many more countries will be rich by today's standards, and fewer will be poor or middling. Does it follow that the next four decades will witness the deindustrialisation of the world?

In a word, yes. The share of industry (and agriculture) in GDP will fall. But that does not mean the absolute level of farm and factory output will also drop. The 9.3 billion people alive in 2050 will, after all, need more food and manufactured items than the 7 billion alive today. The number of cars on India's roads, to take one example, will increase by 3,880% by 2050, according to Goldman Sachs.

But farming and factory output will still fall as a percentage of GDP over the next four decades, just as they have over the past four. As people grow richer, they spend a smaller share of their incomes on food and manufactured trinkets, and a larger share on services. This is partly because manufactured goods become progressively cheaper, relative to services (which is in turn because the scope for improving productivity in manufacturing is so much greater than in services).

But even when prices are constant, spending shifts to services as incomes rise. This is such a regular pattern as to be close to a natural law, rooted perhaps in the "hierarchy of needs" identified by Abraham Maslow, a psychologist, in 1943. Once we are adequately fed, watered and sheltered, we turn to satisfying higher needs, such as recreation and culture (see Figure 11.6). Many of these needs can be met with things. But eventually we have enough stuff and seek other kinds of fulfilment, amusement and edification. Since there is no limit to the ways we can become more useful to each other, and no limit to the accumulation of human knowledge, there is no limit to growth. But as economies become richer and more sophisticated, they devote more of their energies to providing services, rather than making things.

Emerged markets

The industrialisation of the EMs has marched in step with their globalisation. Their manufactured goods have conquered overseas markets, claiming an ever expanding share of world trade. As their economies continue to grow and prosper in the coming decades, it is tempting to assume their share of world exports can only grow.

But countries trade with each other partly because they differ. Portugal traded wine for English cloth, in the classic example, because

FIG 11.6 **More money, more choice**

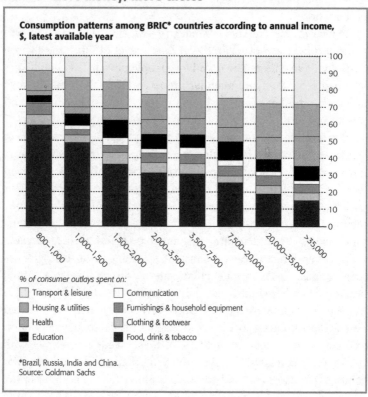

Consumption patterns among BRIC* countries according to annual income, $, latest available year

% of consumer outlays spent on:
- Transport & leisure
- Housing & utilities
- Health
- Education
- Communication
- Furnishings & household equipment
- Clothing & footwear
- Food, drink & tobacco

*Brazil, Russia, India and China.
Source: Goldman Sachs

its climate differs from England's. China buys high-tech components and sells laboriously assembled manufactures because it has a lot of nimble-fingered workers relative to its stock of capital and know-how.

As the emerging economies catch up with America, Europe and Japan, they will also become more similar to them. That will weaken one motivation for trade. There is no point in America importing labour-intensive goods from China if labour becomes almost as scarce in China as it is at home.

But whereas trade in goods may slow, two-way trade in financial assets has lots of potential to grow. Thirty years after van Agtmael started pitching his Third World Equity Fund, the combined value of EM stockmarkets has reached about $14 trillion, or 31% of the value of all the stockmarkets in the world. That total could rise to $80 trillion by 2030, according to Goldman Sachs, 55% of global market capitalisation.

To reach these figures, EM stockmarkets will have to grow by over 9% a year. That is twice the rate of more mature markets, but rather slower than the EMs have appreciated over the past 20 years, when they expanded at the breakneck pace of almost 16% a year.

But that does not mean that anyone holding EM stocks today can expect 9% returns. Of the $66 trillion gain in the value of EM stockmarkets over the next 20 years, about 40% will reflect new stocks that list on the market and increase in value thereafter. Existing EM shares will increase in value by only 7% a year or so.

Emerging-market stocks now account for only about 6% of the equity holdings of asset managers in the developed world. Over the next 20 years, according to Goldman Sachs, these institutional investors will purchase another $4 trillion of EM equities, raising their weight in their portfolios to 18%.

Capital can flow both ways of course. Because they save so much, EMs are already net exporters of capital, investing more in the rest of the world than the world invests in them. China is the biggest single contributor to this savings glut: its excess savings, reflected in its current-account surplus with the rest of the world, amounted to almost $1.7 trillion from 2006 to 2010.

This thrift partly reflects China's demography. China now has many people of working age relative to the number of dependants (young and old). That gives it scope for thrift. Demography also gives it the motivation to save. Because the population is ageing quickly, it makes sense to set aside money now in anticipation of the day when China's workers begin to retire in droves.

As China ages, it will have less scope to save. It will stop adding to its foreign assets at such a clip and may start to draw them down. China now has 7.9 people of working age (ie, aged between 20 and 64) for every person over 65. By 2050, it will have only 2.2. No country has ever supported so many elderly people per worker. Even Japan, the greyest country on the planet today, has 2.6 workers to support every retiree.

China's workers will therefore be stretched thin. That will make

TABLE 11.1 **Countries of the future compared with today's**

	2050 GDP per person (2011 $)	Nearest equivalent today	2050 median age	Nearest equivalent today	2050 average years of schooling[a]	Nearest equivalent today
Bangladesh	6,749	Colombia	41.3	Greece	10.1	Chile
Brazil	49,051	US	44.9	Japan	10.3	Cyprus
China	57,158	Sweden	48.7	Japan	10.7	Netherlands
Egypt	17,178	Slovakia	36.9	US	11.5	Russia
India	21,399	Taiwan	37.2	Georgia	9.5	Bahrain
Indonesia	24,107	Bahrain	41.6	Bulgaria	10.4	UK
Mexico	48,820	US	41.8	Austria	10.8	Hong Kong
Nigeria	9,864	Venezuela	23.1	Paraguay	10.3	Cyprus
Pakistan	7,327	Suriname	34.7	Ireland	9.1	Croatia
Philippines	21,549	Oman	32.5	Mauritius	12.3	Canada
Russia	73,022	Switzerland	43.1	Italy	12.6	Japan
Vietnam	21,808	Saudi Arabia	45.8	Japan	8.8	Colombia
US	98,086	Norway	40.0	Spain	12.2	Canada

a Of workforce.

Sources: Goldman Sachs; IMF; UN; author's calculations based on IIASA projection

them all the more grateful for the present saving of their parents and grandparents. That saving will allow China to accumulate extra physical capital at home as well as an impressive hoard of foreign assets abroad. The extra capital will make its overstretched workers of tomorrow more productive. And its foreign assets can help it pay for imports, releasing some of the labour now dedicated to earning foreign exchange through exports. That will leave China's dwindling domestic workforce free to concentrate on doing the things that can only be done in China – such as caring for granny.

Over the next four decades, today's upstart economies will prosper, age and slow down. Even a desperately poor country like Bangladesh can look forward to a Colombian standard of living (see Table 11.1). Others will enjoy a per-person income comparable to that of today's Gulf states. All the EMs except Nigeria will become middle-aged societies, with a population older and better schooled than many present-day European societies (provided the additional quantity of schooling is matched by improvements in quality). And only Nigeria's economy will still be growing faster than 6% a year; China's growth will be more like 2.5%.

"Why isn't the whole world developed?" asked Richard Easterlin, an economic historian, 30 years ago. The basic technologies of industrial capitalism are there for all to copy. And an abundant pool of global capital is there for all to tap. Wherever capital is scarce, returns should be high, and wherever returns are high, investment should flow. If poor countries can borrow the capital and copy the ideas required for development, why haven't they all had an industrial revolution of their own?

Even by 2050 the whole world will not be developed. Some countries will no doubt remain poor and stagnant, beset by bad geography, which is more or less impossible to escape, or bad politics, which can be surprisingly hard to change. Others may have begun to grow at the kind of rates that excite emerging-market investors today. But the next wave of industrialisers will be too small to qualify for trendy acronyms. The biggest of today's poorest countries (the Democratic Republic of the Congo, Ethiopia, Tanzania) will have sizeable populations by 2050 – about the size of Russia's in 2011. But even if one or two of them do take off, none will make the splash that Brazil, India or China are making today.

By 2050, then, the big economies will no longer be emerging, and the emerging economies will no longer be very big. Forty years ago, emerging markets did not exist. Forty years from today, they may disappear again from view.

12 Globalisation, growth and the Asian century

Laza Kekic

Any backlash against globalisation will not send it into reverse in the coming decades. Indeed, globalisation will coincide with Asia's re-emergence as the dominant force in the world economy

"GLOBALISATION" IS SHORTHAND for the integration of markets across the world. Its driving force is both the technological changes that reduce transport and communication costs, and the policies that liberalise trade and investment rules and make migration easier. Simply put, globalisation is the extension of markets across frontiers. But it need not refer only to economic processes. It represents also the declining importance of national boundaries and geographical distance as constraints diminish on the mobility not just of people, goods, capital and technology but also of ideas, culture and values.

A crude graph of globalisation over time would resemble a roller coaster. It rises to a peak in the early part of the 20th century, and falls steeply before starting another climb in the decades towards the turn of the millennium. Then, in recent years, it flattens out, giving the world a frisson of tension about what will happen next. Whether it resumes its rise or plunges again has big implications for the shape of the global economy between now and 2050.

The roller-coaster ride

Economic globalisation is one of the most powerful trends since the second world war. Yet the rapid expansion in international integration over the past six decades is not unprecedented. Between 1870 and 1914, international trade in goods and services was as free as it is today. The breakthroughs in transport and communication that have facilitated globalisation had already happened by 1900: the railway, the steamship, the telegraph and refrigeration. International lending and borrowing were also highly developed and subject to few official restrictions. The mobility of people, including international migration, was much less restricted during the "golden era" of globalisation than it is today. As John Maynard Keynes famously commented, looking back on that era in 1920:

> What an extraordinary episode in the progress of man that age was which came to an end in August 1914! The inhabitant of London could order by telephone, sipping his morning tea in bed, the various products of the whole earth ... He could at the same time and by the same means adventure his wealth in the natural resources and new enterprise of any quarter of the world.

War wrecked all this. Global markets were disrupted, technical advances petered out and stagnant consumption discouraged innovation. The years between the start of the first world war in 1914 and the end of the second in 1945 saw a prolonged retreat from economic globalisation. This period of instability and downswings brought two world wars, hyperinflation in Germany, the Great Depression and the end of the gold standard. The economy that emerged in 1945 was far more fragmented than that before 1914. By 1945, international trade was more than 40% below its 1913 level.

Globalisation's recovery after 1945 was steady but slow. One crude measure is the ratio of foreign assets to world GDP. As globalisation slumped, this ratio fell from 17% in 1914 to 5% at the end of the second world war. The 1914 ratio was not attained again until 1980, and the 1913 ratio of global goods exports to GDP was not regained until 1970.

Only after 1990 did trade growth relative to GDP accelerate appreciably; world export volume has tripled since the early 1990s, substantially outpacing growth in GDP. Several developments have driven this trend: rapid industrialisation in Asia; trade liberalisation (including China's accession to the World Trade Organisation in 2001); and the expansion of trade between emerging markets ("south-south trade"). All these factors have propelled export volumes in developing economies to rise fivefold from their levels two decades ago (albeit from a relatively low starting-point), with particularly steep gains over the past decade.

The celebration of globalisation reached its high point in the 1990s: communism had collapsed, American productivity was surging and a technological revolution was under way. Eulogies to this brave new globalised world and its seemingly limitless possibilities were legion. Commentators pronounced that distance and national borders no longer mattered, that the nation-state and geography were no longer economically relevant. Globalisation, they declared, had become irreversible.

So much for the conventional wisdom of the time. The bursting of the dotcom bubble at the end of the 1990s, the terrorist attacks in America on September 11th 2001 and the 2008–09 financial crisis have, cumulatively, now set a different tone. More sober assessments are the norm today.

Global limits

In truth, globalisation has not gone as far as people tend to think. In his book, *World 3.0*, Pankaj Ghemawat, a professor at IESE business school in Barcelona, argues that we live in an era of "semi-globalisation", at most. He notes that many indicators of global integration are surprisingly low. Foreign direct investment (FDI) accounts for less than 10% of all fixed investment. Only 2% of the world's students are at universities outside their home countries, and only 3% of people live outside their country of birth. Today's levels of emigration pale beside those of a century ago. The immigration rate per 1,000 people in the United States was 10.4 in 1910, and only 1.7 in 1970 and 2.6 in 1990. America's foreign-born population was 15% of the total in 1910, and only 4.7% in 1970 and 7.9% in 1990.

But even the "semi-globalisation" achieved in recent decades suffered a setback during the 2008–09 economic crisis, as international trade and capital flows slumped. The shock was worldwide in scope. And because international supply chains had become much more complex and integrated, the effects of disruptions were magnified.

There was a dramatic drop in world trade in 2009. World exports fell by 22% in US dollar terms – by far the sharpest annual decline since the end of the second world war. Air-cargo traffic fell by 23% year-on-year in December 2008 (by comparison, traffic fell by only 14% following the September 2001 terrorist attacks). Nearly a quarter of North American and European companies shortened their supply chains in 2008. It now takes three times longer to process a lorry-load of goods crossing the Canadian-American border than it did before September 11th 2001.

Even before the crisis, criticism of globalisation was mounting. Some opponents focused on the supposed negative impact on developing countries. Others worried about environmental issues, national sovereignty and the exploitation of workers. Meanwhile, the rise of emerging markets was starting to have increasingly uncomfortable implications for the West, in the shape of takeovers of Western firms by emerging-market competitors, increased competition for jobs and pressure on wages. The great recession and its aftermath have dented the West's confidence and widened the gap in terms of economic growth between most Western economies and the leading emerging markets.

With growth slow and unemployment high, many countries have resorted to protectionist measures of various sorts. Although such measures number in their hundreds according to those who keep tabs on such distortions and restrictions, they are not yet serious enough to pose a threat to global trade, which recovered by 14% in 2010. But the trend indicates an erosion of the discipline that kept world markets open through the downturn and prevented protectionism from further impeding global growth.

Globalisation and growth to 2050

So where does globalisation go from here? Many of the forces that underpin the phenomenon remain powerful. Businesses depend on international supply chains to stay competitive and on expansion beyond their home markets to grow revenues. Countries today are more interdependent than in the past, export lobbies wield more power and successive global trade agreements provide greater legal stability for trading relations. Many emerging markets have only relatively recently embarked on liberalisation, and reforms are likely to continue, even if often at a slower pace than would previously have been expected.

However, the risks to globalisation are considerable. As we have seen, previous episodes have been reversed and new barriers to trade and capital flows could yet proliferate. Given the tortuous progress of the WTO's Doha round, further advances in the multilateral liberalisation of trade in goods and services look unlikely for a long time to come. The days of unfettered capital markets may well be over, as evidenced by tighter regulation of the financial sector and the growing popularity of controls to dampen excessive inflows of speculative capital. The European Union remains the single outstanding example of integration across borders, and yet here too there are centrifugal forces at work, putting into question the survival of Europe's single currency. And if the euro zone breaks up, the European Union and its single market would be in severe danger too.

So even if a generalised retreat from openness is avoided, over the next few decades the global business landscape will be characterised by greater caution and tighter regulation than in the final decade of the 20th century. There is a risk of what has been called "murky protectionism": industrial subsidies, requests that banks lend only to local companies, or the invocation of environmental concerns to discriminate against foreign goods and services. The share of exports of goods and services in global GDP has recovered after the temporary decline in 2009, but has now reached a plateau at about one-third, where it is likely to remain for a long time to come.

Despite the concerns and risks, trade flows will continue to increase, especially in emerging markets, but the rate of increase will slow compared with recent decades. Many of the gains in open trade have already been achieved and there will be an increasing emphasis on domestic demand within the high-growth markets. The most rapidly growing cross-border trade involves emerging markets. During the decade to 2010, trade among mature economies grew at an annual rate of 4.6%; between emerging markets and advanced economies it grew by 10.8%; and trade among emerging markets increased by 17.6%. Moreover, trade among advanced countries by 2010 was smaller than that among emerging markets. The main stimulus for the emergence of these new trade patterns has been China, which – as the world's largest exporter (overtaking Germany in 2009) – is set to dominate trade in the 21st century.

Three scenarios and a baseline

The baseline forecast from the Economist Intelligence Unit assumes a "controlled globalisation": a significantly less open world than at one stage seemed likely. Worse scenarios are possible, based on a partial reversal of globalisation ("globalisation in retreat") or its unwinding ("globalisation sunk"). The Economist Intelligence Unit has traced through the quantitative effects of the various scenarios, by making assumptions about changes in the factors that drive growth, such as the extent of trade integration, and regulatory, institutional and technological developments (all of which are influenced by the degree of openness).

The scenario of "globalisation in retreat" sees protectionist sentiment thriving in a climate of insecurity. Throughout much of the developed world, economic weakness and high unemployment breed angst and fuel protectionism. This would shave a percentage point from annual global growth in 2010–30, relative to the baseline forecast of "controlled globalisation", amounting cumulatively to a large loss in world output. "Globalisation sunk" is akin to the 1914–45 period of retrenchment (turning away from globalisation). Were this to be repeated, the consequences for growth would be disastrous. Global growth would drop to about 1% per year, implying a fall in world income per head. The hardest hit would be the emerging markets, especially the poorest ones.

American policy will remain a key determinant of which model will prove dominant. The United States may no longer be an unambiguous champion of the further freeing of markets. That is because in future other countries will stand to gain relatively more than America from globalisation.

In the light of these trends, and assuming a scenario of "controlled globalisation" in the decades ahead (see box) – that is, neither a rampant revival of liberalisation nor a headlong retreat from it, but

TABLE 12.1 **Variable speeds**
Annual average growth, %

	GDP			GDP per person		
	2011–30	2031–50	2011–50	2011–30	2031–50	2011–50
World	3.7	3.8	3.7	3.2	3.4	3.3
Rich world						
North America	2.5	2.1	2.3	2.0	1.8	1.9
Japan	1.0	0.9	0.9	1.1	1.2	1.1
Western Europe	1.8	1.9	1.8	1.7	1.9	1.8
Emerging markets						
Developing Asia	5.5	4.8	5.2	5.0	4.5	4.7
Middle East & north Africa	4.7	4.7	4.7	3.9	4.0	3.9
Eastern Europe	3.3	3.1	3.2	3.3	3.2	3.2
Latin America	3.6	3.7	3.7	3.1	3.4	3.3
Sub-Saharan Africa	5.5	5.5	5.5	4.3	4.5	4.4

Sources: Economist Intelligence Unit; author's calculations

rather a wary continuation – what might the world economy of 2050 look like? Long-range forecasts are of course only a very rough guide to the future. But the numbers paint a revealing picture of the sort of change that lies ahead, and its scale.

The GDP projections in this chapter are based on Economist Intelligence Unit projections for 2010–30 extended to 2050 by the author. According to this forecast, real world GDP, measured at 2010 purchasing-power parity (PPP), will grow at an annual average rate of 3.7%, and growth in real GDP per person will rise by 3.3% a year over the same period. The projected growth in annual average world real GDP is lower than in 1950–70 (4.9%) or in the eight-year period to the 2008 crisis (4.2%). But, because of slower population growth, the growth rate per head in 2010–50 will actually be slightly faster than in 1950–70 and 2000–08.

The fastest-growing regions over the next four decades in terms of real GDP per head will be developing Asia (4.7%), followed by

TABLE 12.2 **How rich by American standards?**
GDP per person[a], US =100

	2010	2030	2050
World average	22.7	30.3	42.3
Western Europe	71.9	71.3	74.2
Eastern Europe	27.4	37.7	50.6
Middle East & north Africa	20.0	30.6	48.5
Latin America	23.4	30.9	43.4
Developing Asia	11.9	22.6	38.9
Sub-Saharan Africa	4.7	7.8	13.7
South Korea	63.1	87.8	105.0
Germany	76.2	82.9	87.7
France	72.1	70.1	75.2
Russia	33.5	50.4	71.9
UK	73.9	69.5	71.1
Italy	62.2	54.7	60.1
Japan	71.8	63.7	58.3
China	15.9	32.0	52.3
Brazil	23.8	33.1	49.1
Thailand	19.4	29.8	48.5
India	7.1	14.8	34.5
Indonesia	9.3	16.4	29.5

a At purchasing-power parity.
Sources: Economist Intelligence Unit; author's calculations

sub-Saharan Africa (4.4%) and the Middle East and north Africa (3.9%). Latin America (3.3%) and eastern Europe (3.2%) will lag behind the fastest-growing of the emerging-market regions. Growth in today's rich regions will be far slower.

The world's two most populous states, China and India, will remain among the fastest-growing countries, although Chinese growth will slow significantly from its present spectacular rate. Although they will increase their share of global income, both China and especially India will remain poor countries in terms of income per person.

Nonetheless, there will be a substantial closing of the income gap per head between countries that are rich today and countries that are poor today. Many emerging markets have opened up and reached the level of institutional development needed for fast growth and rapid catch-up. Some of these markets will also reap a "demographic dividend" thanks to a rapid increase in their populations of working age. And the quality of human capital – the health and education of the workforce – in much of the developing world will continue to improve.

The Asian century

In 1950, the developed world accounted for more than 60% of global GDP in PPP terms. By 1990, that share had still fallen only slightly, to 55%. But in the past two decades emerging markets have surged: by 2010, developing Asia's share of world GDP had risen to 28%, from 14% in 1990 and 9% in 1970.

Over the next four decades this trend will gather pace, with a stunning shift in the distribution of global GDP and economic power. The share of world real GDP (at PPP) accounted for by North America and western Europe will fall from 40% in 2010 to just 21% in 2050, while developing Asia's share will almost double. The share of China alone is likely to increase from 13.6% in 2010 to 20% in 2050.

TABLE 12.3 **Half-Asian**
Share of world GDP[a], %

	2010	2030	2050
Developing Asia	27.9	39.5	48.1
North America	21.5	16.9	12.3
Western Europe	18.7	12.8	8.9
Latin America	8.7	8.5	8.5
Middle East & north Africa	4.8	5.8	6.9
Eastern Europe	7.0	6.5	5.6
Sub-Saharan Africa	2.6	3.6	5.1
Japan	5.8	3.4	1.9

a At purchasing-power parity. Figures exclude Australia, New Zealand, Israel and Turkey, so do not add up to 100.
Sources: Economist Intelligence Unit; author's calculations

Back to the future

Economic historians will come to see Asia's economic eclipse by first Europe and then America as just a temporary blip. Figure 12.1 shows the European, American and Asian shares of global GDP over the past thousand years, and plots the implications of the forecast to 2050. Asia (here meaning not just the emerging giants but Japan and the rest of the continent too) is surging back to its historical position as comfortably the planet's biggest economic region. By 2050 it will be back to roughly the share of the world economy that it had in 1820.

FIG 12.1 **Asia rises again**

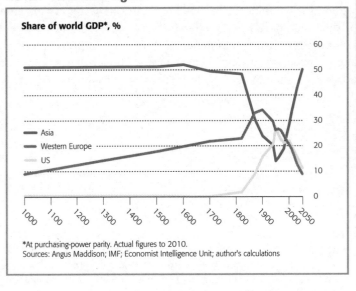

Share of world GDP*, %

*At purchasing-power parity. Actual figures to 2010.
Sources: Angus Maddison; IMF; Economist Intelligence Unit; author's calculations

But for China to achieve this, global market access, which has made China the greatest beneficiary of globalisation, will remain essential. This means ready access to world markets for funds, expertise and ideas as well as for commodities. China's economic prospects appear strong. Certainly, its projected real GDP growth rate of just under 5% per year in 2010–50 will be a considerable slowdown on present rates, but it will still be one of the fastest growth rates in the world. Large amounts of research and development and rising levels of education will further improve its already impressive pool of human resources (entrepreneurship appears to be flourishing despite obstacles to the expansion of private business). These factors will offset barriers to growth such as unemployment, corruption, environmental degradation and social tensions arising from income inequalities.

From a historical perspective, China's emerging status as the world's leading economy will not be a novelty. It was by far the world's largest economy until the 19th century (in terms of purchasing-power parity), accounting for 20–30% of the world's output. Along with India, it dominated the world economy for nearly two millennia before its temporary decline (see box). By 2050, these two countries will have resumed that dominance. If the forecast presented here is anywhere near right, developing Asia as a whole will by mid-century account for something close to half the world's output. Prepare for the Asian century.

A note on methodology

The projections of GDP growth to 2030 are from the Economist Intelligence Unit and are based on a cross-section growth model in which growth in real GDP per head is related to its key determinants. The projections are extended by the author to 2050 on the basis of a growth-accounting framework. A country's labour-force growth in 2031–50 is assumed to be equal to growth in its working-age population; the growth in the capital stock is based on 2000–30 trend rates; and total factor productivity growth (TFP) is derived from the following equation: $1.3\% - b*\ln(\text{GDP pc}/\text{GDP pc US})$, where 1.3% is assumed to be the long-term growth rate of TFP in the technological leader, the United States, and b is the relative speed of convergence assumed to be 1.5%; ln denotes the natural logarithm. The demographic projections of total and working-age populations are from the UN population projections and the US Census Bureau.

13 The great levelling

Zanny Minton Beddoes

The gap between the world's rich and poor will be far narrower in 2050. It will depend much less on where you live than on how educated you are

IN THE EARLY 20TH CENTURY, the vast gap between rich and poor spawned political upheaval and social reform in many of the world's big economies. America's Progressive era brought a slew of policies, from trust-busting to the introduction of income and inheritance taxes, to prevent the Vanderbilt, Carnegie, Rockefeller and other great fortunes of the Gilded Age from forming an entrenched elite. In Britain, Lloyd George's government introduced an array of welfare reforms, from old-age pensions to unemployment insurance.

A century later, worries about income disparities are back on the political agenda, this time around the globe. In America, long a society where people admired the wealthy and aspired to join them, polls now suggest a majority of people consider inequality to be a pressing problem. The "Occupy Wall Street" protest movement, which sprang up in 2011 to rail against it, was copied in cities around the world. The question of whether to raise taxes on the rich looms large in America's 2012 presidential election campaign. In Europe, concerns about fairness are colouring an era of budget austerity. Britain introduced a top tax rate of 50% in 2010, and France, Spain and Italy expanded surtaxes on the rich. Talk of new, and tougher, wealth taxes is becoming commonplace.

Though the economic outlook in emerging markets is rosier, many politicians there share similar worries. China's outgoing president, Hu Jintao, has fretted publicly that widening income gaps, particularly between the rural poor and urban affluent, threaten progress towards a "harmonious society". Indian politicians debate furiously about how to make the country's growth more "inclusive".

Technocrats have come to share the politicians' concerns. Bastions of economic orthodoxy, such as the International Monetary Fund (IMF), used to pay little attention to income disparities, arguing that in most cases it was far more important to focus on lifting all boats with faster economic growth. The standard view was that trying to reduce inequality might be counterproductive, if redistributive taxes sapped the incentive to save or invest. But a spate of new research, including at the IMF, suggests that income inequality can be economically damaging in itself, leading to weaker, less sustainable and more volatile growth. Some economists argue that the roots of the 2008 financial crisis lay with widening income gaps: as their living standards were squeezed, poorer people resorted to debt-fuelled spending.

Inequality, in other words, has leapt towards the top of the global agenda. A 2011 survey by the World Economic Forum, a Swiss-based club of the global elite, found that its members regarded widening income disparities as one of the two main global risks for the next decade (alongside failings in global governance).

Look at the numbers, and you can see why. Over the past few decades inequality has risen in many countries, often dramatically (see Figure 13.1). In more than three out of four advanced economies, income disparities are higher than they were in the 1980s. Many poorer countries have grown less equal too. China has gone from being one of the world's most egalitarian (albeit impoverished) societies 30 years ago to having some of the biggest income disparities. Following the collapse of communism, inequality has soared in eastern Europe and the former Soviet Union. All told, a majority of the world's citizens now live in countries where the gap between the rich and the rest is a lot bigger than it was a generation ago.

But the past is not necessarily prologue. The future evolution of income disparities will turn out to be more nuanced than recent history suggests. More countries will see wider inequality, particularly poorer parts of Africa and Asia that are still in the early stages of development. But in those countries where income gaps are already wide, such as America and China, they are likely to stabilise or even

FIG 13.1 **Far from perfect**

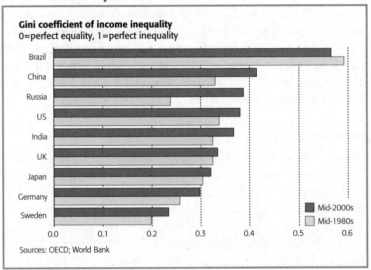

Gini coefficient of income inequality
0=perfect equality, 1=perfect inequality

Brazil / China / Russia / US / India / UK / Japan / Germany / Sweden

Mid-2000s
Mid-1980s

0.0   0.1   0.2   0.3   0.4   0.5   0.6

Sources: OECD; World Bank

narrow over the coming decades. By 2050 national income disparities will have converged, for many countries at a higher level than they were in the 20th century.

These national trends will be what attract political attention. But from a global perspective, they will not be the main determinant of inequality. That is because the global distribution of income depends not just on the gaps within a country, but also on those between countries, in terms of average living standards. And over the coming decades the wealth gap between rich and poor countries will narrow dramatically as emerging economies grow faster than advanced ones. This will stand in stark contrast to the experience of the past 200 years, when richer countries in Europe and North America typically grew faster than poorer ones.

The narrowing of disparities between countries will be greater than any widening of disparities within countries. As a result, overall global inequality – the income gaps between all people, regardless of where they live – will fall, probably rather sharply. The coming decades will see a great levelling of global living standards.

At the same time the nature of inequality will change. Today the gaps between the richest and poorest within any country are still far smaller than the gaps between countries. Around 70% of global income inequality comes from the fact that poor countries lag so far behind rich ones. By 2050 that picture will be quite different, with a large and growing global middle class coinciding with big income gaps within countries. Wealth disparities will depend less on where people live than on what they do.

Measuring the gap

Most discussions of inequality are contentious; and many are confused. That is because there are lots of ways to define income disparities and even more ways to measure them. Economists argue about whether differences in living standards are best captured by differences in consumption or in income. They have developed several technical gauges of inequality, which do not always paint the same picture. The pattern can change depending on what disparities you are trying to measure: inequality between races or sexes, for instance, or between regions, or among citizens of one country or among all people in the world. The figures are also influenced by whether you derive income distributions from household surveys or tax statistics; how you marry national distributions with cross-country income measures; and how you adjust for differences in purchasing power between countries. The subject, in short, is a statistical minefield.

To keep things simple, let us focus on two kinds of disparities: inequality at the global level and that within individual countries. And let us look at two common measures of inequality: the share of overall income going to different sections of the population (such as the top 1%) and the so-called Gini coefficient.

Created by an Italian statistician, Corrado Gini, in 1912, the Gini coefficient provides a summary measure of inequality that ranges from 0 (if everyone has exactly the same income) to 1 (if one person gets all income). In practice, of course, it is impossible to reach either of the two extremes. At the country level, Gini coefficients range from about 0.25 for egalitarian places such as Norway or Sweden to over 0.65 for highly unequal ones such as South Africa. America's Gini score is 0.38. Small movements in that number – of a few hundredths

FIG 13.2 **A world of difference**

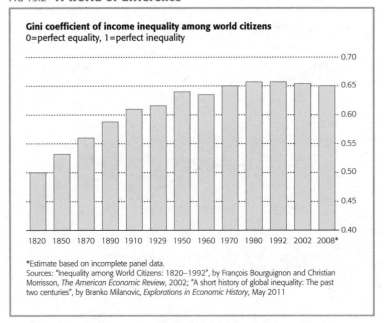

Gini coefficient of income inequality among world citizens
0=perfect equality, 1=perfect inequality

*Estimate based on incomplete panel data.
Sources: "Inequality among World Citizens: 1820–1992", by François Bourguignon and Christian Morrisson, *The American Economic Review*, 2002; "A short history of global inequality: The past two centuries", by Branko Milanovic, *Explorations in Economic History*, May 2011

– translate into big changes in income disparities. The average Gini measure for the mostly rich-country OECD club, for instance, has risen from 0.28 in the mid-1980s to 0.31 today.

Global inequality is much higher than inequality within almost any country. A spate of recent studies has put the global Gini coefficient between 0.63 and 0.68. Branko Milanovic, an economist at the World Bank, who has assembled the most complete database, reckons that the global Gini, using historically comparable figures, is currently around 0.65 (see Figure 13.2). Using the latest purchasing-power-parity measures it is closer to 0.7.

Using some clever statistical sleuthing, two French economists, François Bourguignon and Christian Morrisson, put together estimates for global inequality as far back as 1820. Their research suggested that at the dawn of the Industrial Revolution the global Gini coefficient was around 0.5. Most of that inequality was thanks to a big divide within countries, between a small rich elite and the poor proletariat.

FIG 13.3 **Rich pickings**

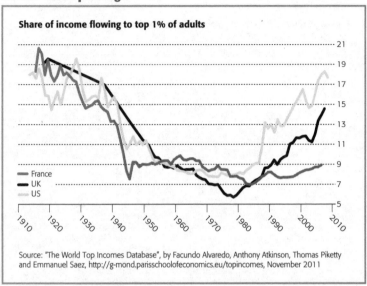

Share of income flowing to top 1% of adults

— France
— UK
— US

Source: "The World Top Incomes Database", by Facundo Alvaredo, Anthony Atkinson, Thomas Piketty and Emmanuel Saez, http://g-mond.parisschoolofeconomics.eu/topincomes, November 2011

By contrast, the gap between countries was modest: income per head in the richest ten countries in the 19th century was only six times that of the poorest ten.

Over the past two centuries global inequality has steadily worsened. This is because for most of that time richer countries grew faster than poorer ones. After the Industrial Revolution, economic growth in Europe and then North America sped up, while staying stagnant in much of the rest of the world – a divergence that continued for most of the 20th century. As a result, income per head in the richest ten countries is now more than 40 times higher than it is in the poorest.

That widening gap between countries outweighed the narrowing of income disparities that occurred within many of them during the 20th century. The reasons for this narrowing differ. Communism imposed a brutal and destructive equality in many countries. But even in Western economies, Gini coefficients fell along with the share of income going to the richest 1% (see Figure 13.3). Widespread access to education played a big role; so did mass-production manufacturing and other technological advances that spurred demand for mid-skilled factory jobs. Progressive taxation was important too, as was the growth of unions and other institutions that regulated markets and boosted workers' clout.

These trends lasted long enough for people to believe they were permanent. In the mid-1950s Simon Kuznets, a Russian émigré economist, famously argued that inequality tends to follow an inverted U-shaped pattern as countries grow richer. At the early stages of development, inequality increases as people move from subsistence agriculture into industry. Then, as societies mature, the gap between rural and urban incomes shrinks, governments redistribute more and inequality declines. This "Kuznets curve" became economists' rule of thumb for understanding inequality.

Unfortunately, it proved a poor guide to recent history. Starting in the late 1970s, the two trends that had, until then, characterised global income trends in the 20th century – widening gaps between countries and declining gaps within them – both began to reverse.

The onset of China's economic reforms in 1978 and India's in the early 1990s marked the turning-point for income gaps between countries. Though a few poor countries had started to grow faster earlier (particularly Asian Tigers such as South Korea and Taiwan), it was the acceleration of growth in the world's two most populous economies that shifted the global picture from divergence to convergence. And as more countries adopted market reforms and technology boosted globalisation, that convergence has become stronger. Since 1990 a majority of emerging economies have grown faster than America, and the pace of catch-up has quickened.

Yet the widening of income gaps within countries began around the same time, and has proved almost as ubiquitous. Among rich countries, it began first, and has been most extreme, in Anglo-Saxon economies, particularly America. America's Gini coefficient has risen from 0.31 in the mid-1970s to 0.38 today. That widening of inequality occurred partly because the income of poorer people fell behind that of those in the middle, but it has been mainly thanks to a surge in the share of income at the top. Including capital gains, the portion of national income going to the richest 1% tripled from 8% in the 1970s to 24% in 2007. It has fallen since the financial crisis. Nonetheless, the richest 1% of Americans now take about as big a slice of national income as they did a century ago. So much for Kuznets.

The same thing has happened even in Europe, where economies are more egalitarian. Inequality has risen sharply in Germany and Sweden, for instance – again thanks mainly to a surge in incomes at the top. Among emerging economies, China and Russia have seen by far the biggest rise in income gaps, but disparities have also risen in India and parts of Africa. The only emerging region to buck the trend is Latin America, where many countries have seen income disparities fall. Brazil, long one of the most unequal countries in the world, has seen a big decline in inequality in the past decade.

At a global level, these two trends have pushed in opposite directions. But the narrowing of income gaps between countries has been the more powerful of the two. This is why the world's Gini coefficient has started to fall.

A more equal future

What will happen in the coming decades? The safest prediction is that the emerging economies' catch-up growth will continue. Economic theory suggests that poorer countries should grow faster than richer ones, provided their economies are open, stable and well-run. And as ever more countries fulfil these prerequisites, and as the diffusion of innovation and technology becomes ever easier, catch-up will continue. Some countries will slow from their recent roaring rates: China, in particular, will see growth rates come down as it becomes a middle-income country and its population ages. But India, poorer and with a younger population, will have room for rapid expansion. So will many parts of Africa. With advanced economies weighed down with big debts and greying populations, the growth gap between today's rich and poorer countries could, if anything, widen.

This will dramatically narrow the gap in global living standards. Calculations by Laza Kekic of the Economist Intelligence Unit in the previous chapter suggest that by 2050 average GDP per person in developing Asia will be 40% of America's, compared with just 12% today. The average Chinese person's income will be half that of the average American's, compared with only 16% today. The average Indian will quintuple his income relative to the average American, from 7% to 35%. Average incomes in sub-Saharan Africa will be 14% of those in America, compared with less than 5% today.

Whether all this translates into a big reduction in global inequality depends on how disparities develop within countries as well as between them. If the gains from rapid growth in emerging economies flow largely to an elite, then the "great levelling" will be much less positive than if those gains are disbursed more broadly. And it will be less politically sustainable.

China's recent experience seems to suggest that spectacularly fast growth in a very poor country implies large increases in inequality. That would be consistent with Kuznets's hypothesis: as people move away from the land, inequality widens. But in China's case, this "natural" increase in inequality occurred from an artificially low base thanks to decades of communism. More important, its effects were exacerbated by specific distortions imposed by the Communist Party: massive rewards for party insiders and limits on internal migration. Because of the *hukou* system of residency permits, people in China cannot freely move from poor rural provinces to urban areas. As a result, regional inequality is huge: average incomes in China's richest coastal provinces are some ten times higher than in the hinterland. This gap would surely decline if people were freer to move.

Part of China's experience is likely to be repeated elsewhere. Poor, still largely agrarian economies will see a rise in income disparities as they industrialise and urbanise, particularly those whose inequality is now reasonably low. This group includes most countries in Africa and South Asia. An analysis by Maurizio Bussolo, Rafael De Hoyos and Denis Medvedev, three economists at the World Bank, which looks only at the impact of underlying economic shifts, such as industrialisation, suggests that two-thirds of poor countries will see income inequality widen in the coming decades.

But the degree of inequality in such countries will also depend on their specific policies and starting points, just as it has in China. Those emerging economies that already have high inequality, such as many countries in Latin America, could combine rapid growth with a diminution of income disparities. Brazil is a case in point. It has long been one of the most unequal societies on Earth, thanks largely to the vestiges of its colonial past. But in recent years Brazil has managed to combine fast growth with a sharp reduction in its income inequality. Its Gini coefficient fell from 0.6 in the mid-1990s to 0.54 today, a spectacular decline, thanks, in roughly equal measure, to rapid job growth, investment in education and a policy of providing cash transfers to the poor.

China itself is likely to see its income distribution stabilise or even improve. Its rapidly ageing population will mean workers' wages rise fast; a shortage of workers will probably lead to a relaxation of restrictions on mobility; and a rebalancing of the economy towards domestic consumption will boost incomes at the bottom. Meanwhile, China's politicians are already building a social safety net, and the government's need for tax revenue will eventually spur greater reliance on a Western-style income tax.

Perhaps most important, rapid overall economic growth in most emerging economies is itself likely to fuel political pressure for the kinds of policies that improve domestic income distribution. According to the World Bank, the ranks of the global middle class – those with incomes between the average of Brazil and Italy today – will swell from fewer than 500m (7% of the world's population) now to more than 1.1 billion (17% of the global population) in 2030. By 2050 it will be even bigger.

This global middle class will not only be the backbone of a huge consumer market, but is likely to exert disproportionate influence on the economic policies of developing countries. Historically, growing middle classes have resulted in greater public investment in education, for instance. Better education, in turn, is the best way to narrow income disparities. With luck and good policies, therefore, many emerging economies have the potential to create a virtuous cycle between rapid and broadly shared growth. If that happens, global inequality will fall sharply.

A new progressive era?

What happens in today's rich economies matters much less for the contours of global inequality than what happens in the developing world, since these rich countries will have a far smaller share of the world's population and its income in 2050. But since the advanced world still has a disproportionate influence on global economic policymaking, inequality trends in countries such as America will have a big impact not just on Americans but also on the global policy environment. Years of widening income gaps and a squeeze of the middle class could easily prompt a protectionist backlash, which would darken the outlook for all.

So will inequality within rich countries continue to widen? The answer, as with the emerging economies, will depend on a combination of policy decisions and underlying economic trends.

Over the past three decades, fast technological innovation and globalisation – the two big forces that have driven the catch-up by emerging economies – have also caused a widening of income disparities within rich countries. Job markets have become more polarised as many of the mid-skill jobs that developed during the 20th century, particularly in manufacturing, have been eliminated by new technologies or outsourced to emerging economies. Since the demand for skills has risen faster than education levels have improved, skilled workers have commanded higher wages. The effect of these underlying economic pressures has been exacerbated by the decline of many of the institutions and regulations that evolved during the 20th century to favour workers. Trade unions, for instance, have lost clout across the rich world – particularly in America, where only 6.9% of private-sector workers are now union members.

Technology, skill gaps and the weakening power of workers explain why poorer people are falling behind. But that does not fully explain why the share of income going to the richest has risen so much. Other factors must be at play too.

Economists have come up with several possibilities. One is that the market for those at the top of their field – the best actors, CEOs or lawyers – is now global and far bigger than it used to be. This has fostered a "winner takes all" environment that widens the gap between those at the top of any profession and others below. Another possibility is that the disproportionate growth in financial services over the past three decades has itself fuelled inequality, since many of the highest incomes are in that industry. Even as income disparities widened, government policies, by and large, became less redistributive. Punitive tax rates were slashed. Though rich countries still narrow income differentials with taxes and spending, the impact is smaller than it used to be.

Over the coming decades these trends are likely to evolve differently. The disproportionate influence of finance will probably wane, as the industry is tamed by new regulations. But the secular economic forces – a larger global marketplace, continued rapid technological change – will continue to favour the highly skilled. Whether this means ever more inequality will depend most on whether people can improve their skills as rapidly. And this in turn depends above all on education. Countries that invest more successfully in education will see smaller rises in inequality.

The biggest uncertainty lies with how much governments will redistribute. For the past quarter-century they have reinforced the trend of the market. Public policy has become relatively less progressive even as inequality has widened. It is possible that this will continue, particularly if the wealthy elite have disproportionate political clout. But it seems unlikely, for the simple reason of budget arithmetic.

Most rich countries have huge public debts and face the fiscal burden of ageing populations. Fixing their public finances will demand some combination of more tax revenue and an overhaul of pension and health-care costs. Two obvious routes to doing so are to raise taxes at the top while means-testing public benefits such as health care and pensions. Both would help to balance governments' books. They would also help to narrow income disparities. Designed poorly, punitive tax rates would cause economic harm. But done smartly, for instance with an emphasis on eliminating tax deductions rather than on raising rates, they could even make the economy more efficient. In other words, rich countries, like emerging ones, could make policy choices that improve both their economies' outlook and their income distribution.

Today's focus on inequality, in both advanced and emerging economies, suggests that policies will shift to tackle the most glaring disparities. This could happen crudely, in ways that damage growth; or it could be done the smart, efficiency-enhancing way. With luck the coming years will see an echo of the reforms of the early 20th century, but this time on a global scale and in parallel to a tendency for poorer countries to catch up with richer ones. That would be a "great levelling" to look forward to.

14 Schumpeter Inc

Adrian Wooldridge

Businesses can expect the storms of creative destruction to rage even more furiously in future – largely for the better

EVEN BY THE STANDARDS of the Harvard of the mid-20th century Joseph Schumpeter was a bit of a fuddy-duddy. He neglected to learn to drive, avoided aeroplanes and, apart from a single unhappy experiment, refused to take the subway that links Cambridge with Boston. Obsessed by the idea of being a perfect gentleman, he spent an hour every morning dressing himself. Impatient with new-fangled devices like photocopiers and carbon paper, he dispatched the only copy of his masterpiece, *Capitalism, Socialism and Democracy*, to his publishers by post.

Yet this strange man, this part cock-of-the-walk and part Austro-Hungarian stick-in-the-mud, was one of the most acute prophets of social change that the 20th century produced. For Schumpeter capitalism was above all a "perennial gale of creative destruction" – a gale that was forever sweeping away old ways of doing things and replacing them with new ones. He believed that entrepreneurs were the agents of disruptive innovation – the people who saw the future first and translated it into viable businesses. And he argued that history was speeding up. Old ways of doing things were being discarded faster. Change was becoming more discontinuous. Businesspeople were constantly finding the ground disappearing from beneath their feet.

Schumpeter was often ignored during the era of managed capitalism that followed his death in 1950, an era when his great rival, John Maynard Keynes, ruled the roost, and when Keynes's disciples, such as J.K. Galbraith, argued that the economy was planned by a handful of giant companies. But today he is rightly regarded as a prophet who saw deeper and farther than the likes of Karl Marx (who predicted communist calm at the end of the capitalist storm) or Max Weber (who saw history becoming ever more rational, bureaucratic and predictable): so much so that Lawrence Summers, who served as Bill Clinton's Treasury secretary and Barack Obama's chief economic adviser, has argued that Schumpeter may well prove to be the most important economist of the 21st century.

It is a commonplace that we live in a period of unusual turbulence. Just look at the titles of the business books that pour from the presses: *Faster, Blur, Out of Control, Blown to Bits, Fast Forward, Speed of Thought, Wake Up!*. But Schumpeter suggested that this turbulence had a hidden logic. Entrepreneurs are constantly generating innovations that give them a temporary advantage over their competitors. And these innovations send waves of disruption through the economy as their competitors try to adjust to the new business landscape and institutions scrabble to adjust to new realities. The price of improved productivity is perpetual change.

Tempestuous times

Businesspeople might be forgiven for thinking that the weather cannot get any stormier than it has been of late. Business has seen a succession of disruptions unleashed by the powerful combination of technological innovation and global integration. The internet has spread more rapidly than any previous innovations and has rewritten the rules of business more completely, putting billions of people into instant contact with each other, transforming information-intensive industries and creating companies, such as Google, that give away their products for free and yet somehow contrive to make billions of dollars.

The internet has turbo-charged a process that has been sweeping through the physical economy for decades: globalisation. Today's Davids can shake up long-established Goliaths: look at the way that Julian Assange of WikiLeaks has out-scooped media giants like the BBC or the *New York Times*. And companies from exotic corners of the world can come knocking on your door: Ponoko, a New Zealand-based company with clever software, will arrange to have your ideas turned into products and then delivered to your customers wherever they might be in the world.

As if this were not enough, the capital markets are adding to the turbulence. Financial institutions are more powerful than ever before and more intrusive (investors put constant pressure on companies to perform). They are also injecting ever more uncertainty – unleashing whole flocks of "black swans", as it were. In 2007–08 problems with arcane securities traded by often-obscure financial institutions shook "real" companies to their foundations and threw millions of people out of work.

The most obvious result of all this has been a radical reduction in the life expectancy of businesses. In 1956–81, an average of 24 companies dropped out of the *Fortune* 500 list every year. In 1982–2006, that number jumped to 40. But the upheaval is producing radical changes in business models, too. Businesses have been forced to transform themselves from fortresses to switches in networked systems. At the most basic this means encouraging outsiders to produce ideas for products. Procter & Gamble gets more than 50% of its ideas from outsiders. Other companies have gone further and introduced "collaborative consumption". Netflix and Zipcar have revolutionised markets in renting entertainment and cars respectively. CouchSurfing connects people who have a spare couch with people who are willing to pay for the privilege of using it. Flickr, Twitter and Linux specialise in taking the shared efforts of thousands or even millions of people and then using them to create online communities.

This turbulence will become far more dramatic in coming years. The internet revolution is going into warp speed. Google is experimenting with super-high-speed networks that operate more than a hundred times faster than regular broadband. Cisco claims that its latest router can deliver the entire printed collection of three American Libraries of Congress in just over a second. Facebook took five years to attract 350m users (in December 2009) but has more than doubled that number since then (800m in November 2011).

And globalisation is closer to the beginning than the end. Pankaj Ghemawat, a professor at IESE Business School in Spain, points out that foreign direct investment (FDI) so far accounts for only 9% of all fixed investment and cross-border internet traffic accounts for only about 20% of all internet traffic. The speed at which the world's emerging markets have grown has taken even passionate supporters of globalisation by surprise: their share of global GDP rose from 20% in 1990 to almost 50% today. But again we are merely at the beginning of the turbulence created by this great transformation: turbulence caused by these countries' demands for changes to the architecture of global institutions, and turbulence caused by political ructions, as restive populations demand more say over their futures. The 2011 "Arab spring" reminds us that many emerging markets suffer from fragile and dysfunctional political regimes.

Tidal waves of change

The coming decades will see the biggest revolution in manufacturing since the arrival of mass production. Mass production created a world of huge organisations and gigantic conglomerations of people: Henry Ford's River Rouge plant employed 100,000 workers and covered 16m square feet. Three-dimensional printing or "additive manufacturing" will turn manufacturing inside out and upside down. Inside out because three-dimensional printing creates products by addition rather than subtraction – building up objects by adding material, one layer at a time, rather than taking a lump of stuff and hacking away at it. Upside down because three-dimensional printing makes it as cheap to produce a single copy as 1,000. This will help to create a world much more like the one that fierce critics of mass manufacturing, such as William Morris and his fellow members of the Arts and Crafts movement, dreamed of: a world of independent craftsmen flourishing in Elysian peace. Small manufacturers will be able to service the global market from the back of beyond. And ordinary people will be able to design and print their own products, rather than buying them off the shelf.

Three other innovations will add to the sense of radical change, sending ripples through the world economy. First, the "internet of things" will allow people and objects to communicate via millions of sensors embedded in physical objects. Fridges will reorder food; wine glasses will warn us that we have had too much to drink; medicine bottles will advise us to take our medicines. Second, the world envisaged by so many science-fiction writers will soon be upon us, as robots take on a growing number of tasks that humans are reluctant to do: difficult, dirty and dangerous ones, such as cleaning nuclear plants, and routine ones, too, such as housework. In a decade or so, personal robots will be available for elderly or disabled people for as little as $10,000. And third, robots will acquire cousins, in the form of electronic secretaries, which will organise the torrent of information that comes our way, manage our timetables, set up meetings and arrange business trips.

This tidal wave of innovations will spread to the public sector as well as the private sector, as governments try to get more value for their taxpayers' money and citizens demand the same quality of services from the state as they get from private providers. The remarkable reduction in the cost of collaboration, brought about by the internet, will arguably transform the public sector even more radically than the private. State institutions will transform themselves from bureaucratic empires to "platforms", working hand in hand with voluntary organisations, private businesses and active citizens. Schools will routinely use computers to deliver basic instruction – thereby giving teachers more time to spend with individual pupils. Doctors will monitor patients over the internet and call them into their surgeries when they spot something wrong. Universities will be able to plug themselves into a bank of star lecturers and state-of-the-art courses. This transformation will provoke a bitter war with professional guilds, as academics and doctors fight to preserve their comfortable niches, but the pressure on governments to improve the productivity of the public sector will be irresistible.

The emerging world will become a cauldron of innovation as high-growth economies challenge the rich world for brainwork as well as manual work. Emerging-world giants will produce ever more sophisticated goods. Rich-world companies will move more activities to the emerging world in order to exploit local brains and bring their factories close to growing markets. The result will be that an activity that has been a monopoly of the West since the 16th century – business innovation – will become global. Emerging economies will produce a growing number of "breakthrough" innovations.

Emerging models

The emerging world will challenge the dominance of the traditional public company – the corporate form that was introduced in the middle of the 19th century and, for most of the 20th century, swept all before it. The developing world has already produced new corporate forms such as state-dominated companies (which enjoy the backing of the state at home but venture freely abroad) and highly diversified companies. And there may be more new varieties on the way as private companies mate with philanthropies and as Western multinationals mate with emerging-market multinationals.

The emerging world will also continue to produce new business models as it grapples with what might be politely called "uneven development": islands of modernity surrounded by seas of backwardness. Indian software companies such as Infosys and Wipro have applied the Toyota manufacturing system, with its emphasis on continuous improvement, to software development. Li & Fung and other Chinese companies excel in rapidly turning out products in response to customer orders rather than producing them first and trying to find customers second. In other words, they are adapting the old bespoke model to the age of mass production.

Other companies have added a new version of economies of scale: instead of requiring their employees to work in a factory or office (and possibly move to the city), they are using modern technology, particularly mobile phones, to bring jobs to scattered populations. For example, Nutriset, a French manufacturer of fortified food for malnourished children, has outsourced production to local franchises in Africa, many of them based in villages.

China is already becoming a world leader in the "internet of things", embedding sensors in manufactured products; Kenya is leading the world in "mobile money" (using mobile phones to make payments);

Asian countries in general are leading the world in video gaming.

The emerging world will also be setting the pace in a new kind of innovation – so-called "frugal innovation", driven by the desire to cut the cost of products not just incrementally, by 10%, but dramatically, by 90%. We have already seen a few examples of this: Tata's $2,200 car; General Electric's $400 electrocardiogram; Godrej & Boyce's $70 fridge, "the little cool". But much bigger things are on the way, from a $300 house that will revolutionise life in the slums to cheap genetically modified foods. These innovations will change life in the rich world as well as the poor one: emerging-world countries will produce a wave of products that will force rich-world companies to reduce their costs, produce more value, or go out of business, and they will do this on more and more fronts.

Emerging markets will lead the world in thinking creatively about the delivery of human welfare. Indian entrepreneurs have applied mass-production techniques to health care. Devi Shetty has created a focused hospital in Bangalore that has dramatically reduced the cost of heart operations without any loss of quality through a combination of specialisation and economies of scale (the hospital performs 600 operations a week). LifeSpring has reduced the cost of giving birth in a private hospital to $40 by looking after many more mothers. Aravind, the world's biggest eye-hospital chain, performs some 200,000 eye operations a year and takes the assembly-line principle literally: four operating tables are laid side by side and two doctors operate on adjacent tables. When the first operation is done, the second patient is already in place. MedicallHome, a Mexican company established by telemarketers, has reorganised the medical profession around the telephone: the company connects its customers to its network of 6,000 doctors over the phone for just $5 a month, paid with the phone bill. More than 60% of cases are resolved over the phone and the other 40% are immediately seen by company doctors.

Surfing through the storms

This turbulence will add to long-term trends that are reshaping the world of work, such as the feminisation of the workforce, the spread of flexible working and growing life expectancies. The traditional career will not disappear entirely: companies will continue to employ core workers who join when they are young and try to climb to the top of the ladder. But in general careers will become much more complicated. Companies will be surrounded by a large penumbra of contract workers who might well sell their work to several different employers.

Many people will pursue complicated careers. Feminists have created the phrase "off-ramping" and "on-ramping" to describe the way that women leave the full-time workforce to have children and then rejoin as their children grow up. Off-ramping and on-ramping will spread to men as life expectancies grow and voluntary breaks (through sabbaticals and the like) and involuntary ones (through job churn) become more common. Lynda Gratton, a professor at London Business School, suggests that we should abandon the image of ladders in favour of "a series of ascending bell-shaped curves – or what's termed carillon curves, in which energy and the accumulation of resources grow and then plateau, only to grow again".

How will we cope with all this creative destruction? Will we be able to harness it to improve the quality of our everyday lives? Or will it tear apart our societies and degrade the quality of life? For most companies the great problem of the coming decades will be how to innovate as quickly as their competitors. But for a growing number of ordinary people the great problem will be coping with the social and psychological impact of all these innovations.

Several things are already creating tensions. The cognitive elite is pulling further ahead of the rest of the population. Brainworkers of various descriptions – not just bankers but also consultants and surgeons – are soaking up a greater proportion of national income. And within the cognitive elites intellectual stars are pulling further ahead of their less stellar (or more modest) peers. This is happening not only in America, which has led the trend, but also across the industrial world, even in countries that have more communitarian instincts than America such as Japan and Germany.

Many brainworkers have supersized jobs to match their supersized salaries: they spend their youths commanding ever more demanding bodies of knowledge and their careers working long hours. These pressures will only become greater as knowledge advances. But the burden of work is also increasing for more modest people: the combination of globalisation and the internet means that work has become omnipresent and all-consuming. Evenings and weekends can be eaten up by e-mails and conference calls from far-flung parts of the world. The problem of information overload will only get worse as the cost of communications continues to fall and as work is dispersed along global supply chains.

Striking a sustainable balance between the imperatives of creative destruction, on the one hand, and the demands for a manageable life, on the other, will be one of the great themes of the next 40 years. This will lead to some interesting growth industries.

IT companies will produce lots of clever ideas for coping with the information overload that they are themselves creating. Bright people will devote more effort to "managing themselves" – learning how to deal intelligently with dramatic changes in their careers and the humdrum pressures of their lives. Educational entrepreneurs will recognise that there is a huge market among middle-aged people wanting to upgrade their knowledge and older people wanting to pursue second careers as philosophers and writers. "Free agents" will form all sorts of networks and associations in order to provide themselves with security as well as to escape from loneliness. Freelancers are forming "virtual associations" such as LawLink (for lawyers), Sermo (for physicians), NewDocs (for dentists) and H-Net (for social scientists) as a means of keeping their skills and knowledge up to date. Entrepreneurs are also creating office complexes – variously dubbed hubs, sandbox suites and citizen spaces – to provide freelancers with places to go.

These developments may add up, as they gather momentum, into something bigger and more surprising: the recreation of something like medieval guilds. One of the great battles in coming years will be about the nature of guilds: will they be closed shops, like today's academic and medical professions? Or will they become friendly societies that help all-comers to keep their skills updated and their social connections in good order?

The struggle to strike a balance will also produce some significant continuities during all this *Sturm und Drang*. Companies will survive in a recognisable form not just because they are powerful economic institutions but also because they salve the human desire to form associations with other people (the term company is derived from two Latin words, *cum* and *pane*, meaning breaking bread together). That may help to explain why, even in a technology sector that is notable for its nerds and characterised by extraordinary degrees of volatility, a remarkable number of companies are founded by partners rather than lone wolves.

It is also important to remember that people will win more than they lose from all these changes. Schumpeter's phrase about "creative destruction" is attractive because it seems to capture the dynamism of the modern economy. But in many ways it is deceptive. Creative destruction creates far more than it destroys: e-books supplement physical books, rather than replacing them, for example.

Schumpeter once observed:

> *Queen Elizabeth [I] owned silk stockings. The capitalist achievement does not typically consist in providing more silk stockings for queens but in bringing them within the reach of factory girls in return for steadily decreasing amounts of effort ... The capitalist process, not by coincidence but by virtue of its mechanisms, progressively raises the standard of life of the masses.*

By 2050 more people than ever before will have access to silk stockings in the form of computer tablets that can deliver the world's books at the touch of a screen, miraculous drugs that can control today's killer diseases, and sundry other technological marvels that have not even been thought of. The storms of creative destruction are blowing us to a better place.

15 Market momentum

Philip Coggan

Economies and markets move in cycles – as investors will discover, sometimes to their cost, between now and 2050

CONSIDER TWO INVESTORS. One placed his nest-egg in American equities in 1965, confident in the long-term prospects for shares, and then adopted a life of quiet contemplation, ignoring the financial headlines. In 1982, he checked his portfolio for the first time, only to find that its real value had declined by more than 40%. The shock duly killed him.

His heir followed the same tradition, leaving the money in equities for the next 17 years. But when he checked the valuation in 1999, he found that its real value had increased more than fivefold.

In short, the rewards for thrift vary greatly over time. When you are born, and when you start saving, make an enormous difference to your long-term returns. In valuation terms, the American equity markets had four peaks in the last century: in 1901, 1929, 1965 and 2000 (see Figure 15.1).

There are cycles in bond markets and in property as well, and these three asset classes interact. Generally, good news for shares and property tends to be bad news for government bonds and vice versa.

These longer cycles have many possible explanations. They may simply be an intrinsic feature of markets. Hyman Minsky, an American economist who died in 1996, suggested that the financial system worked in three phases. In the first, which he dubbed hedge finance, investors tend to be conservative; to the extent that they use borrowed money (for example, to buy a house), they put up a large deposit and have enough cash to both meet the interest payments

FIG 15.1 **Equities' bumpy ride**

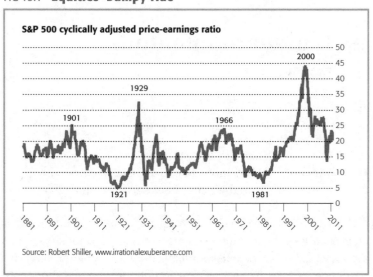

S&P 500 cyclically adjusted price-earnings ratio

Source: Robert Shiller, www.irrationalexuberance.com

and repay the principal. The second stage, dubbed speculative, occurs when asset prices have been rising for several years. The level of the deposit is lower and the borrower may have only sufficient cash flow to cover the interest payments; it is assumed by borrower and lender alike that asset prices will keep increasing.

By the time the market becomes a bubble, which Minsky dubbed the Ponzi stage after a notorious 1920s fraudster, investors are no longer able to meet the interest payments on the loan. They are buying the asset with the explicit intention of selling it to a "greater fool" at a higher price. The American housing market in the mid-2000s was a classic case: witness "negative amortisation" mortgages, where unpaid interest was added to the value of the loan, and "condo flipping", where apartments were bought and sold before completion.

Minsky's point was that this cycle was a natural progression. The longer the period of economic or financial tranquillity, the greater the incentive for investors to take risks with borrowed money; there is no factor more likely to make someone bullish on property than to have a friend or neighbour who has made a huge profit. Initially, as investors take risks, they reinforce the trend by increasing demand. But eventually prices are driven so high, and the supply of new investors runs so low, that a collapse becomes inevitable.

The reflexivity theory of George Soros, a hedge-fund manager, pursues a related line of reasoning. At some point, people's perceptions of fundamentals alter the fundamentals themselves. A cycle thus feeds on itself. Rising property prices make banks more willing to lend money against property, and the greater availability of finance makes property prices rise still further.

The bull phase of the cycle is often marked by extreme investor confidence and can be associated with some new trend that makes people believe that "this time is different". In his book, *Boombustology*, Vikram Mansharamani notes that the Dutch tulip mania of the 1630s and the Wall Street boom of the 1920s followed their countries' victories in major wars. Optimism was a natural result.

Another common theme is the emergence of a new industry that seems to promise both faster economic growth and extra returns to early investors. That was true of both canals and railways in the 19th century and of internet companies in the 1990s. In fact, history suggests that the gains from such changes end up in the pockets of consumers rather than investors; so many businessmen spot the trend that their excess competition drives down profits. Warren Buffett, possibly the world's most successful investor, quipped that the right response to the development of the car was not to buy the shares of auto manufacturers but to short the price of horses.

Some people have even argued that these bubbles are necessary to fuel economic growth. Societies may need technological change at regular intervals to drive long-term growth, and those changes have to be financed. That means having a supply of "suckers" in the form of investors willing to gamble on quick profits.

Demography may also play its part. In the developed world, rising populations are likely to be accompanied by a faster nominal increase in GDP. In property, where the supply of land is restricted, a growing population will lead to higher house prices. In the West, the baby-boomers piled into property in the 1980s and 1990s, driving up house prices to the ultimate benefit of their parents, who already owned their homes. They may have had a similar effect in the stockmarket; the prime earning years of the boomer generation, 35–54, coincided almost perfectly with the bull market of 1982–2000.

The deteriorating demography of Japan, where an ageing population has brought about a shrinking workforce, has led to two decades in which equity and property prices have both been depressed, while inflation and government bond yields have remained at very low levels.

A prolonged period of population decline, a prospect faced by Germany, Italy and Russia, has not been experienced in the developed world since the Middle Ages. Perhaps the best-known example was the Black Death, which led to a shortage of agricultural labourers who could work the land; the result was higher wages and falling property prices.

Do these cycles interact in a way that is predictable? Various economists have attempted to quantify the process, most notably Nikolai Kondratiev, a Russian who proposed a 40–60 year cycle (and was executed by Stalin for his trouble). Given that the Wall Street crash occurred in 1929, many saw the sharp share price falls of 1987 (dubbed Black Monday) as the herald of a new depression – but that turned out not to be the case. Few take the Kondratiev view seriously now. It is particularly hard to see why technological innovation should be in any way predictable.

The ineluctable credit cycle

If there is one factor that seems to drive market cycles, it is the availability of credit. The use of borrowed money has featured in every bubble in history, whether it was shoeshine boys buying shares on margin in 1929 or janitors buying $500,000 homes in 2005.

There is an underlying economic rationale at work. Easy credit and lower interest rates tend to be associated with economic booms; restricted credit and rising interest rates are associated with busts. Low rates and easy credit make it easier to set up businesses, and make it easier for existing businesses to expand. They also allow borrowers to service their previous debts and take on new debt, not least with their credit cards.

Eventually, however, either increased demand by consumers pushes up prices or increased competition among businesses reduces their profit margins. If the former happens, the central bank will tighten policy to reduce inflationary pressures. If the second happens, companies will find it harder to service their debts and banks will be more wary of extending credit.

When this point of the cycle is reached, the higher rates or tighter credit will dissuade people from setting up new businesses or expanding existing ones. But then the price pressures will lessen and the economy will slow – and so the central bank will cut rates. In other words, the whole cycle will start again.

The credit cycle appears in both short-term and long-term versions. The longer-term version is associated with changes in monetary regimes. For example, the late 19th century was marked by adherence to the gold standard and very low inflation. Although there were panics in 1890 and 1907, there were no clearly identified bubbles in asset prices.

The cost of financing the first world war drove nations off the gold standard. When the war ended, they were slow to return. Rather than restore gold at the pre-war parity, which implied a massive deflation, some countries chose to adjust the money supply to higher prices. Germany suffered hyperinflation.

The return to the gold standard in the mid-1920s did not have an immediate effect, in part because America's Federal Reserve lowered interest rates to help its British counterpart. But the constraints of the standard, which limited credit growth, help to explain the subsequent bust in the 1930s.

Moving forward to 1971, the last formal link to gold was abandoned as the Bretton Woods system began to unravel. Bretton Woods had created a trade constraint: persistent trade deficits put pressure on the currency and forced the central bank to tighten policy. That caused the "stop-go" cycle that marred Britain's post-war economic record.

Once Bretton Woods ended, there was an immediate dash for growth among developed economies, which resulted in an inflationary bust in the mid-1970s. Eventually a new system emerged from the rubble. The Europeans tried to reconstruct a fixed exchange-rate system among themselves but the big currencies – the dollar,

Deutschmark, yen and sterling – fluctuated against each other. Without an exchange-rate peg to defend, countries were able to run persistent trade deficits without severe consequences. After the Federal Reserve led the way in squeezing inflation out of the system in the early 1980s, bond yields declined and equity markets surged.

The stage was set for the "Great Moderation", a two-decade period – roughly from 1987 to 2007 – marked by steady growth, low inflation, buoyant asset markets and rapid credit growth. That made the fortune of our lucky investor who started buying equities in 1982.

The bursting of the dotcom bubble in 2000 was an early indicator that the long-term trend might change. Equity valuations peaked that year and investors suffered a miserable decade. But central banks reacted as they had done before by slashing interest rates; the subsequent recession was mild and was followed by a housing boom.

In that sense, the credit cycle had not been broken. Borrowers found it easy to get loans and interest rates stayed low. Crucially, perhaps, the integration of the Chinese, Indian and eastern European economies into the global system created a benign supply shock, boosting growth while keeping inflation low.

Matters came to a head in 2007–08, of course, with the bursting in America of the subprime housing bubble and the implosion of Wall Street. Once again, central banks were forced to intervene dramatically. Interest rates were cut almost to zero. When that measure proved insufficient, central banks used "quantitative easing", purchasing financial assets in an attempt to add liquidity to the market and to reduce long-dated bond yields. At the same time, budget deficits soared in an attempt to stimulate the economy in a Keynesian fashion. In some European countries, these deficits fuelled a sovereign-debt crisis, as markets balked at supplying the sums demanded. The European Union was obliged to mount financial rescues for Greece, Ireland and Portugal.

Changing trends?

It is possible that this moment marked the culmination of two very long-term trends. The first is the decline in interest rates. Treasury-bond yields peaked at nearly 16% in 1981 and dropped to as low as

1.9% in 2009. That provided a great fillip to the economy and to equity markets. Falling bond yields lowered the cost of finance for business, reduced the pressure on government budgets, and encouraged investors to switch out of the safety of bonds and into riskier assets such as equities and property.

This trend might not yet have reached its zenith. The history of Japan's attempts to stimulate its economy suggests that bond yields can fall as low as the 1–2% range. But unlike Japan, America and Britain have to finance a good deal of their deficits from overseas – and it may be difficult to fob investors off with low yields. To attract them with rising rates might be damaging for the economy, since it would increase the cost of finance for business and make it harder for borrowers (including home-owners) to service their debts.

The second trend relates to the ability of governments to support the markets. The huge deficits recorded from 2008 to 2010 in the developed world may have exhausted the ammunition of governments. The work of Carmen Reinhart and Kenneth Rogoff suggests that government debts are associated with slower economic growth once the ratio of debt to GDP reaches 90%. Many Western governments have either reached that level or, in the absence of a programme of fiscal reform, are heading towards it.

So developed-world governments may face a tricky problem. Rather than hand out goodies to the electorate, in the form of tax cuts or spending increases, they will be allocating pain, raising taxes and cutting services. This could lead to an era of political turmoil, as it did in the 1920s and 1930s, with extremist parties gaining ground.

A further problem for the developed world is a phenomenon that began well before the financial crisis: the rise of commodity prices. For much of human history, economic events were driven by the agricultural cycle, with a good harvest meaning prosperity and a bad one revolution. But other raw-material prices, from oil to copper, can have boom and bust phases. That relates to the difficulties and costs involved in discovering and exploiting them.

When a raw-material price is low, there will be little incentive for producers to search for more of it (and indeed they may not have the cash to do so). Supply growth will thus be constrained. Eventually demand will grow and put pressure on supply, encouraging producers

FIG 15.2 **What goes up ...**

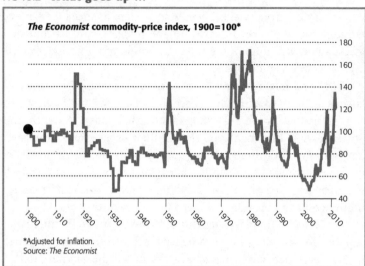

The Economist commodity-price index, 1900=100*

*Adjusted for inflation.
Source: *The Economist*

to search for new sources. But since it takes time to find and develop them, prices will keep rising, perhaps for as long as 20 years. That prolonged price surge will only encourage more prospecting – and the eventual result will be a glut, prompting prices to plummet. In this way, the commodity-price boom of the 1970s was followed by the disinflationary 1980s and 1990s (see Figure 15.2).

The low point in this cycle was reached in 2002. From then on, growing demand from China and India caught up with supply, leading to a remarkable surge in prices. Jeremy Grantham of the fund management group GMO created an equally weighted index of 33 commodities. From 1900 to 2002, this fell by 70% in real terms (with occasional revivals in the two world wars and the late 1970s). But from 2002 to 2010, in just eight years, all that lost ground was regained.

What is particularly striking is how quickly commodity prices recovered after the recession of 2008–09. In past cycles, falling commodity prices often gave developed economies a leg-up out of recession, acting as the equivalent of a tax cut. But as demand surges in developing countries such as China, the developed economies are no longer the price-setters for commodities; they have become the price-takers.

Some observers, including Grantham, think high commodity prices are here to stay. They argue that mankind has tended to develop those natural resources that are easiest to find and cheapest to develop. New discoveries, such as the oilfield deep under the sea near Brazil or the tar sands in Canada, are more expensive to exploit. In effect, this is a supply shock for the developed economies, resulting in slower growth and higher inflation than would otherwise have been the case.

The contrary argument is that such warnings have proved false many times in the past, as they did in the 1970s. Mankind is ingenious enough to get around the problems (by using alternative sources of energy, for example). Furthermore, some analysts believe that the rise in commodity prices was driven not by the fundamentals of supply and demand but by speculators and institutional investors moving into the markets. Buying commodities, they point out, has been a way for investors to hedge against inflation and to link their portfolios to the growth of the Chinese economy.

Looking to the future, which view of the commodity cycle turns out to be right could be highly significant for the other cycles mentioned in this chapter – and so for Western economies already suffering from deteriorating demography and the debt burden of the credit crunch. Without decent economic growth, it will be hard to generate credit growth, and thus harder for asset bubbles to appear. In that case, sluggish Japanese-style markets might endure for an extended period. The more bullish interpretation is that higher commodity prices are merely a teething problem in the great boom that Chinese and Indian growth is unleashing on the world. The historical parallel would be the late 19th century, when the development of America and Argentina led to an agricultural depression in Europe but eventually boosted global prosperity.

Momentum

Throughout all the bull and bear cycles of the past 100 years, some investors have still been able to make money. This is in part because

FIG 15.3 **Momentous**

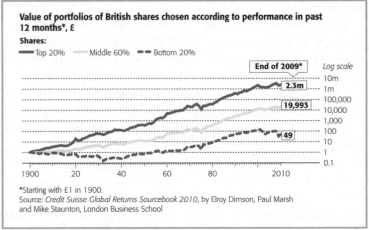

Value of portfolios of British shares chosen according to performance in past 12 months*, £

Shares:
Top 20% Middle 60% Bottom 20%

End of 2009*

2.3m

19,993

49

Log scale
10m
1m
100,000
10,000
1,000
100
10
1
0.1

1900 20 40 60 80 2010

*Starting with £1 in 1900.
Source: *Credit Suisse Global Returns Sourcebook 2010*, by Elroy Dimson, Paul Marsh and Mike Staunton, London Business School

of an odd stockmarket phenomenon: momentum. Shares that have performed well in the recent past have a pronounced tendency to continue to do so.

The cumulative effect is quite startling. Elroy Dimson, Paul Marsh and Mike Staunton of London Business School looked at the largest 100 stocks in the British market since 1900, calculating the return from buying the best 20 performers over the previous 12 months and rebalancing every month. Such a strategy would have turned £1 in 1900 into £2.3m by the end of 2009; the same sum invested in the worst performers of the previous 12 months would have grown into just £49 (see Figure 15.3).

The same effect has been seen in other markets. AQR Capital Management, a hedge-fund group, found that American stocks with the best momentum outperformed those with the worst by more than ten percentage points a year between 1927 and 2010.

So what can explain the phenomenon? Momentum runs counter to the idea that markets are "efficient" and that past price movements tell investors nothing about the future. But it seems unlikely that this is a mere quirk of the data, like the supposed link between stockmarket performance and the winning team in the Super Bowl. Academics first noticed momentum in the mid-1980s and it was still apparent 25 years later. Nor can it be argued that the potential gains from such an approach would be dissipated in trading costs.

It is possible that investors are slow to adjust to new information. They may have a mental image of a company, judging that its management is poor or that it is operating in a dull sector. They may thus dismiss any initial set of good results as a blip. But if the trend continues, more investors may realise that the change is substantial and long-lasting.

At that point, there may be a bandwagon effect. Portfolio managers have to report to their clients every three months or so. They may wish to "window dress" their performance by including stocks that have done well, often buying them at the end of the quarter. Paul Woolley, who founded a centre for Capital Market Dysfunctionality at the London School of Economics, suggests that a "principal-agent" effect may be at work. Investors give money to fund managers who have recently performed well; those managers then buy more of the stocks they like, causing the momentum of such stocks to accelerate.

But explaining the effect is not enough. The question is: why has it not been arbitraged away? If it makes sense to buy the best performers of the last 12 months, some investors would presumably buy after 11 months to get a jump on the rest; and then others would buy after 10, and so on. Perhaps the reason that this has not happened is that there are moments when the trend can sharply change – in which case a momentum strategy can produce big losses, as was the case in 2009.

Another issue is that the momentum effect does not last forever. Clearly, it could not, or share prices would rise indefinitely. At some point in a 2–5 year period, share prices start to revert to the mean. The high-flyers fall back. This may well be because investors get over-optimistic about a company's prospects: all the good news is then (more than) reflected in the price and the supply of new buyers starts to dwindle.

At that stage, a contrary phenomenon known as the value effect kicks in. Some companies become overlooked and undervalued, and trade, for example, at a discount to the value of their assets. Bargain-hunters spot the opportunity and buy the stocks. Over the long run, this strategy too has produced market-beating returns, although some academics argue that this is simply a reward for taking extra risk (companies in the value category are more likely to go bust).

Some observers have divided stockmarket investors into "value" and "growth" stock-pickers. Caricaturing the two types, value investors do not care about the nature of a company's business as long as its shares are cheap, while growth investors do not care about the price of a company's shares provided that its business is attractive.

Cycling into the future

Like the other trends mentioned in this chapter, value and growth styles go in and out of fashion. The growth school tends to be associated with the headiest stages of bull markets, such as the dotcom bubble of the late 1990s; the value school tends to do best as the economy emerges from a recession.

If the developed world is going to get out of its debt trap, then it will need a few industries that inspire the growth school into another burst of enthusiasm. Big profits will be made by those who can spot such industries (biotech, say, or alternative energy) early.

So where will these trends take us by 2050? Since there was the great recession in the early 1930s, the collapse of the Bretton Woods system in the early 1970s and then the subprime crisis of 2007-08, it is tempting to think that the world will be due for another crisis around 2050. Tempting, but rather facile. There is no reason for these cycles to operate like clockwork.

It can be stated with rather more confidence that we will probably have seen more than one cycle by the time we get to 2050. In 2011, credit conditions were still fairly tight in some parts of the market and several European governments were facing a funding crisis. Such periods of tightness cannot last forever. Either the economy recovers, and the bankers ease their criteria, or the lack of credit leads to defaults, and a rearrangement of the economy. Similarly, it is implausible that commodity prices can keep rising for 40 years. At some point either new sources of supply will be found or demand will collapse (possibly with disastrous economic repercussions).

Demography is another matter; trends are much slower to adjust. Nevertheless, it is possible that the developed world could see another baby boom like that of 1946–64 or, less cheerfully, that disease (or the impact of obesity) could cull the ranks of retirees.

In financial-market terms, the cycles between now and 2050 will probably last longer than their economic counterparts. The equity bear phase of 1966–82 was followed by the bull run of 1982–2000, for example. So we will have had a few more booms and busts by 2050. One thing is certain: during those booms, stockbrokers will tell their clients that the old valuation measures are no longer relevant. The smart investors will not listen. The most dangerous words will remain "this time is different".

PART 4

Knowledge and progress

The frontiers of science, space and technology

16 What (and where) next for science

Geoffrey Carr

Mankind's quest for knowledge will enter new territories, explored and captured more by the liberal and disorderly West than the hierarchical East

IN SCIENTIFIC TERMS, the future belongs to biology. As an intellectual discipline, chemistry is exhausted. The periodic table has been extended into realms where the lifetime of atoms is measured in mere seconds, and the fundamental nature of the chemical bond has been elucidated. There will be no more chemical surprises – though there will, one hopes, be lots of practical discoveries.

Physics is only slightly more hopeful. Though there is much still to be learned about the fundamental structure of the universe, the machines needed to do the exploring are getting bigger and more expensive all the time. Diminishing returns may be setting in – and while a true breakthrough with the latest toy, the Large Hadron Collider near Geneva, might reinvigorate the field and persuade politicians and taxpayers that it is still worth backing, little science applicable to humanity's quotidian comfort is likely to come from the search for universal fundamentals.

Biology, though, is different. It really is still terra incognita and it promises and terrifies in equal measure. There will be discoveries here aplenty. Biology will also link up with two fields that are not quite traditional science, but will serve both to illuminate it and to allow it to be turned into technology. These fields are nanoscience and information science. For biology is both. Cells operate in the nano realm – bigger than chemistry, but smaller than traditional mechanics. And living things are, essentially, information-processing systems.

Exactly how biology, nanoscience and information science come together will drive much of the innovation between now and 2050.

The other big change that may happen to science is not intellectual, but geographical. As non-Western countries catch up economically, many are seeking to catch up scientifically. If they succeed, they will transform the field, by bringing vast amounts of extra brainpower to bear on it. But that success is by no means certain, for to achieve it some of these countries will have to pay a social price which their leaders may not like.

Unravelling life

Biology is now getting into its stride for several reasons. The first is the recently developed ability to sequence DNA rapidly and in huge quantities. The second is improvements in microscopy that enable cellular processes to be understood more perfectly. The third is better techniques for examining the brain, which is the most interesting biological object and probably the most interesting thing in the known universe. And the fourth is the spread among biologists not just of a belief in evolution (few would dissent from that), but also of an understanding that this belief needs to inform the process of biological research.

The next couple of decades will see a filling in of the genetic stamp album similar to the filling in of the list of species on Earth that happened in the glory days of taxonomy, the 19th century. By 2030, or thereabouts, most of known life will have been sampled, and the process of sampling may, itself, reveal much unknown life. (Many biologists, for example, think a reservoir of specialised bacteria lives deep inside the Earth.)

That is of obvious intellectual interest. It will help biologists understand life's history, by making accurate connections between the myriad types of single-celled organisms that dominate life on Earth but are as yet barely studied. (A recent foretaste of this was the discovery by genetic means of what looks like an entire new domain of living creatures, of equal standing to the three domains of archaea, bacteria and eukaryotes that are the top level of biological classification.)

That will be fascinating. But the new biology offers more than just academic fascination. The huge new pool of genes, and the biological understanding that will come with them, should also open the subject to the sort of industrial exploitation that happened to chemistry in the 19th century, when the periodic table was discovered and the real nature of chemical reactions explained.

Part of this opening up will come from the interaction of biology with nanoscience and information science. Nanotechnology, much hyped over the past couple of decades, has proved a false start. Scattering tiny crystals in materials to improve their properties, which is all it really amounts to at the moment, is a far cry from the collaborative armies of microscopic machines that were promised by visionaries in the 1990s. But that will change as the behaviour of cells is understood better. Proteins and DNA are huge molecules, and fall slap-bang into the remit of nanoscience: not traditional chemistry, but too dominated by short-range electrostatic effects to be tractable by traditional mechanics. It was these forces that did for the visionary version of nanotechnology. The cogs and sprockets that the early nanotechnologists dreamed of do not work when they are so small that van der Waals forces and other ill-understood electric effects come into play. Living systems, however, obviously do work. Once they are properly analysed, a whole range of technological applications will be opened up – either highly modified organisms, or completely artificial systems that simply borrow their ideas from biology: perhaps robots of the sophistication imagined by the playwright Karel Capek, who introduced the word to the world in 1921.

Such robots would require the intersection of information science and biology, too: a better understanding of how brains function allied with more sophisticated artificial computing power. New brain-scanning techniques will reveal how the various parts of the brain link up right down to the cellular level. Faster, more powerful computers will allow the consequences of those discoveries to be modelled in software. That will reveal how the brain really works. And it will allow the construction of artificial brains that work on the same principles. Not only will this permit advanced robotics, it will also give science a fair chance of cracking what is, perhaps, the one natural phenomenon left about which it has no real clue at all: consciousness.

Know thyself

Understanding consciousness would be the ultimate self-knowledge. But even if that particular breakthrough in self-awareness does not happen by 2050, plenty of others will. Some will come from genetics. Some will come from new discoveries in the fossil record. And some will come from a growing understanding of the brain, even if the problem of consciousness is not cracked. Together, they could change mankind's view of itself – and in ways that could be politically explosive.

Humans will learn, soon, for example, which genes make them different from Neanderthals: the core, in other words, of what it is to be *Homo sapiens*. DNA from other fossil human species, as well as from living great apes, will add to the picture. It will also become clear whether there really are any important and systematic mental differences between populations from different parts of the planet – races, to use the politically loaded term – or whether humans actually are brothers and sisters under the skin.

Researchers will find out, too, how much of an individual's likely success in life is predestined by his genetic make-up, and how much can be enhanced by education (a field that will, itself, be transformed by the new brain science). They may even, though this may prove too complicated, be able to tweak the genetic make-up of people's offspring to improve these children's chances.

Even if tweaking for intelligence proves impossible, genetic tweaks for better health and longer life seem likely. That area of controversy has gone quiet recently, because genetics has proved a lot more complicated than was originally hoped or, indeed, expected. But as the processes by which genes control cells, and thus bodies, are disentangled, the controversy is certain once more to grab the headlines.

Manipulating brains will, though, be possible through other methods than tinkering with the initial genetic blueprint. For with a true understanding of how human brains work will come one of what they are really for – and that is not always what traditional philosophers, divines, economists and other non-scientific intellectuals have assumed they were for. Pre-biological thinking has emphasised human uniqueness. Even those who do not believe in divine creation tend to compartmentalise people as being somehow separate from nature. That kind of thinking will be challenged as the evolutionary and genetic origins of *Homo sapiens* are laid bare, and as even his uniqueness is explained in terms of evolutionary adaptations whose function is, at bottom, just survival and reproduction.

This process will illuminate both the bad and the good about humanity – and the good (which traditional philosophy has always had a hard time explaining) more so than the bad. The biological origins of selfishness are easy to imagine. The biological origins of the co-operativeness and, on occasion, extraordinary self-sacrifice that characterise humans and have led to their ascent are less easy to elucidate. Yet they are now being studied. As is how people actually behave in complex, modern economies, rather than how the simplified (and often ideologically loaded) models of economists dictate that they ought to behave. Even religion is not off limits to students of human evolution. And the next 40 years will certainly see progress in many of these areas, if not all of them. Expect, then, both well-meaning political theories based on the new knowledge, and manipulative politicians who try to take advantage of it.

The outward urge

Fundamental knowledge will pour in from other directions, too. The end of the space age as it used to be understood (the grand plans of the 1950s and 1960s, for wheel-like space stations, bases on the moon and human colonies on Mars are unlikely to be revived any time soon) does not mean the end of space exploration. But this will mostly be done remotely, using sophisticated telescopes either based on Earth or in orbit around the planet. Such instruments will seek to answer two questions: "Why are we here?" and "Are we alone?"

The likely end of accelerator-based particle physics will not be the end of fundamental physics *per se*. Instead, the subject will go back to its roots by studying what is naturally there (as Ernest Rutherford and Paul Villard studied alpha and beta particles, and gamma rays) rather than by seeking to create from scratch things like exotic quarks and Higgs bosons that do not exist naturally. That will mean looking outward into the universe. In particular, the search will intensify for dark matter (fundamental particles that interact with other forms of matter almost exclusively through the force of gravity) and for gravitational waves (which may help to link the force of gravity, currently explained by the splendid isolation of Einstein's general theory of relativity, with the quantum theory that explains the rest of physics). Both of these phenomena should be detectable by reasonably cheap ground-based equipment – cheap at least compared with a new, monster particle accelerator. The other known unknown of physics, so-called dark energy, which is pushing the universe apart, requires a theoretical breakthrough for its explanation more than it needs new data. That is completely unpredictable. Perhaps a bored patent clerk somewhere in the world is wrestling, Einstein-like, with the problem as you read these words.

But it is, once again, in the field of biology that astronomy may make its greatest contribution – for by 2050 it should be clear whether life is abundant in the universe or if, rather, it is so rare that humans might reasonably regard what has happened on Earth as unique. The key to that knowledge is the recent discovery of planets orbiting other stars. Studying these is one piece of fundamental science that is pretty much guaranteed to get funding for the future, for it truly can answer the question: is anybody out there? It will do so using spectroscopy. Just as the composition of the sun and other stars can be read from the light they emit, so the composition of a planet's atmosphere can be read from the light it absorbs. When an alien planet passes in front of its parent star, a good enough telescope is able to read that signal from Earth.

It is clear, already, that most stars have planets. Enough such planets that are visible from Earth will pass before their stars for thousands to have been logged by 2050. Any planet with free oxygen in its atmosphere will be a dead giveaway – or, rather, a live one (oxygen is too reactive to hang around unless it is constantly replenished, and no non-biological way of doing so is known). Conversely, if there is no sign of oxygen, or of atmospheres that seem out of chemical equilibrium in some other way, there is probably no life out there.

Which leads to one of the biggest questions of all: how did life on Earth originate? Looking at other planets should tell us whether the origin of life is easy or difficult, but it will not explain exactly how it happened. Experiments on Earth, however, should do just that.

The answer will come from drilling down into the workings of modern cells, to see which bits are truly primitive and thus likely to have come about when life first got going, and from experimentation in laboratories to find the simplest chemical systems that, given only an input of raw materials and energy, can reproduce themselves with reasonable fidelity.

Re-creating life-as-we-know-it – based on nucleic acids to carry the genetic information and proteins to do the heavy lifting – would be a huge step forward. It would also allow biologists to ask if other forms of life could come into existence: other types of gene, perhaps, or other workhorse polymers than proteins. The metabolism of those truly artificial life forms might, in turn, answer the question of what sorts of atmospheres the exobiologists' telescopes should be looking for, if not just for oxygen.

Galileo's children

So much, then, for the "what" of the future of science. But there is a second question, and that is "where?". Will science remain mainly a Western activity, or will the rising powers of Asia take it up as well?

That might sound an odd query – even a slightly racist one. It is not. It is, rather, a query about the sorts of society that curiosity-driven research can flourish in.

One thing that has been true about science until now is that it is almost exclusively a product of the modern West. It is fashionable, in these multicultural days, to praise the caliphate of Baghdad and the Song dynasty of China for their innovative scientific endeavours. Similarly, the Western scientific revolution is said to owe much to the ancient Greeks. And even the pre-Columbian science of the Aztecs, Incas and Maya is lauded by some. But these apparent historical precedents are misleading.

The rediscovery of Greek thought did, it is true, stimulate the scientific side of the European Renaissance. But it is important to remember that, apart from their mathematical ideas, the Greeks got almost every explanation of what they saw in nature wrong. Their theories, from the Earth-centred astronomy of Ptolemy to the humour-based medicine of Galen, were up the spout, and a lot of early Western science was actually concerned with removing the dead hand of received Greek wisdom from the academies of Europe, so that the real truth could out. As for the pre-Columbian science, it may have been mathematically impressive, in the way that Ptolemaic astronomy is, but beyond creating accurate calendars, it was wrong too (and its technology was pathetic: the Incas failed even to invent the wheel).

The cases of Arabia and China are equally misleading. Both produced lots of data and much useful technology. Neither (again, excepting mathematics) produced much theory. And, crucially, neither encouraged the idea of testing theory by experiment and, if necessary, rejecting the wisdom of the ages as a result. Good science, by contrast, is anarchic and respects only data, not authority.

And therein lies the dilemma. Asian countries, China in particular, say they want to encourage science. Indeed, science was one of Deng Xiaoping's four modernisations. But science works by challenging authority, not by accepting it. Even Japan, the main non-Western technological power at the moment, has difficulty doing truly fundamental science. Only 15 Nobel science prizes have gone to Japanese researchers. That is just two more than have been won, for example, by Austrians – and Austria has less than 7% of Japan's population. One reason often given for this is the unwillingness of young Japanese scientists to challenge the ideas of their elders. In the West, by contrast, such challenges are the foundations of careers. And more than just individual careers are affected by this disrespect for authority. Western science has risen to pre-eminence hand-in-glove with the liberal modes of thought that lead to political transformation, and scientists from Galileo to Darwin have upset the prevailing social norms on which the settled power of the time depended.

The rising powers of Asia have feasted on the innovation that four centuries of the Western scientific revolution have provided without, so far, having to deal with the disruptive ways of thinking that this innovation required. They have poured capital into their under-employed labour forces to create economic growth rates unheard of in the places that did the original innovating. But, once they have caught up, what will they do next?

Let a hundred papers bloom

China's attempt to become a scientific power has certainly produced a flurry of wood pulp and electrons. In 2000 the country was eighth in the number of research papers published. Now it is second, behind only the United States. Extrapolating (always a dangerous technique, as any good scientific researcher will tell you), it would catch up with America in 2015.

What is less clear is how influential all this science is. Measured by the number of citations in other researchers' papers (a common index of the impact of a piece of scientific work), China is still nowhere. Not a single one of the 100 most-cited scientific papers in history has had a Chinese researcher as its principal author.

By 2050, then, on present trends, China will be the top scientific nation, measured by names-on-papers. Whether that translates into invitations to receive gold medals from the king of Sweden is another matter.

FIG 16.1 **China gets scientific**

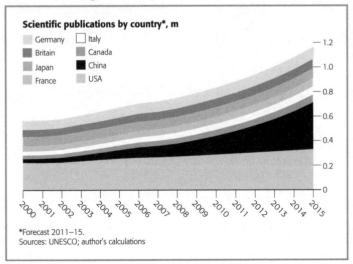

Scientific publications by country*, m

*Forecast 2011–15.
Sources: UNESCO; author's calculations

In the answer to that question lie both the future of science and the future of humanity. If the new powers permit the development of the sort of liberal, intellectual environment, so hard-won in the West, that allows science to flourish, then they will flourish themselves – and not only scientifically, but socially and politically too. If they do not, or cannot, they will have the same fate as Japan, drifting along with a comfortable standard of living, but unable to do much that is truly new. It is this reality that makes the long-term prospects of democratic, disorderly India (another country with a strong mathematical tradition) more promising than those of its perennial rival, authoritarian China.

Winston Churchill once said that scientists should be on tap, not on top – and it is true that the black arts of politics do not mesh comfortably with the naive honesty required to do good science. But it is also true that the constant intellectual ferment which modern science has created is responsible for a good part of the West's social and political advantages as well as its creature comforts. The last scientific trend to watch for, then, is the actions of scientists themselves. Will they fight the stifling embrace of illiberalism, or will they be co-opted by the political authorities, to the detriment of both science and society itself?

17 *Ad astra*

Tim Cross

Man's exploration of space will be less starry-eyed

SPACE EXPLORATION, the headline-writer's favourite stereotype of futuristic high technology, inspires plenty of emotions, but nostalgia is not usually one of them. Yet a slew of anniversaries and milestones in 2011 – 50 years since a Soviet cosmonaut, Yuri Gagarin, became the first man in space, the same half-century since John F. Kennedy kicked off the Apollo moon-shot programme, and the final flight of NASA's venerable space shuttle – prompted reveries about the glory days of can-do cold warriors and the "steely-eyed missile men" who blazed the trail into the great dark beyond.

Back then, at the dawn of the space age, humanity's imminent conquest of the high frontier was taken for granted. The rocket men promised orbiting space stations that would conduct undreamed-of scientific research. Space-based factories would revolutionise manufacturing by turning out exotic materials that could be made only in zero gravity. The moon missions – which would soon result in a permanent base – were to be mere practice runs for much more ambitious manned trips to Venus and Mars.

Others made darker predictions. Generals on both sides of the cold war were fascinated by the strategic possibilities of space, particularly the idea of stowing nuclear weapons in orbit. The Strategic Defence Initiative (derisively called "Star Wars" by its many critics) proposed protecting America from nuclear attack by deploying satellite-mounted lasers to zap incoming warheads.

Of course, most of those predictions never came to pass. Rocket science has not brought about a futuristic Utopia, and the real world can seem mundane when compared with the glittering visions of a few decades ago. Yet the nostalgics overstate their case. The space age arrived – just not quite in the way its most vigorous prophets predicted. The commercial value of the swarm of satellites gazing down upon the planet was reckoned to be $160.9 billion in 2009, an 11% increase on the year before despite the economic difficulties in much of the developed world. Parts of the industry are growing fast: one report suggests that the market for navigation services, mostly based on America's global positioning system (GPS), is growing at 20% a year, and will be worth about $75 billion by 2013.

Communications satellites bounce phone calls, television channels and internet traffic around the globe. Armies, particularly America's, consider space the "fourth battlefield", but their focus is more on reconnaissance, intelligence-gathering and navigation than on using orbiting bombers to incinerate their enemies.

Other satellites monitor the Earth in more peaceful ways, keeping track of everything from weather patterns and the changing climate to soil fertility and deforestation rates. Freely available satellite imagery allows house-buyers to stroll round a neighbourhood from their sofas, or oil traders to monitor activity in Saudi Arabia's secretive fields. Scientific spacecraft, most famously NASA's *Hubble* space telescope, have made fundamental discoveries about the nature of the universe. Meanwhile, although the orbiting factories have yet to come to pass, the International Space Station (ISS) – magnificent white elephant that it is – has hosted a continuous human presence in space for over a decade.

Half a century after men landed on the moon in 1969, attitudes to space exploration, especially manned exploration, are still dominated by the glorious exploits of the Soviet and American space programmes (see Figure 17.1). But the space race was a product of its time: of cold-war paranoia, of the developing military technology of ballistic missiles, and of a life-or-death struggle between two competing political and economic systems. Nothing similar exists today. That poses a problem for fans of manned space exploration; with no ideological opponent to compete with, there will be little motivation in the coming decades to send humans, at great risk and expense, out to the planets. But closer to home there is money to be made, and so the immediate

FIG 17.1 **Mission possible**

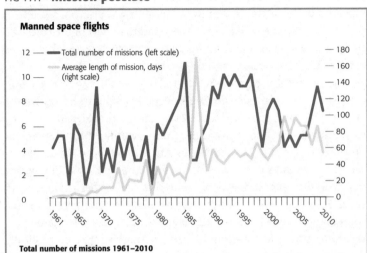

Manned space flights

Total number of missions (left scale)

Average length of mission, days (right scale)

Total number of missions 1961–2010

US	USSR/Russia	China	Private
165	114	3	3

Sources: www.braeunig.us; NASA; National Earth Science Teachers Association

environs of Earth will remain busy, with new satellites offering new services to the humans on the ground.

Space is also an astronomer's dream. Free from the interference of the atmosphere, telescopes can see billions of light years into the distance, and billions of years back in time, gathering the data to test scientific theories. And with so many planets out there – and the ability now to detect them directly – it seems almost certain that at least one will be found to harbour life.

The space race rerun

Yet advocates of the heroic form of space exploration, in which gutsy astronauts blast off to tread on other worlds, have always been an optimistic lot. In some quarters, nostalgia for the past is spiced by anticipation of a new, 21st-century space race, with China or perhaps India providing the competition. President Barack Obama fuelled such talk in his 2011 state-of-the-union address when he talked of the rise of those two nations as modern America's "*Sputnik* moment", a reference to the Soviet launch of the world's first artificial satellite in 1957. Coming at the height of the most paranoid part of the cold war, *Sputnik* was seen as a disaster for America, which feared that it was being left behind by its communist rival.

Squint and it is possible to see today's parallels with the 1960s: China and India are rising powers, developing rapidly and, outwardly at least, full of confidence; America is uncertain, weighed down by its recent history and a misfiring economy. Indeed, the retirement of the space shuttle in 2011 leaves America without the ability to send its astronauts into space for the first time since 1981. The nation that won the space race is now reduced to renting berths on Russian spacecraft to get its astronauts to the ISS. Of America's potential competitors, China has advanced the farthest. In 2003 it became only the third country to put a human being into orbit atop a domestically developed rocket (plenty of people from other countries have hitched rides on American or Russian spacecraft), when Yang Liwei, then a lieutenant colonel in the Chinese air force, spent 21 hours in orbit before landing on the Inner Mongolian grasslands.

Since then, two further missions have taken five more of China's "taikonauts" into orbit. But the country has much bigger ambitions. Besides launching a slew of satellites and trying to attract commercial business for its Long March rockets, its plans include a space station of its own. Two parts of a test station successfully docked together in November 2011. An unmanned sampling mission to the moon is pencilled in for 2017, with the objective of gathering lunar soil and returning it to Earth. By 2025, the goal is a manned mission (see Table 17.1).

China's prowess should not be overstated. Its capacity still lags behind Russia's. And even without the shuttle America's spending on manned space flight will be higher than that of any other nation, at least for the foreseeable future. Clearly, landing a taikonaut on the moon would be an unmistakable signal of China's status as a fledgling superpower; but although it would be an admirable feat of organisation and technological competence, it might not capture the imagination in the same way as America's Apollo programme of the 1960s – the magnificent shadow of which still dominates popular imaginings of space travel. Assuming the Chinese mission arrives on time (a big assumption), it will get there over half a century after the Americans left. There would be saturation press coverage and much portentous speechmaking. But America will stay in the history books as the country that did it first.

That feeling – that a return to the moon would simply be rehashing an old accomplishment – was one of the reasons behind America's decision in 2010 to cancel its own moon-return missions, and it may yet scupper China's plans, too. To really make a mark on history, you need to set your sights farther afield. NASA has tentative plans to send astronauts to the asteroids; but although scientists would love to know more, it is hard to extract inspiration from a landing on a small hunk of itinerant rock. For that, you have to go to Mars, the El Dorado of manned space flight. Plans for such a trip have existed for decades. After the triumph of the moon landings there were plenty of people in NASA who saw it as the agency's next logical step.

TABLE 17.1 **Boldly going**

The past …

1961	Yuri Gagarin becomes first man in space
1969	Neil Armstrong and Buzz Aldrin land on the moon
1971	*Salyut*, the first space station, arrives in orbit
1981	Space shuttle completes maiden flight
1990	*Hubble* space telescope deployed
2001	Dennis Tito becomes first space tourist
2004	*SpaceShipOne* completes first private sub-orbital spaceflight
2011	Final shuttle mission

… and the future?

2013	Virgin Galactic starts paid suborbital tourist flights
2014	SpaceX launches first manned orbital flight
2017	*James Webb* telescope, *Hubble* successor, launched
2020	International Space Station abandoned
2025	Crewed Chinese mission to the moon
2035	Manned American mission to Mars

Will it finally happen by the middle of this century? Astronauts journeying to Mars will have to spend six months aboard their spacecraft (as opposed to three days for the moon voyagers). Along the way they will be zapped by cosmic rays and risk being cooked by solar flares, those unpredictable eruptions of energy from the sun. Upon arrival, they will be so far away that messages to their controllers on the ground will take tens of minutes to arrive, and the same amount of time to come back, meaning that the astronauts will have to be much more self-reliant than were the moonwalkers, whose actions were constantly cross-checked by experts on the ground.

However, manned space flight has always been about less tangible things than can be fitted into a cost-benefit analysis. When Richard Nixon's administration was pondering pulling the plug on the 16th and 17th Apollo missions, Caspar Weinberger, one of his advisers, opined that to cancel the missions would amount to "confirming, in some respects, a belief that I fear is gaining credence at home and abroad: that our best years are behind us, that we are turning inward and voluntarily starting to give up our superpower status." The moon landings provided an undeniable boost to America's standing in the world and its opinion of itself. Anyone who doubts the psychological benefits of such adventures should imagine the headlines the next day, if the Chinese do indeed manage to beat the Americans to the Martian surface.

Not all space races have to be peaceful, of course. Space is very useful for armies, since it allows them to keep tabs on the enemy, keep their own troops in contact with each other, and even, through systems like America's GPS, guide bombs and soldiers accurately to their targets. There is plenty of competition happening even now. Russia is building its own version of GPS (it is already operational), as is the European Union, and China is planning something similar. In 2007 a Chinese missile destroyed an old weather satellite in a thinly veiled demonstration to the Americans that China now has the capacity to remove other nations' satellites from orbit. Alarmed, Russia began boasting about similar capabilities, and a few months later America shot down an old satellite of its own – merely a safety precaution, insisted the government, pointing out that the satellite was about to fall back to Earth. Few believed that story.

That kind of competition will continue, with spy satellites becoming more and more advanced (there are already rumours of "stealthy" satellites that are invisible to radar). In the long run, there may be more dramatic possibilities. America is currently flying an experimental military spaceplane that is, essentially, a smaller, robotic version of its space shuttle. It will not say what it is for, but theories range from surprise reconnaissance (avoiding the predictability of orbiting satellites) to dropping bombs from orbit, long an air-force ambition. Starry-eyed generals talk of dropping tungsten-penetrating rods on targets from orbit which would hit at thousands of miles an hour, faster than even the swiftest artillery shell. All this and more may lie in the future, particularly if the rivalries between established powers and the newcomers get a little less friendly. But for the coming decade, at least, it is likely that the future of space will more closely resemble the present reality, where the name of the game is information-gathering and intelligence, as it has been for the past five decades.

Ex astris, pecunia?

Another promise from the 1960s was that space would lead to untold commercial opportunities. Again, these have proved overblown. Dreams of zero-gravity manufacturing in orbiting factories have turned to dust. Beaming solar power from orbiting satellites, another sci-fi favourite, is simply too expensive, although it may have a few uses in beaming power to isolated army bases or research establishments. And the modern era has dreams of its own. A small but noisy caucus (supposedly including the chief scientist of China's lunar programme) advocates building the necessary infrastructure to mine helium-3 from the surface of the moon (produced by cosmic-ray bombardment, the substance is not available on Earth), since helium-3 is a potential source of energy for fusion power. That we still do not know, after 50 years of trying, exactly how to build fusion reactors does not dim such enthusiasm.

But there will indeed be money made in space. Back in the 1960s, when Gagarin and Alan Shepard were riding into space atop modified ballistic missiles, rocketry was an exciting new technology. Today there are dozens of launches a year and a dozen designs of rocket. Knowledge has migrated out of government bureaucracies like

Finding alien life

For most of its history, astronomy has been closely allied with physics. But the biologists may get their day beneath the stars, too. The discovery of extraterrestrial life would rank as perhaps the most important in the history of science.

Detecting alien life is not easy, particularly if the life in question consists of relatively simple microbes rather than fully fledged alien civilisations. The question of whether there is – or was – any life on Mars is still not resolved, three decades after the first robot missions landed on the planet. And there are other planets in the solar system that could, just conceivably, harbour alien critters, including Europa, an ice-bound moon of Jupiter hypothesised to host a planet-wide ocean beneath its surface, kept warm by the moon's gravitational interaction with its parent planet. Titan, a Saturnian moon, is another candidate. Data from the *Cassini-Huygens* mission, which arrived at Titan in 2004, have reported chemical traces in the moon's atmosphere that are consistent with, but do not prove, a tentative hypothesis that some form of life may exist in the cold methane in the lakes that dot the moon's surface.

Admittedly, those are long shots. Earth may well prove to be the only life-bearing planet in our solar system. But for as long as

NASA, which in any case has always relied on private contractors to do much of its engineering work. There already exists a competitive market for rocket launches, even if it contains only a few big players, such as Europe's Arianespace consortium and a Russo-American joint venture, International Launch Services (although China is again keen to make inroads with its Long March series of rockets). The satellite business is both big and mature, carrying telephone conversations, internet traffic, TV channels and the like around the world. America's government is intimately involved, since it controls the GPS system of satellites that has helped revolutionise everything from the international freight business to driving your car on holiday.

they have known that stars are merely other suns, astronomers have suspected that there are plenty of other planets out there in the galaxy. In recent years we have been able to detect these "exoplanets" directly. NASA's *Kepler* space telescope, launched in 2009 to hunt for such planets, has so far found evidence for about 1,200. Extrapolating from that number suggests that planets are as common as muck. The Milky Way alone may host as many as 50 billion scattered among its roughly 100 billion stars. If even a small fraction of those lie within the "habitable zone" of a star – close enough that water can stay liquid, not so close that it boils – then there may well be millions of worlds on which life could have developed.

Rather than relying on statistical arguments about how common aliens might be, we will soon be able to check for their presence directly. Technological advances will make it possible to analyse the composition of their atmospheres, looking for the telltale chemical by-products of metabolism. The plenitude of planets and the onward march of telescope technology mean that, for someone looking for a profitable long-run wager, the discovery of alien life at some point in the next few decades looks a pretty attractive bet.

America's government is about to become a bigger customer, too. President Obama's space strategy, unveiled in 2010, envisions a much bigger role for privately run missions, which he hopes will relieve NASA of the burden of flying supply missions to the ISS and, in the next few years, will fly astronauts there as well – and do it for much less than a typical NASA launch. Several firms have received money from NASA to develop their products, but the one that has grabbed the most headlines is SpaceX, a California-based firm run by Elon Musk, an internet entrepreneur. In December 2010 it launched its Dragon capsule into orbit and recovered it successfully. A cargo visit to the ISS (alongside another by a competitor named Orbital Sciences) would follow.

The next development in truly private space flight, with no real government involvement, will come from tourism. Russia has blazed the trail. Its *Soyuz* spacecraft have taken several people into Earth orbit and to the ISS, at a cost thought to be somewhere in the region of $30m per flight. Virgin Galactic, a grandiosely named firm run by a British serial entrepreneur, Richard Branson, is hoping to use an aircraft-launched rocket ship to take tourists on the sort of short suborbital hop that made Shepard the first American in space. It hopes to start flights in the next couple of years, and a seat will go for the still-eye-watering cost of about $200,000. If those costs can be brought down, via innovative rocket design, mass-production and economies of scale, then it may be that in a couple of decades' time space tourism will become "affordable", at least for the very well-off, and that a trip beyond the atmosphere will be the 21st-century equivalent of a trip to a particularly posh ski resort.

Oddly, not all those in the private-spaceflight industry are pure, hard-headed businessmen with ambitions limited to making money. Musk freely admits that he is in the business because, he says, in the long run, humanity will have to spread itself beyond Earth if it is to survive. Only the private sector, he thinks, can make space travel cheap and reliable enough to make a manned mission to Mars – and eventually the colonisation of other worlds – a reality.

Ex astris, scientia

Those who see manned spaceflight as risky and expensive have always preferred that space agencies' budgets should go on science missions instead. Humans have been studying the night sky for thousands of years, but one of the most sobering achievements of modern astronomy is to make it clear how little we can see. Specifically, the visible matter and energy that we can see through our telescopes seems to account for only about 5% of the total amount of stuff in the universe. The missing material has been dubbed "dark matter" and "dark energy".

Take dark matter first, thought to account for about a fifth of the total amount of stuff in the universe. The gravitational pull exerted by all the matter visible from Earth is insufficient to explain the movements of large-scale structures such as galaxies and clusters of galaxies. To square that circle, scientists have postulated a large amount of hidden matter lurking in the void (the planet Neptune was discovered in the same way, after oddities in the orbit of Uranus suggested to astronomers that there was another planet out there).

This stuff, scientists believe, falls into two categories. Some is simply cosmic detritus: failed stars, sunless planets, wandering asteroids and the like that are too dim to be seen from Earth. But most of it is thought to be made of a ghostly new type of particle that interacts only weakly with normal matter (and is therefore dubbed a WIMP, for weakly interacting massive particle), making it difficult to detect directly. A few physicists have suggested an even more exciting possibility: that there is no missing matter at all, and that Albert Einstein's theory of relativity, one of the best-tested theories in the history of science, is nevertheless wrong, with gravity behaving in strange new ways when applied over intergalactic distances. Various experiments – both Earth-based and space-based – are probing the mystery, but, so far at least, the nature of dark matter remains elusive. Whoever eventually manages to explain it will almost certainly get a Nobel prize for the trouble.

Dark energy, which accounts for the remainder, is more mysterious still. In 1999, evidence from supernovas – exploding stars – suggested that the rate at which the universe expands is accelerating. That was a startling result: gravity should slow the expansion of the universe over time, so the fact that it is getting faster implies there is a force out there strong enough to overcome the combined gravitational pull of everything the universe contains.

One possible explanation is to resurrect the cosmological constant, a repulsive force opposed to gravity and postulated by Einstein to make his relativity theory accord with the assumption, current at the time, that the universe was of a fixed size. That force could be powered by "vacuum energy", a prediction of quantum mechanics that says that even empty space contains a certain quantity of energy. The trouble is that the size of the vacuum energy predicted by quantum mechanics is enormously bigger than what is observed from the expansion of the universe – so big that the universe would have ripped itself apart billions of years ago. That embarrassing discrepancy between theory and observation (which is something in the region of a hundred orders of magnitude, the biggest in the history of science) has led some physicists, as with dark matter, to tinker with existing models of gravity. Cue for another 21st-century Nobel, waiting in the wings for the first to disentangle the mystery.

18 The web of knowledge

Kenneth Cukier

The internet has transformed society in a remarkably short time. Even faster change lies ahead as the amount of data that is produced and processed increases at an exponential rate

IN THE WANING DAYS of the second world war, Vannevar Bush, science adviser to America's President Roosevelt, penned an essay in the *Atlantic Monthly* entitled "As We May Think". He conceived of a machine, called the "memex", that would contain all human knowledge and could be summoned in an instant. An operator would sit before a keyboard and monitor – a small mental leap from the mechanical typewriters and library microfilm screens then available – and interact with information. The memex would make associations among documents, just as people find patterns among ideas. The machine was designed to automate human thought. Bush described a typical fellow using it in ways that, in the light of the internet today, are remarkably prescient:

> First he runs through an encyclopedia, finds an interesting but sketchy article, leaves it projected. Next, in a history, he finds another pertinent item, and ties the two together ... He branches off on a side trail which takes him through textbooks ... He inserts a page of longhand analysis of his own. Thus he builds a trail of his interest through the maze of materials available to him.

Coming from almost anyone else, the idea would have been dismissed as science fiction. But as one of the most eminent scientists of his day, Bush inspired the best minds to think big about how information could be harnessed by technology. The engineers who later developed the internet and precursors to the world wide web have expressed their debt to his vision. The future may not have turned out exactly as he predicted: the strait-laced New Englander would bristle to learn that porn has long been the most dominant "trail of interest" among web users. And his conjectures completely missed the computer revolution that by changing the way information is generated, processed and transmitted would bring his prediction to reality. Yet his memex neatly foretold how people have extended their ability to think, discover and share knowledge.

Over the next 40 years, two main developments will flow from this remarkable transformation in how we interact with information. First, the technology will continue to improve at an accelerating pace, making things like today's iPad seem more akin to the memex than an icon of engineering excellence. Second, because the technology will be so powerful and ubiquitous, the emphasis will shift from the technology itself to the way it is used (just as, for example, the incredible advances of the early printing presses paled in significance beside what the devices unleashed, such as mass literacy, the reformation and democracy).

Ancient and modern

It is worth bearing in mind that the world has always been awash with information. Its perfect accumulation has been a timeless pursuit. In the third century BC, Ptolemy III of Egypt stocked the Library of Alexandria by demanding that all travellers surrender their scrolls to be copied and preserved (with the library astutely keeping the originals and returning the copies). After September 11th 2001 an American government initiative called Total Information Awareness sought to compile everything from phone-call and web-surfing records to credit-card purchases and even medical records, before privacy concerns forced it to change form. In the delightful short story "On Exactitude in Science", Jorge Luis Borges describes an empire in which cartographers became so obsessive that they produced a map as big as the empire itself (becoming so cumbersome that future generations left it to disintegrate). "[I]n the western deserts, tattered fragments of the map are still to be found, sheltering some occasional beast or beggar."

Yet three factors set the modern age apart from previous eras. First, the microchip revolution means that the ability to generate, store and process information increases, while the price of doing so declines. Second, the extraordinary degree of economic development around the world in the 20th century has significantly increased the number of people who interact with information. Third, wireless sensor technology, albeit in very early stages, ushers in a world in which information will be created less by people and more by machines, our bodies or even the environment itself.

Together, these trends suggest that the growth of data will accelerate. Where for most of our history we have suffered from a shortage of information, tomorrow we will struggle with a surfeit. Already today the chief difficulty is not so much obtaining information but finding the relevant bits. For instance, one of the most valuable companies in the world is Google, which a decade after its founding in 1998 reached a market capitalisation of $200 billion. Its value is not derived from doing anything more than helping people find the information that is already publicly available. Yet because there is so much of the stuff, the main constraint is relevance not access. And, ironically, by doing this, Google ends up generating a ranking of search results, which amounts to still more information.

As a starting point, consider how much information exists in the world and the degree to which it is increasing. The experts disagree a bit, because they count different things. But they tell the same story: there is a lot of information around and it is growing fast. For example, in the 50 years from 1453 to 1503 about 8m books were printed, which is considered to be more than all the scribes of Europe had produced since the founding of Constantinople 1,250 years earlier, notes Viktor Mayer-Schönberger of the Oxford Internet Institute (analysing data from Elizabeth Eisenstein, a historian). "A staggering 25-fold output increase," he says.

Yet modern technology makes even that dramatic development seem quaint. According to IDC, a research firm, the quantity of stored information in the world doubles about every two years. The amount reached 1.8 zettabytes in 2011 (a zettabyte is 1 followed by 20 zeros), or 1.8 trillion gigabytes (see Table 18.1 for an explanation of what all these bits and bytes mean at human scale). Meanwhile, the cost of generating

TABLE 18.1 **Data inflation**

Unit	Size	Description
Bit (b)	1 or 0	Short for "binary digit", after the binary code (1 or 0) computers use to store and process data.
Byte (B)	8 bits	Enough information to create an English letter or number in computer code. It is the basic unit of computing.
Kilobyte (KB)	1,024 bytes; 2^{10} bytes	From "thousand" in Greek. One typed page of typed text is 2KB.
Megabyte (MB)	1,024KB; 2^{20} bytes	From "large" in Greek. The complete works of Shakespeare total 5MB. A typical pop song is about 4MB.
Gigabyte (GB)	1,024MB; 2^{30} bytes	From "giant" in Greek. A two-hour film can be compressed into 1–2GB.
Terabyte (TB)	1,024GB; 2^{40} bytes	From "monster" in Greek. All the printed information in America's Library of Congress totals 15TB.
Petabyte (PB)	1,024TB; 2^{50} bytes	All letters delivered by America's postal service in 2010 amounted to around 5PB. Google processed around 1PB every hour in 2009.
Exabyte (EB)	1,024PB; 2^{60} bytes	Equivalent to 10 billion copies of *The Economist*.
Zettabyte (ZB)	1,024EB; 2^{70} bytes	The total amount of information in existence in 2011 was estimated to be around 1.8ZB.
Yottabyte (YB)	1,024ZB; 2^{80} bytes	Currently too large to imagine.

Note: The prefixes are determined by an intergovernmental group, the International Bureau of Weights and Measures. Yotta and Zetta were added in 1991, but terms for larger amounts have yet to be established.
Source: *The Economist*

and storing information today is around one-sixth of what it was in 2005. The price of a gigabyte of computer memory is tumbling from $19 in 2005 to an estimated 66 cents by 2015. There is every reason to think these trends will continue at as quick a pace, if not faster.

Within ten years, by 2020, the amount of information that needs to be actively "managed" is expected to grow 50-fold. Or, to return to Mayer-Schönberger's examination of the information revolution of medieval times, whereas Europe about doubled its stock of knowledge in 50 years, today society increases it 50-fold in roughly

Moore's law

The underlying principle of the information age was inadvertently defined in 1965 by an engineer named Gordon Moore at Intel, a big computer-chip company. He observed that the number of transistors incorporated in a chip will approximately double every year. This was later revised to every 18 months, and has remained fairly consistent ever since (as Figure 18.1 shows). In the decades since, the conjecture known as Moore's law has become one of the few articles of faith in Silicon Valley, even as its demise has been regularly predicted every few years. The idea has evolved far beyond what Moore originally stated, and it now claims that not only will the performance increase, but also the price will drop, the size will shrink and the speed will increase at similar rates. By and large, they have. Moore's law has decreased the cost of computing and increased performance by a factor of 1 billion, nine powers of ten. As James Gleick writes in *The Information: A history, a theory, a flood*:

> *All that information capacity looms over us, not quite visible, not quite tangible ... Heaven must once have felt this way to the faithful.*

FIG 18.1 **Moore and more**

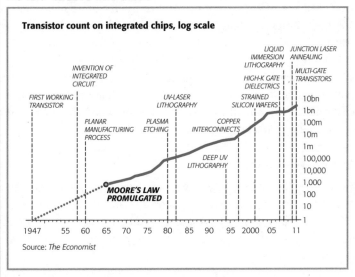

Source: *The Economist*

ten. Moreover, like the images in Plato's cave, the stored information is a mere shadow of what is out there. IDC estimates that every gigabyte of stored data can generate a petabyte (just over 1m gigabytes) or more of transient data, such as phone calls and television signals, that go unrecorded and simply disappear into the ether.

Martin Hilbert of the University of Southern California's Annenberg Centre goes beyond stored data to look at all the information that surrounds us at any time. That would include television, video games, phone calls, even car navigation systems and letters via the post. He calculates that by 2007 the world was flooded with 2.25 zettabytes of data. But because in his model the amount of information doubles roughly every three years and four months, by 2011 there were more than 600 exabytes of stored data alone. If all that information were placed into books, they would cover the entire surface of America 26 layers thick. If on CD-ROMs, they would stretch to the moon and back and then halfway to the moon again. Relatively, the quantity is equal to giving every living person as much information as was stored in the Library of Alexandria 160 times over.

Hence it is understandable that information overload is a very real phenomenon of our times, even if there has always been a cornucopia of data to fret about. To put it in a more classically imaginable way, the amount of information storage grows four times faster than the world's economy, and computer computation grows nine times faster. The bad news is that we are being more and more swamped. The good news is that this also suggests a way out. The tools to help us handle it are improving. For instance, the dramatic fall in the cost of computation and communications has made spam a regular feature of modern life – but it has also improved the performance of spam filters to get rid of most of it. Technology giveth and technology taketh away.

Getting ever smarter

The same trends appear when we look at telecommunications. Two shifts have been under way for years: data traffic subsuming voice calls, and mobile phones overtaking fixed-line phones. These trends totally transform the business of telecommunications, and change the way that people interact with information and with one another. Because so many people have lived through the revolution, we sometimes fail to see just how profound these changes are.

Think first of telecoms as a business activity. Starting in the 19th century, because the cost of deploying the technology was so high, and because most governments had wanted some control over the communications of citizens, the phone company was a state-run affair. (France maintains governmental oversight of carrier pigeons even today.) By the end of the 20th century, the newly privatised phone companies were usually the biggest firms in their respective countries. America's AT&T and Japan's NTT used to compete for the title of biggest company in the world in terms of revenue, market value and employees.

How the mighty fall. There are lots of measures to illustrate the demise of the former monopoly operators, but the most interesting is the waning importance today of all traditional telecoms carriers in handling calls. From 1990 onwards the growth of international voice traffic grew by around 13% a year, with a spike during the business boom of 1999–2001. Yet starting in 2005 something odd happens: growth plummets to below 5%. Are people making fewer international calls? Absolutely not – they are making more of them. But this is not being measured in the figures recorded by the telecoms carriers, according to TeleGeography. The missing volume is being handled by Skype, a software-based phone service. Today, internet calls account for around a quarter of all international phone traffic. But the increase in international calls sees Skype's growth exceeding that of all the world's telecoms carriers by a factor of two to one. In other words, the opportunity for new revenue from voice calls goes to the software start-up, not the infrastructure provider. The entire industry has been transformed – obliterated, some might say – in the space of a decade.

Next, consider mobile phones. Not so long ago they were an exotic novelty. These days it is fixed-line phones that are becoming the anomaly. In 2008 more calls were placed to mobile phones than landline phones, while the volume of calls that originate on mobiles is expected to exceed that placed from traditional phones by 2012. Just as the telephone replaced the telegraph, cell phones will over time push out fixed-line phones. The impact of this is that communications and mobility will be forever interlinked. And because the devices do much more than make calls, everyone will have a digital device to assist them (and track them) at all times.

Evolution and revolution

One of the next steps in this development will be to push aside voice calls for video ones. In many cases this makes lots of sense: more information can be transmitted through images than by voice alone, particularly the emotional content of conversions. Seeing the other party's eyes, for one thing, is considered essential for trust. But video calls do not make sense in many other contexts. So just as radio flourished despite the advent of television, so too voice calls will probably be commonplace even as video chats become more regular. However, a more substantial evolution in telecommunications will be to get rid of the discrete device, by integrating mobile phones into what we would ordinarily carry anyway (a ring, a bracelet) or actually embedding them in our bodies. This is not as far-fetched as it might seem.

We may have considered the trends of the silicon and telecoms revolutions separately, yet in fact the two technologies are increasingly joined at the hip. The world produces more than 10 billion microprocessors annually, and they go into everything from computers and cars to coffee-makers and credit cards. The vast majority of them are able to "think" but not "talk": they perform specific tasks but cannot communicate. This will change. Remember Moore's law? The chips are getting smaller, more powerful, faster and cheaper. As this happens, they have more "space" on them to add new features that do new things.

The history of mobiles and microchips over time has been that functions handled on separate components get bundled into the chip itself. That is one reason why today's phones are far smaller than ones a few years ago. If you crack open the casing, you will notice far fewer doohickeys stuck on the green circuit board: all those tiny transistors, resistors and capacitors have been integrated into the chip itself. Today's chips are more than "computing" devices: they use their abundant transistors to be things like radios, too (though they still need adjacent physical things like a crystal and an antenna).

Called by many names – the internet of things, ubiquitous computing, the embedded internet, sensor networks, machine-to-machine communications – the development will mark the biggest change in how people live over the next four decades to 2050. David Clark, a computer scientist at the Massachusetts Institute of Technology (MIT) who helped develop the internet, believes that in ten or 15 years' time the network will need to accommodate 1 trillion devices. That is a far cry from roughly 13 billion networked devices that are estimated to have existed in 2010, according to a study by Cisco, a communications-equipment firm. But it is conceptually feasible, particularly considering all the RFID (radio frequency identification) tags that are cropping up in everyday use, from clothing tags to traffic-management systems. Basic ones cost fractions of a penny, the smallest fit into the groove of a fingerprint, and it is only a matter of time before they are fully networked. The MIT engineers who pioneered sensor networking referred to it as "smart dust", since they envisioned the chips someday being just as small, cheap and ubiquitous. Making the same point, Jim Gray, who was a database pioneer at Microsoft, liked to talk about "the penny PC".

The exponential future

All this technical gobbledygook has profound implications. What it suggests is that there is a fundamental disconnect today between how people understand the world and its future trends, and how they will unfold over time. We experience a linear world when we interact with nature, but the technical world we have created develops at an exponential rate. For instance, our forebears hunted by watching an animal run and knowing when to throw a spear by predicting where the creature would be a few seconds later: a linear process. We do something similar when we pass cars on the road. But the silicon revolution operates on an entirely different scale. Progress is measured in exponential increases, and at this point – around 60 years since the transistor was invented by AT&T as a replacement for fragile vacuum tubes – information technology has evolved to such a degree that the new iterations are leading to far more changes than were anticipated even just a few years earlier. This forces people to think anew; and we will have to do so with much greater frequency.

One aspect of society to be shaken up will be economics. The powerful technology and new types of data that were impossible to collect before will enable new markets to form. For instance, economists today treat many items as indirect costs because there is no way to attribute the use of a resource to a particular person or entity. Sensor communications can change this by making it possible to base things on a person's actual usage. The technologies bring visibility, accountability and measurement. For example, few roads are capable of charging people based on use. But as wireless modules are integrated into vehicles, as they are in German lorries, this is possible. In recent years, insurance companies have begun to sell car-insurance premiums based on when and where people actually drive, not just on an annual basis. The system has yet to base its fees on how safely they drive as measured by driving behaviour or the time it takes to travel distance – but it probably will.

Business, too, will undergo a transformation. Two savants of the silicon tsunami are John Hagel III, a consultant, and John Seely Brown, a former director of Xerox PARC, a legendary research lab that invented (but failed to exploit) everything from computer networking to the computer mouse. In their view, the modern corporation will need to shift its appreciation of "transaction costs" to include the cost of acquiring knowledge and sharing it within the firm. Learning, and innovation based on it, will define businesses in the future. So companies need to do everything they can to ensure employees can access and exchange information easily. Whereas a century ago the central challenge for a company was to control operations and information through hierarchical structures, today and in future the technology seems to beg firms to cede some central control and encourage autonomy.

The new order

The societal changes will be perhaps the biggest of all. Wikipedia, built almost entirely by self-organising volunteers, has already become a repository of the world's knowledge, albeit with all the imperfections of the world it describes. Whereas it took around 70 years after the Gutenberg printing press for Martin Luther's criticism of the church and translation of the Latin Bible into vernacular German to spark the reformation, it was only four decades after the first internet message in 1969 before the 2011 "Arab spring" exploded across the region, fuelled in part by social-networking sites like Twitter and Facebook.

This is all very new. Yet the rate of adoption of new technologies has been increasing over the past century. Compare the rate of growth of the web with that of previous technologies. One way to measure it, from Ray Kurzweil, a father of artificial intelligence, is to examine the time it took for various technologies to become mass-mediums – defined as reaching a quarter of the American population, which was typically the lead market (see Figure 18.2). By this measure, it took the telephone 35 years after it was introduced in 1876. Radio and television needed increasingly less time. But once silicon took over, adoption sped up dramatically. By the time the web was born in 1991 it took a mere seven years to reach a quarter of the American population.

Kurzweil takes the trends a few steps further. He foresees a time in the not-too-distant future (2045 according to one estimate) when computers attain superhuman intelligence – which he calls "the singularity". Many people dismiss the idea as fanciful. And to be sure, considering how often computers crash or cell phones drop calls, it is hard to take seriously that all the technical goodies will one day actually work as advertised. Still, it is certain that something special is going to happen as the level of computing power grows exponentially over the coming decades.

One fear is that of machines running amok, akin to the creepy HAL in 2001: A Space Odyssey. But an argument can be made that the computers are already out of control. In 2010, thanks to "high-frequency trading", two-thirds of the shares traded on the New York Stock Exchange happened via computer algorithms. We have laws and institutions that are designed to regulate behaviour by implicitly taking into account human motivations (be they rational or not). But how do you begin to regulate a software program?

Ultimately, we cannot predict how all the information and nascent technologies will be used, but we can appreciate the ways they

FIG 18.2 **Inventions increasingly for all**

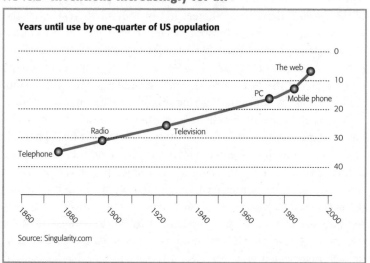

Years until use by one-quarter of US population

Source: Singularity.com

will exist as platforms for subsequent technical revolutions. Just as electrification was built for one purpose, the light bulb, but eventually was used for powering all sorts of devices including the PC, so too sensor networks, artificial intelligence and the data deluge will be exploited to do things that outstrip their creators' ken.

If these trends point to anything, it is that we ought to approach the future with a heavy dose of humility. Technology rarely evolves in the way that people think it will. When Marconi invented his wireless telegraph in the 1890s, he never imagined broadcast radio. A decade earlier Heinrich Hertz had famously declared: "I do not think that the wireless waves that I have discovered will have any practical application." To the men at Bell Labs in 1947 the transistor was simply an efficient replacement for vacuum tubes in radios; they had no inkling of its use in computers. Even Vannevar Bush's memex is somewhat comical, foreseeing audio via records (but not magnetic tape) and never conceiving of digitisation.

Before we get too excited about our informational prowess, it bears recalling that our processing and storage technology is nothing compared with nature itself. The DNA inside the roughly 60 trillion cells of every person about equals the information stored in all our computer gadgets. "Compared to mother nature, we are but humble apprentices – she is still way ahead," stresses Martin Hilbert of USC. And the computational power of all the world's computers combined in 2010, measured in processing instructions, amounted only to what the brain can process about every five minutes, in terms of the maximum number of nerve impulses. "The human brain is the most impressive information-processing machine of them all," Hilbert says. That should be good news for us all, that we will not be replaced so quickly.

Distance is dead. Long live location

Ludwig Siegele

Technology has killed distance. Yet as people become ever more connected, where they are will matter more than ever

ARE WE WITNESSING the "death of distance"? That was the question Frances Cairncross, at the time a senior editor at *The Economist*, asked in her 1997 book of that title. She concluded:

> The death of distance as a determinant of the cost of communications will probably be the single most important force shaping society in the first half of the next century. It will alter, in ways that are only dimly imaginable, decisions about where people work and what kind of work they do, concepts of national borders and sovereignty, and patterns of international trade.

She found it remarkable that MCI, then America's second-largest long-distance telephone operator, would allow its regular customers to make free calls on Mother's day – and predicted that at some point in the future it would be Mother's day every day and everywhere.

Talk is cheap

For many this future is already here – thanks to internet-based services such as Skype and Google Talk. Download their software on your personal computer or laptop or smartphone and you can chat away as long as you want, free, if your interlocutor has the same program. Calls to regular landlines and mobile phones cost next to nothing (on Skype, as of June 2011, a mere 2 cents per minute for calls from Britain to America). Even for those who prefer to make calls on a regular phone, talk has become ultra-cheap. When Cairncross's book was published, an average peak-time one-minute call between the United States and other OECD countries cost 81 cents.

Cheap talk is just the beginning. Technological prophets have been forecasting the triumph of video calling ever since 1936, when Germany's Reichspost launched the first public videophone service. Now it is actually happening: Skype, for example, lets its users make free video calls, and in the first half of 2010 these accounted for about 40% of the 95 billion minutes that people spent on the service.

Video calls on Skype or Google or Apple's iChat may be good enough to beam home grandma, but their quality and reliability are not yet sufficient for professional communications of the kind that could replace face-to-face meetings. This is why several firms, Cisco and HP among them, have developed "telepresence". Cameras, microphones and speakers are placed in a special studio in such a way that users literally see eye-to-eye and voices come from the direction of the large monitors on which speakers are shown. Fast networks and clever data-compression techniques ensure that communication is instantaneous. After a few minutes the participants start thinking they are in the same room.

Such studios are still expensive. But as their price comes down, in the corporate world this type of communication will quickly become commonplace. Expect to make many fewer business trips in the decades to come – but at the cost of staying up late or getting up early to attend telepresence meetings with colleagues in other time zones.

Eventually telepresence technology will make its way into the living room, probably built into television sets, which will become ever larger and flatter. And consumers will come up with new ways to use it. Already some families host "Skype dinners", with relatives calling in. Others never hang up, thus turning a display in the kitchen into a window on somebody else's home. Both habits indicate what the future may hold: homes will have video walls that connect rooms and other places with each other virtually.

Personal velocity and perpetual motion

Another way to kill distance is to travel super-fast. Phileas Fogg needed 80 days to circumnavigate the world. In future his options will range from supercars to high-speed trains and supersonic jets: Concorde may no longer fly, but at least one company is developing a "supersonic business jet" which could get passengers from New York to Paris in about four hours at a speed of up to Mach 1.6.

It is not just people's maximum speed of travel that has been rising, but also the average "personal velocity" (a concept popularised by Dopplr, a website, which calculates users' average speed based on their travels). Take air travel: the number of global revenue passenger miles (the number of revenue-paying passengers aboard an aircraft multiplied by the distance travelled) has grown ninefold since 1970. Or cars: in the rich world, the number of motor vehicles per 100 inhabitants is approaching 50. There were only 5.5m vehicles on China's roads in 1990; now there are more than 90m.

Will these trends continue? Only up to a point, for they face headwinds. The faster and the more cheaply bits and bytes can move, the less atoms will have to. Videoconferencing can slice travel budgets. And the number of cars cannot keep going up without dire environmental results. According to some estimates, if China had the same number of cars per person as America, the country's fleet would emit twice as much carbon dioxide as that produced by all the cars in the world today – even if fuel consumption were to fall below average.

Given such concerns people may not move around much faster in 2050 than in 2012 (unless someone invents Star-Trek-style teleportation). Yet life will still keep speeding up in other ways. Smartphones and other mobile technology will allow people to be continually on the move while remaining continually connected. Welcome to the age of the digital nomad.

FIG 19.1 **Walking the talk**

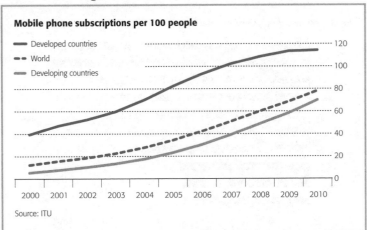

Mobile phone subscriptions per 100 people

Source: ITU

The mobile miracle

Whereas ever cheaper voice calls and ever better video communication clearly bring people closer, it is mobile technology that truly knits them together. "Many people will carry mobile telephones as unthinkingly as they carry a wallet or a watch," wrote Cairncross. In the rich world this has been true for years: most developed countries now boast many more mobile numbers than people. And with remarkable speed, mobile phones are becoming ubiquitous in poor countries too (see Figures 19.1 and 19.2).

This mobile miracle has been possible because processors and other electronic components have become ever cheaper and more powerful. They will continue to do so. Simple mobile phones now cost as little as $10. Mobile talk time has become affordable even for many in poor countries. In India, a minute can be bought for less than 1 cent.

Mobile technology will not only bring the world's excluded closer to the global mainstream. It will also be a tool to make markets more efficient, allowing poor countries to leapfrog much of the infrastructure that has been built in the developed world. Bad roads, for instance, are much less of a problem when farmers can make a

FIG 19.2 **On the move**

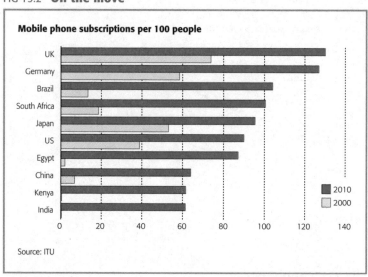

Mobile phone subscriptions per 100 people

Source: ITU

call to see when and where it is best for them to sell their crops. An additional ten phones per 100 people in a typical developing country boosts GDP growth by as much as 0.8 percentage points, according to the World Bank.

Another powerful tool is mobile money: transferring cash by text message. One of the most successful such services, M-PESA, began in 2007 in Kenya. Four years later, it boasted more than 13m users in a country of 38m people. The service is now used for salaries, bills, donations: few things cannot be paid for via a handset.

The next wave of this mobile revolution has already started in the rich world, and will also spread to developing countries. It involves smartphones, wireless handheld computers that come with a touch screen, and tablet computers. The most advanced of these new mobile devices are more capable than the equivalent personal computers of ten years earlier.

However, it is not their impressive number-crunching capacities that make smartphones and tablets so powerful, but the "apps" that run on them – downloadable applications that are often connected to a "computing cloud", a digital service generated in a data centre and delivered over the internet. A popular example is a map app: thanks to GPS, a satellite-based global positioning service, most smartphones can figure out where they are; the app then downloads the necessary maps for the location.

Within just four years of the launch of Apple's iPhone in 2007, such apps were already counted in the hundreds of thousands: from games to information services and book readers. Most give users access to all kinds of information at their fingertips. But some literally do away with the need to overcome physical distance: they allow individuals or groups of people to stay constantly connected.

One of the most popular such "group messaging" services is BlackBerry Messenger (BBM), which runs on the eponymous smartphone made by RIM, a Canadian firm. Users form groups and then broadcast messages, which can include images and are free of charge, to other members. These usually arrive within less than two seconds – worldwide. Before BBM and other such services, people had to come physically together to have a similar kind of interaction.

BBM is hugely popular among Western teenagers (in the summer of 2011 it proved handy for helping some of them organise riots in British cities), particularly in countries where texting is still expensive. But the number of users is also growing rapidly in many developing countries, not least because the service allows people to circumvent laws that limit the freedom of assembly. In the real world it is relatively easy for governments to keep citizens from meeting in public; barring people from gathering in groups of more than three is a popular part of the toolkit of authoritarian regimes. In the virtual realm such bans are much harder to enforce.

In the coming decades more and more such services will tempt the consumer, creating an ever denser web of communications. And the telecoms infrastructure will expand to accommodate a massively growing demand for "real-time" virtual services.

Location, location, location

We will increasingly live in a world that is "always on", where people are constantly connected and distance has in many ways ceased to matter as it once did. Yet a strange thing will happen as distance dies.

Really?

Photos that move and talk have until recently been enjoyed only by Harry Potter and fellow imaginary magicians. But in early 2011 such pictures hit the muggle word of reality, thanks to Aurasma, a service provided by Autonomy, a British technology firm (which was acquired by HP, an American computer-maker, later that year). Users download to their smartphone an application that allows the device to recognise objects and then display related information around them on the device's screen. Hold the smartphone up to a picture of Roger Federer and it will play a video of his latest triumph.

Aurasma is an intriguing example of what is called "augmented reality". But it also shows how, in the decades to come, humans will interact with the world around them: the distance between the virtual world and the physical world will shrink. In some cases, these realms will merge.

Brainwave controllers are already marking the convergence of the virtual with the real. Although not – yet – as sophisticated as in *The Matrix*, a film in which humanity is enslaved by machines inside a virtual world, these devices are in use in areas as diverse as health care, market research and entertainment.

But researchers are going further, implanting brainwave sensors directly into people's heads. Scientists at Intel are developing a chip that will allow users to operate computers by thought alone. Gone will be the need for a keyboard or mouse. Other boffins talk of putting miniature mobile phones into people's heads. Maybe, in a few decades, newborns will be chipped straight after birth

Physical location, of people and of things, will in some respects start to matter more than ever.

Take the sort of communications services that will develop in the coming years. Many of the most inventive of these are likely to take advantage of the ability to provide people with highly relevant information based on where they are: the street they are looking at, and enter the world with a unique telecom number (which could double as an ID number). Embedded or not, smartphones are likely in future to receive and transmit data from sensors in their owners' bodies (health care would be an obvious beneficiary). And by 2050 the phones' batteries, thanks to kinetic energy, will surely never die.

Meanwhile, contact lenses will become displays, so that people will see the world with data superimposed on their visual field – like Arnold Schwarzenegger's character in the Terminator movies. Scientists at the University of Washington in Seattle have already built a contact lens with one light-emitting diode, which can be controlled wirelessly. No doubt the number will multiply.

Look forward, then, to universal, instantaneous, super-wideband communications. Today's separate world of data, visible through the windows of laptop and smartphone screens, will be layered over the real world.

And what if everything is connected to every other thing and everybody? Every nut and bolt, book, painting, film, photo, video, and so on could have its own internet address. In such a world, people could educate themselves – at home or in a virtual 3D world – using the collected wisdom available from everywhere. Oxbridge and the Ivy League would be accessible to all.

So by 2050 muggles could be living in a world in which the borders between the virtual and the real have blurred dramatically. People will then be nodes in a global hybrid network of humans and computers.

the road they are driving on, the town they are travelling to. Such "augmented reality" marries the real world and the virtual, not so much to kill distance but to harness it into a service.

Or take the communications networks themselves. Certainly, they are becoming ever faster and cheaper. But as they do so, their physical location becomes more important, at least for certain applications.

Operators of online games, for instance, think long and hard about where they put their data centres – so that the response time for users is as short as possible.

Those who build computer systems for investment banks and other financial institutions have to be even pickier when it comes to location: being a microsecond slower than the competition in high-frequency trading can add up over a year to tens of millions of dollars in lost profit. "We now all know how much time it takes for light to travel 1 foot in a fibre-optic cable," says the chief technology officer of one big American exchange. As long as there is more money to be made, this digital tortoise-and-hare race will continue.

More importantly, when people can log in (and thus work) from wherever they are, they are much freer in the choice of where they live. This means that they can move away from urban centres. But it also allows other forces to take effect, notably the fact that people prefer to live in communities of like-minded people. In particular, those whom Richard Florida, an American theorist of urban life, has labelled the "creative class" (for the most part highly skilled professionals) can now more easily live in places they find attractive rather than where their company is based. Depending on how these forces play out, a cheaper and better communications infrastructure may actually drive people together – and not apart.

What is more, in a world that has been flattened by data networks, things that keep people apart become more visible and important, in particular cultural differences. A few years back, big software firms offshored programming work to India and other countries because labour costs were lower. Although this is still the case, the divison of labour is becoming increasingly discerning. Product development will more and more be split in such a way that certain jobs are done in places where the conditions are most favourable in terms of culture and regulation. SAP, a German software giant, for instance, tends to rely on its labs in Silicon Valley to come up with innovative user interfaces and marketing strategies, two areas in which the Californian high-tech region is hard to beat. Indian developers, who are in abundant supply, excel at using the latest programming languages and tools, which is why many of SAP's new products are written there. And German developers, known for their rigorous thinking, focus on the business rules and the overall architecture of SAP's enterprise applications.

Finally, there is growing evidence that electronic communications, instead of bringing people closer together, isolate them in new ways. At least in America, people seem to be losing interest in talking to others. The amount of time mobile subscribers speak on their handsets dropped in the four years from 2007 by more than 100 minutes to 700 minutes a month (including incoming calls), according to Nielsen, a market-research firm. And a survey by CTIA, a trade group, shows that the average length of a call plummeted from 3:08 to 1:40 minutes over the same period.

More interestingly (or perhaps worryingly), teenagers, instead of spending time with their friends, manage their relationships with others online, often via Facebook, the world's largest social network. Some scientists have argued that this type of activity is changing our brains, making them focus on short exchanges rather than long-term relationships. The digital gadgets on which we now depend have already begun rewiring our brains, writes Nicholas Carr in his book *The Shallows*. He mainly worries about the effects on thinking of "hypermedia" – clicking, skipping, skimming – and especially on working and deep memory. There is evidence, he says, that digital technology is damaging the long-term memory consolidation that is the basis for true intelligence. Hypermedia may have a similar effect on personal relationships.

Whether you agree or not, there will be heated debates about such issues. And it would not come as a surprise if the world saw the emergence of a group of people that could be called "The Disconnected": those who willingly "cut the cord" because they have come to the conclusion that digital communications are inhumane.

All this means that the death of distance will have surprising consequences. In terms of the cost of communications and the time it takes for information to get from one end of the world to the other, distance is largely now a thing of the past in rich countries, and is rapidly becoming so in poor ones too. But in some senses physical location will become more important. And it may be that technology creates a new type of distance between people – something that will require another wave of ingenuity and inventiveness to overcome.

20 Of predictions and progress: more for less

Matt Ridley

Man's ingenuity and inventiveness will prove all soothsayers wrong, pessimists especially

THE MOST UNWITTINGLY PROFOUND THINGS that have been said about predicting the future were said by two sportsmen, neither renowned for his conventional intellect. Yogi Berra, an American baseball player, said: "I never make predictions, especially about the future." Paul Gascoigne, a British footballer, went one better: "I never make predictions and I never will."

Prediction is a mug's game. Everybody who has ever done it has proved to be terrible at it – and (I confidently predict) always will be. Yes, even the ones with reputations as great seers were actually hopeless most of the time. Arthur C. Clarke, for example, saw geostationary satellites coming, but also said (in 1962) that hovercraft were going to dominate land transport to the point that by the 1990s a common sign would read "No wheeled vehicles on this highway".

So, before issuing more of my own predictions, here are some of the reasons that they will fail. First, many trends are non-linear, so things that are mere smudges of cloud on the horizon in one decade (mobile telephony and the internet in the late 1980s) can turn into hurricanes in the next. Second, as Tim Harford argues in his book, *Adapt*, blind trial-and-error is responsible for most of the innovations that change the world, not intelligent design or planning. Third, as Dan Gardner argues in his book, *Future Babble*, status–quo bias means that forecasters tell you much more about their own times than about the future. In the mid-20th century, after 50 years of little change in communications technologies, but astonishing innovations in transport, futurologists were all babbling about routine space travel, personal gyrocopters and jetpacks, but not one of them foresaw the internet or ubiquitous mobile telephony.

What will not happen

The next 40 years will not see the end of anything: not history, science, oil, war, capitalism, books or love. With remarkably few exceptions (trebuchets, antler retoucheurs), old technologies and ideas persist alongside new ones. Even trebuchets have been revived – for throwing flaming pianos at rock concerts. The nature of human society is to accumulate ideas, more than to replace them. Likewise, it is a mistake to rule any outcome impossible, as Ernest Rutherford did atomic power ("moonshine"), or the British Astronomer Royal did space travel two weeks before *Sputnik* ("bunk"). Arthur C. Clarke again – on target this time: "When a distinguished scientist ... states that something is impossible, he is almost certainly wrong." Yet to forecast the rise or fall of any specific technology is as good as impossible. If I could predict the invention of the teletransporter, then I could invent it.

By far the sharpest lesson to draw from past forecasts is that planetary pessimism is usually wrong. The field of futurology is littered with cataclysmic prognostications that failed. Go back 40 years to 1971 and recall the continual dirge of dire doom that those of us who became teenagers that year were subjected to over the next four decades. The grown-ups told us with terrible certainty that the population explosion was unstoppable; global famine was inevitable; crop-yield increases would peter out; food aid to India was futile; a cancer epidemic caused by pesticides in the environment would shorten our lives; the desert was advancing at two miles a year; nuclear fallout was a growing risk; nuclear winter was an inevitable consequence of an inevitable nuclear war; Ebola, hanta virus and swine flu pandemics were overdue; urban decay was irreversible; acid rain was going to destroy whole forests; oil spills were increasing; economic growth was ceasing; global inequalities would rise; oil and gas would soon run out; and so would copper, zinc, chrome and many other natural resources; urban air pollution was getting worse; the Great Lakes were dying; dozens of bird and mammal species would become extinct each year; a new ice age was coming; sperm counts were falling; mad cow disease would kill hundreds of thousands of people; genetically modified weeds would devastate ecosystems; nanotechnology would run riot; computers would crash at the dawn of the millennium, bringing down parts of civilisation with them; winter snow would become a rarity; hurricanes would increase in frequency; malaria would get worse; climate change would wipe out species; weather would kill more people and sea-level rise would accelerate. All these were trumpeted loudly in the mainstream media at one time or another: I am not picking obscure cases.

Here are some quotations to show that I am not exaggerating. U Thant, director general of the UN, in 1969: "If such a global partnership is not forged within the next decade, then I very much fear that the problems I have mentioned will have reached such staggering proportions that they are beyond our capacity to control." (It wasn't.) A best-selling book, The Limits to Growth, in 1972, on its cover: "Will this be the world that your grandchildren will thank you for? A world where industrial production has sunk to zero. Where population has suffered a catastrophic decline. Where the air, sea, and land are polluted beyond redemption. Where civilization is a distant memory. This is the world that the computer forecasts." A distinguished economist, Robert Heilbroner, in 1974: "The outlook for man, I believe, is painful, difficult, perhaps desperate and the hope that can be held out for his future prospects seems to be very slim indeed." A celebrity ecologist, Paul Ehrlich, in 1974: "The train of events leading to the dissolution of India as a viable nation is already in motion." The New York Times, in 1980, just before oil prices fell: "There should be no such thing as optimism about energy for the foreseeable future ... prices will go up and up." Al Gore, in 2006: "Many scientists are now warning that we are moving closer to several 'tipping points' that could – within as little as ten years – make it impossible for us to avoid irretrievable damage to the planet's habitability for human civilisation."

With the exception of a handful where the jury is still out, every single one of the predictions listed in the last paragraph but one was wrong. Not just off by a few years, but diametrically, 180-degrees, wrong. Over the 40 years after 1971 the population growth rate halved; famine became rare; average crop yields doubled; India became a food exporter; lifespan increased by 25% globally; age-adjusted cancer rates fell; the Sahel grew greener; radioactive fallout levels fell by 90%; two-thirds of nuclear weapons were dismantled; no viral pandemic occurred; many cities flourished; forest cover slightly increased; the amount of oil spilled in the ocean fell by 90%; an unprecedented global economic boom occurred; inequality fell sharply as poor countries grew rich far faster than rich countries; oil and gas reserves ballooned and for a while prices fell (though oil prices have bounced upwards again since 2008); metal prices plummeted; urban air pollution improved rapidly throughout the developed world; the Great Lakes cleansed themselves; the ice age never came; bird and mammal species extinction rates remained low; sperm counts failed to fall; mad cow disease killed at most 172 people in 20 years; genetically modified crops led to increased biodiversity; nanotechnology did nada; computers suffered few and minor problems at the millennium even in countries that did nothing about the Y2K bug (like Italy and South Korea); average winter snow cover in the northern hemisphere increased; tropical cyclone accumulated energy fell to record lows; malaria retreated; not a single species became globally extinct as a result of climate change (golden toads were killed by a fungus); fewer people died as a result of extreme weather; and sea-level rise did not accelerate.

You think I have cherry-picked cases to suit my argument? What doom-predictions would you prefer instead? Arctic summer sea ice retreated in the first years of this century faster than some expected. True, but Antarctic summer sea ice increased slightly over the same period. The seasonal ozone hole over Antarctica failed to recover, true, but the resulting skin cancer and cataract epidemic in Patagonia or New Zealand turned out to be entirely pseudoscientific. As for global warming generally, the warming between 1970 and 2010 was about half a degree centigrade and was slowest in the last decade of the four. It has significantly undershot the predictions made in the 1980s by the likes of NASA scientist James Hansen, the man who first made global warming a celebrity. He said in 1988 that by now temperatures would have risen by 1.4–2.8°C to "well above any level experienced on Earth in 100,000 years". A quarter of a century later they have risen about one-tenth as much.

Forgive me, then, if I take with a pinch of salt the dire dirge of pessimism that my teenage children are being subjected to in their textbooks and in the media today – a dirge that keeps an industry of pressure groups and subsidised corporations in funds. The ability of this Armageddon industry to move on from its mistakes with a shrug of hindsight bias and without the media asking even the simplest of questions about what went wrong with previous predictions is apparently something that one can safely predict will continue. It is a safe bet that in 2050 the media (whatever form it takes) will be dominated by pessimists then too. Disaster will be imminent – still.

The invisibility of good news

There are two simple reasons that these predictions of doom were wrong in 1971 and will be wrong again in 2012 and in 2050. First, bad things will always be much more newsworthy than good things. Good news is smooth, bad news is lumpy: general improvements in human living standards are incremental, and all but invisible, whereas wars, recessions, earthquakes and asteroids tend to strike suddenly out of a clear blue sky. So every time a new scare comes up, the moderate or sanguine voices are drowned out by the more extreme and negative predictions. Yet year by year the world's 2–5% economic growth rate goes on, all but unreported.

The second reason is more fundamental. All the scare stories assume a static response. They assume that humanity is standing on a railway track watching a train coming towards it, rather than moving out of the way. The number of people killed by droughts, floods and storms in the first decade of the 2000s was 93% lower than the number killed by the same causes in the 1920s, despite a much larger population (see Figure 20.1). That is not because weather became less dangerous, but because technologies enabled people to cut their risk of death – technologies of shelter, transport, communication, medicine and more. If food gets scarce, prices rise and farmers plant more crops, use more fertiliser or try more experiments to raise yields; if oil gets scarce, prices rise and new drilling techniques are invented; if whales or copper get expensive, substitutes are found; if pollution gets worse, clean-air laws are enacted; and so on. An otherwise distinguished Victorian economist, William Stanley Jevons, said that "it is useless to

FIG 20.1 **Weather becomes less deadly**

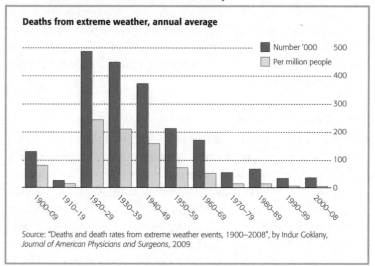

Deaths from extreme weather, annual average

Source: "Deaths and death rates from extreme weather events, 1900–2008", by Indur Goklany, *Journal of American Physicians and Surgeons*, 2009

FIG 20.2 **Metal becomes more affordable**

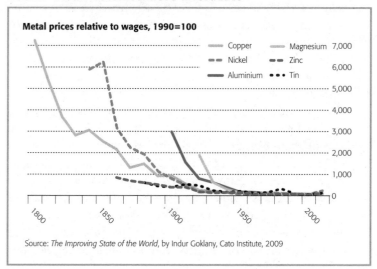

Metal prices relative to wages, 1990=100

Source: *The Improving State of the World*, by Indur Goklany, Cato Institute, 2009

think of substituting any other kind of fuel for coal" – six years after the first oil well was drilled. The relationship between human beings and the resources they need is not that of a man helping himself from a diminishing pile of chocolates; it is a negotiation between human ingenuity and natural constraints in which price signals divert effort into fruitful directions.

The affordable future

Cheaper – that is the key. Economic growth works by reducing the time it takes for people to earn the means of fulfilling their needs and desires (see Figure 20.2). Where an entirely self-sufficient person would take hours to acquire by his or her own efforts even a basic supply of food, shelter or clothing each day, a modern participant in the global division of labour who is on the average wage takes just a few hours each day to earn the money that he or she needs for good meals, fashionable clothes and rent for a decent house. In the 1950s it took 30 minutes to earn the price of a hamburger on the average wage; today it takes three minutes. Nobody loved them, but the robber barons of the late 19th century got rich through cutting the costs of goods. Between 1870 and 1900, Cornelius Vanderbilt cut the price of rail freight by 90%, Andrew Carnegie slashed steel prices by 75% and John D. Rockefeller cut oil prices by 80%. A century later Malcom McLean, Sam Walton and Michael Dell did roughly the same for container shipping, discount retailing and home computing, and nobody loved them either. A technology affects human living standards not when it is invented, but when – decades later – it becomes affordable.

So what goods and services will get cheaper in the next 40 years? Probably energy. Thanks to new technology, natural gas and solar power could both become much cheaper to deliver to customers by 2050. Cheap gas now looks as though it will last for many decades, while solar power is getting steadily cheaper and may soon be affordable without subsidies. Because gas-fired turbines can be switched on and off relatively efficiently, these two can work well together – gas by night, photovoltaic by day. Nuclear may contribute if it can ever get the cost of its safety features under control, get away from the water-cooled uranium-fuelled designs that have dominated its early years and go for inherently safer molten-salt of thorium instead. Wild cards like cold fusion might suddenly emerge, and high-temperature superconductors will help. But whatever the technology, the important point is that energy will probably get cheaper, not dearer. The old-fashioned renewables, like wind, wood and water, have not a snowball's chance in hell of competing on price, or generating the sort of quantities of energy needed in the future (as now), because they need too much land, and land is not going to get cheaper given how many people want to buy it or preserve it. Apart from a few niche applications, they will be white elephants by 2050 and our current enthusiasm for heavily subsidising them will astonish our grandchildren.

Biotechnology is a good bet too for cheapening. A plethora of genetic and molecular breakthroughs in the past 40 years have helped researchers a lot more than they have helped patients or consumers, but that could soon change. One of the most exciting features of stem cells is that they could prove to be affordable once the technology is working well: just hook the patient up to a machine that extracts cells, reprogrammes them and reimplants them. As a way of repairing organs, it could be less costly than surgery as well as less painful. Similarly, cancer treatment stands on the brink of breakthroughs, probably using vaccines and viral gene therapy as a way of delivering large molecules inside cells to where they are needed. (The old-fashioned pharmaceutical approach of seeking small molecules that can cross cell membranes to attack cancer cells is running out of steam.) Again, this could be cheaper than radiotherapy and chemotherapy, as well as more effective. One of the most hopeful trends of the past decade has been a small but noticeable downturn in the age-adjusted death rate from all cancers. By 2050 the cancer death rate could be falling as fast as the age-adjusted death rate from heart disease and stroke is now.

Communication, which has had a spectacular four decades of cheapening, must surely bottom out in the next four decades. Once ultra-broadband-mobile video is costing the square root of nothing per minute, as it almost is, there is not a lot you can do for living standards by making it cheaper still. Transport, whose cheapening in recent decades has come through enterprise more than technology (budget airlines still use basically the same engine designs as they did four decades ago), will probably struggle to get more affordable in coming decades. Congestion, caused by the impossibility of improving infrastructure in crowded cities, will continue to bedevil every attempt to cut its costs.

Cheaper government?

What about government? For the most part, our political masters and their bureaucratic enforcers did little or nothing over the last 40 years to reduce the cost of the services they provide. Indeed, the time it takes average taxpayers to earn the services of their government grew substantially, with barely discernible improvements in that service: any productivity gains were captured in higher pay and pensions in the public sector itself, as is the way with monopolies. There is an excuse for this, which is at least partly persuasive: the things government provides – infrastructure, health care, social services, defence, law and order, and so on – are essentially immune to cheapening. Indeed, as it gets cheaper and cheaper for each of us to clothe, feed, communicate and be entertained (by the private sector), so we are increasingly left with the high-hanging fruit, the things in our lives that cannot easily be made cheaper, like nursing and tax accountancy. Farming and manufacturing are now absurdly cheap, and make up such tiny parts of the cost of fulfilling our needs, that making them cheaper will not make much difference. Gains must come in services. If this is true (as hinted in Tyler Cowen's book, *The Great Stagnation*), then it implies that diminishing returns will have at last arrived.

They are long overdue. Economists have been expecting diminishing technological returns ever since John Stuart Mill, David Ricardo and even Adam Smith. Instead growth just keeps on accelerating – and showing increasing returns. So if global growth were to begin to slow as soon as we have run out of technologies that can be made more productive, it will be a reversal of a trend that has been going since 1800. That is one reason I do not expect it will happen. Another is that somewhere in the world, somebody will work out how to make the quality rise and the price fall in things like medical care and house building and transport and restaurant management. Given that innovation comes from the meeting and mating of ideas, rather than from the thinking sessions of lonely geniuses, it is likely that the internet has accelerated the innovation rate and therefore the chance of finding cheapening solutions.

There is a feature of economic growth that often goes unremarked, namely the larger the political entity, the steadier is the growth. A country is less prone to booms and busts than a city, and a continent than a country. The growth rate of the planet is still steadier, not least because a planet cannot borrow. In only one year since the second world war did global GDP growth dip below zero: 2009, when it was minus 0.6%. Real world GDP per person has doubled since 1970. If it did so again in the next 40 years, the average citizen of the planet would have an annual income of roughly $22,000 in today's dollars – more than that of the average citizen in several European Union countries now.

A more sustainable future

The Malthusian assumption that higher living standards inevitably mean using more resources is wrong. Take land, for example – a limited and vital resource. The amount of land needed to feed, shelter, fuel and clothe a single person keeps going down, not up, as people get richer. Higher farm yields, the use of synthetic fleece instead of wool, the replacement of wood fires with gas-fired central heating, even the use of new building materials like steel or breeze blocks instead of wood – they all cut the acreage footprint of supporting a human lifestyle. The gradual migration of people to cities cuts the amount of land each person needs, even allowing for the rural hinterland that supports each urban dweller's lifestyle. The same is true of many other resources, which are more frugally used by more modern lifestyles. The energy intensity of the world economy, in terms of joules per dollar of output, has been falling for two decades. It is no accident that the greatest threats to wild habitats come in poor countries, not rich ones. Haiti, for example, mostly cannot afford fossil fuels and relies on wood for much of its energy – even bakeries use charcoal – with the result that it has lost 98% of its forest. Next door, the Dominican Republic is much richer and its forest cover is increasing.

An especially revealing measure goes under the name of HANPP – the human appropriation of net primary production. Helmut Haberl of Vienna University calculates that human beings pinch 14.2% of the growth of plants on land for themselves and their domestic animals, and destroy or prevent the growth of a further 9.6% by building roads or unleashing goats, leaving 76.2% for wild nature. But that is only part of the story. Although on balance human beings suppress plant growth, in some places they increase it by fertilising and irrigating the soil. There are even large areas where this enhancement of growth is so great that it roughly matches the human appropriation (as in much of northern Europe) or even exceeds it (the Nile delta). That is to say, even after human appropriation, there is as much or more primary production left for nature as there would be if human beings were not there. Consequently, the net impact of HANPP is lowest in the most industrialised regions. Now imagine that the rest of the world gradually goes further in this direction, steadily raising the amount of plant material that human beings consume, but steadily raising the amount that is left for other animals, too, till eventually 9 billion human beings are living high on the hog without having any net impact on the quantity of wild plant and animal life at all. Incredible? All the evidence suggests that this prospect is eminently feasible so long as energy and water are both plentiful. In other words, by getting energy (and hence water) from some source other than the land, we can spare the land – in contrast to the despoliation of the landscape caused by early, primitive agriculture that had no access to artificial fertiliser and irrigation.

So here is an optimistic prediction about the world in 2050. It will be a time of extensive ecological restoration. Just as rich countries today are regrowing forests at a breakneck pace (New England, for example is now 70% woodland, where it was once 70% farmland), so the world may be doing the same in 2050 – even while feeding a larger population. "Re-wilded" areas in Africa, the American midwest and central Asia may be home once again to migrating herds of wild mammals. Just as rich countries today are bringing some species back from the brink of extinction (it is 160 years since a breeding bird native to Europe – the great auk – became globally extinct; the pied raven was a subspecies, and the slender-billed curlew and bald ibis are not yet extinct), so by 2050 many Asian countries and perhaps even some African ones will be doing the same. It may be too late for some species by then, but perhaps not. Even if the tiger were to die out in the wild, its restoration from captivity by wealthy future Indians seems probable. And one thing that may well have happened by 2050 is the rebirth of an extinct species. The mammoth will probably be the first, partly because of the excellent preservation state of frozen specimens and partly because of the effort that is already going into extracting mammoth cells of good quality. Reprogramming such a cell to become an embryo, implanting it into an Indian elephant and bringing a fetus to term will be a very tall order. But then test-tube babies seemed an impossible dream in 1970 and they were just eight years away.

Acknowledgements

MANY PEOPLE HELPED to make this book possible. First and foremost, the 20 contributors responded gamely to the challenge of peering four decades into the future. James Fransham tended expertly to the charts, with help from Carol Howard, and David Griffiths checked facts. Among the colleagues from *The Economist* who offered insight and support were John Micklethwait, Emma Duncan, Tom Standage, Joel Budd, Fiammetta Rocco and Patsy Dryden.

We are particularly grateful to Stephen Brough and Daniel Crewe at Profile Books for their encouragement, enthusiasm and advice throughout. And we couldn't have wished for a better copy-editor than Penny Williams.

Finally, our special thanks to Gaby Franklin and Hilary Andrews for putting up with megachange at home.

Daniel Franklin and John Andrews

Index